Public Policy and Politics

Series Editors: Colin Fudge and Robin Hambleton

Public policy-making in western democracies is confronted by new pressures. Central values relating to the role of the state, the role of markets and the role of citizenship are now all contested and the consensus built up around the Keynesian welfare state is under challenge. New social movements are entering the political arena: electronic technologies are transforming the nature of employment; changes in demographic structure are creating heightened demands for public services; unforeseen social and health problems are emerging; and, most disturbing, social and economic inequalities are increasing in many countries.

How governments – at international, national and local levels – respond to this developing agenda is the central focus of the Public Policy and Politics series. Aimed at a student, professional, practitioner and academic readership, it aims to provide up-to-date, comprehensive and authoritative analyses of public policy-making in practice.

The series is international and interdisciplinary in scope, and bridges theory and practice by relating the substance of policy to the politics of the policy-making process.

Public Policy and Politics

Series Editors: Colin Fudge and Robin Hambleton

PUBLISHED

Danny Burns, Robin Hambleton and Paul Hoggett, *The Politics of Decentralisation: Revitalising Local Democracy*

Stephen Glaister, June Burnham, Handley Stevens and Tony Travers, *Transport Policy in Britain* (second edition)

Christopher Ham, *Health Policy in Britain: The Politics and Organisation of the National Health Service* (fifth edition)

Ian Henry, *The Politics of Leisure Policy* (second edition)

Peter Malpass and Alan Murie, *Housing Policy and Practice* (fifth edition)

Robin Means, Sally Richards and Randall Smith, *Community Care: Policy and Practice* (third edition)

David Mullins and Alan Murie, *Housing Policy in the UK*

Gerry Stoker, *The Politics of Local Government* (second edition)

Marilyn Taylor, *Public Policy in the Community*

Kieron Walsh, *Public Services and Market Mechanisms: Competition, Contracting and the New Public Management*

FORTHCOMING

Rob Atkinson and Simin Davoudi with Graham Moon, *Urban Politics in Britain: The City, the State and the Market* (second edition)

Robin Hambleton, *Reinventing Local Governance*

Christopher C. Hood and Helen Z. Margetts, *The Tools of Government in the Digital Age*

**Public Policy and Politics
Series Standing Order
ISBN 0–333–71705–8 hardback
ISBN 0–333–69349–3 paperback**
(outside North America only)

You can receive future titles in this series as they are published. To place a standing order please contact your bookseller or, in the case of difficulty, write to us at the address below with your name and address, the title of the series and an ISBN quoted above.

Customer Services Department, Macmillan Distribution Ltd
Houndmills, Basingstoke, Hampshire RG21 6XS, England

Transport Policy in Britain

Second Edition

**Stephen Glaister
June Burnham
Handley Stevens
and
Tony Travers**

First edition 1998
Second edition 2006
First Published by
PALGRAVE MACMILLAN
Houndmills, Basingstoke, Hampshire RG21 6XS and
175 Fifth Avenue, New York, N.Y. 10010
Companies and representatives throughout the world

PALGRAVE MACMILLAN is the global academic imprint of the Palgrave
Macmillan division of St. Martin's Press, LLC and of Palgrave Macmillan Ltd.
Macmillan® is a registered trademark in the United States, United Kingdom
and other countries. Palgrave is a registered trademark in the European
Union and other countries.

ISBN-13: 978-0-333-94882-8   hardback
ISBN-10: 0-333-94882-3   hardback
ISBN-13: 978-0-333-94881-1   paperback
ISBN-10: 0-333-94881-5   paperback

This book is printed on paper suitable for recycling and made from fully
managed and sustained forest sources.

A catalogue record for this book is available from the British Library.

Library of Congress Cataloging-in-Publication Data

A catalog record for this book is available from the Library of Congress

10   9   8   7   6   5   4   3   2   1
15   14 13 12 11 10 09 08 07 06

Printed in China

Contents

List of Tables	viii
List of Figures	ix
List of Abbreviations	x
Introduction	xiii

1 The Historical Context 1

From canals and turnpikes to state-regulated private railways	1
From local to national roads: the creation of the Road Board	5
Road versus rail, 1919–39	7
Post-war nationalization and the switch to roads	12
Coordination and control	14
Rediscovering competition	17
Privatization and deregulation	20
Transport and the environment	27
The rise and fall of an integrated transport policy	32
Conclusion	40

2 The Role of Central Government 42

Central government departments	43
Central government and the transport industries	57
Coordination and control	66
Parliament, the law and the media	74
Conclusion	75

3 Local Government and Urban Transport 77

Local government structures and responsibilities	77
Regional government	79
Local government's spatial and transport planning	80
Local government finance: a key limitation	87
Transport in major urban areas	92
The London congestion charge experiment	99
Conclusion	104

4   The European Union and United Kingdom Transport Policy 106

The common transport policy of the European Union   107
Transport and the institutions of the Community   115
The legal competence of the Community in external affairs   124
Making policy in the European Union   125
The role of the British Houses of Parliament   127
The Europeanization of British transport policy   131

5   Planning 133

Forward planning   135
Spatial planning   146
Conclusion   158

6   Influencing Transport Policy 161

The principles of interest-group action   162
Explaining group influence   168
Characteristics of transport interest groups   171
The context of action   185
Access: insiders and outsiders   188
Political channels of influence: parliamentary committees   189
Conclusion   191

7   Engaging the Private Sector 194

Competition and deregulation of bus services   194
Competition and privatization of rail services   200
The London Underground Public–Private Partnership (PPP)   212

8   Paying for Transport: Appraisal and Economic Issues 218

Government spending on transport   219
Personal spending on transport   220
The distinction between specification and provision   221
National taxation   223
Local forms of taxation   223
Borrowing   228
Transport project appraisal, financing and pricing   232
Road pricing   239

9 Conclusions   245

Two major changes   245
Some theoretical reflections   249
Theory and practice   253
The key issues   258
The policy options   262
Conclusion   269

Guide to Further Reading   271

Bibliography   276

Index   287

List of Tables

2.1	Allocation of governmental responsibilities	44
2.2	Regulation of the transport industries	58
3.1	Delivering sustainable development	84
3.2	Metropolitan transport authorities	95
3.3	Rail passenger journeys, 2003–04	97
5.1	Forecast growth in road traffic and congestion	136
5.2	Road traffic in England: Plan scenarios	138
5.3	Road congestion in England: Plan scenarios	138
5.4	Rail traffic in England: Plan scenarios, 2000–10	139
5.5	Travel in London: Plan scenarios, 2000–10	140
5.6	Vehicle emissions: Plan scenarios, 2000–10	141
5.7	Comparison of outputs from Plan components	142
6.1	Department of transport advisory bodies	166
6.2	Business interest groups	172
6.3	Transport trade unions	175
6.4	Established transport interest groups	177
6.5	'Fire-fighting' or single-issue campaign groups	179

List of Figures

1.1 Transport policy 1555–1914: early development   4
1.2 Transport policy 1914–50: coordination and control   13
1.3 Transport policy after 1951: rediscovering competition   16
2.1 The structure of the Department for Transport, 2005   46
2.2 The structure of the rail industry in 1997   61
2.3 The structure of the rail industry in 2005   65
3.1 Organization of transport in London in 2006   98
4.1 The role and working relationships of the EU institutions   116
4.2 Structure of an explanatory memorandum   128
5.1 Main aims of a Regional Transport Strategy   151
6.1 Seat-belt networks   170
7.1 Hourly earnings of bus and train drivers   196
7.2 Train Operating Company bids and payments   203
7.3 Rail passenger-kilometres, 1908–2004   203
7.4 Train-kilometres, 1987–2003   204
8.1 Public expenditure on transport as a proportion of GDP   219
8.2 Transport prices relative to retail prices   221
8.3 Road schemes appraised by NATA in 1998   237
8.4 Planned public expenditure on strategic roads   238

List of Abbreviations

AA	Automobile Association
AME	Annually Managed Expenditure
APRs	Annual Progress Reports
ASLEF	Associated Society of Locomotive Engineers and Firemen
ATLB	Air Transport Licensing Board
ATOC	Association of Train Operating Companies
ATP	Automatic Train Protection
BA	British Airways
BAA	(formerly known as) British Airports Authority
BALPA	British Airline Pilots' Association
BATA	British Air Transport Association
BIDs	Business Improvement Districts
BTC	British Transport Commission
BUSK	Belt Up School Kids
CAA	Civil Aviation Authority
CBI	Confederation of British Industry
CEC	Commission of the European Communities
CfIT	Commission for Integrated Transport
CNT	*Conseil National des Transports*
COREPER	Committee of Permanent Representatives
CPA	Comprehensive Performance Assessment
CPRE	Council for the Protection of Rural England
CPT	Confederation of Passenger Transport
DBFO	design, build, finance, and operate
DEFRA	Department for Environment, Food and Rural Affairs
DETR	Department of the Environment, Transport and the Regions
DfT	Department for Transport
DG	Directorate General
DoE	Department of the Environment
DoT	Department of Transport
DPTAC	Disabled Persons Transport Advisory Committee
DTI	Department of Trade and Industry
ECAC	European Civil Aviation Conference
ECJ	European Court of Justice

EP	European Parliament
EWS	English, Welsh and Scottish Railways
FHANG	Federation of Heathrow Anti-Noise Groups
FoE	Friends of the Earth
FSS	formula spending share
FTA	Freight Transport Association
GDP	gross domestic product
GLA	Greater London Authority
GNP	gross national product
HACAN	Heathrow Association for the Control of Aircraft Noise
HMSO	Her Majesty's Stationery Office
HSE	Health and Safety Executive
ICAO	International Civil Aviation Organization
IMO	International Maritime Organization
IoD	Institute of Directors
LGB	Local Government Board
LPTB	London Passenger Transport Board
LRT	London Regional Transport
LTPs	Local Transport Plans
LUL	London Underground Limited
mppa	million passengers per annum
NAO	National Audit Office
NATA	New Approach to Appraisal
NATS	National Air Traffic Services
NBC	National Bus Company
NDR	non-domestic rate
nimby	not in my back yard
NNDR	national non-domestic rate
NUMAST	National Union of Marine, Aviation and Shipping Transport Officers
ODPM	Office of the Deputy Prime Minister
OFT	Office of Fair Trading
OPRAF	Office of Passenger Rail Franchising
ORR	Office of Rail Regulation
PFI	Private Finance Initiative
PPPs	Public–Private Partnerships
PTAs	Passenger Transport Authorities
PTEs	Passenger Transport Executives
RAC	Royal Automobile Club
RHA	Road Haulage Association
RIA	Road Improvement Association

RMT	Rail and Maritime Transport Union
Ro-Ro	roll-on roll-off
RoSPA	Royal Society for the Prevention of Accidents
RSPB	Royal Society for the Protection of Birds
RPI	Retail Price Index
RTS	Regional Transport Strategy
SACTRA	Standing Advisory Committee on Trunk Road Assessment
SGCI	*Secrétariat Général du Comité Interministériel pour les questions de coopération économique*
SMMT	Society of Motor Manufacturers and Traders
SRA	Strategic Rail Authority
TENs	Trans-European Networks
TEU	Treaty on European Union
TfL	Transport for London
TGWU	Transport and General Workers' Union
TIF	Transport Innovation Fund
TOCs	Train Operating Companies
TPPs	transport policies and programme submissions
TRL	Transport Research Laboratory
TSO	The Stationery Office
TSSA	Transport Salaried Staffs' Association
TUC	Trade Union Congress
TWA	Transport and Works Act
TWG	Transport Working Group
VAT	value added tax
VED	vehicle excise duty

Introduction

The first edition of this book was written as the New Labour government of 1997 set out to raise the profile of transport policy. John Prescott as Deputy Prime Minister took charge of a large Department of the Environment, Transport and the Regions, promising to shape for the twenty-first century an environmentally sustainable, integrated transport policy. Whilst ministers set out to give greater weight to environmental considerations, many key decisions would lie in the hands of regional and local authorities, independent users and largely privatized providers of transport services, acting within a new framework of economic regulation, much of it at arm's length from central government. The closing years of the twentieth century seemed likely to prove a critical period in British transport policy.

As this second edition goes to print, after nine years under New Labour governments, the wheel has turned, as it so often does in politics. There was indeed a period of several years on either side of the millennium when transport policy was close to the centre of political debate. There were Green Papers and White Papers and 10 Year Plans; parts of the newly privatized railway industry were pulled up by the roots and restructured following a series of railway accidents; the privatizations of air traffic services and the London Underground were hotly contested; a congestion charge was introduced in central London; fuel and vehicle taxation policies were adjusted in the face of strike action which almost brought the country to a standstill; and Secretaries of State came and went in rapid succession. Yet as this second edition was being prepared, there was once again a relatively small Department for Transport, under the direction of Alistair Darling, who kept the low profile traditionally associated with what used to be regarded as a rather unglamorous technical portfolio. Had nothing really changed? Was all the excitement a brief and anomalous departure from the dull, prosaic norm? Or will Douglas Alexander, the sharp young Secretary of State appointed in May 2006, give transport policy the political salience which we think its importance merits?

Every chapter of this book has been completely rewritten as we have observed and reflected on the turbulent events of the past few years. The historical narrative (Chapter 1) has been brought up to date. The scene is set, as before, with a brief survey of the history of

British transport policy which reaches back to the building of canals, turnpikes and railways, and takes us through two world wars to the concentration of power in the hands of the British Transport Commission. We then follow the rediscovery of competition, the policies of privatization and deregulation which have returned almost all the transport industries to the private sector, and finally the debates about the environment and sustainability which dominated the closing years of the twentieth century. Against the background of this narrative, we examine the institutions of central government (Chapter 2) and local government (Chapter 3) which shape policy at the heart of government and implement it at the grass roots. After pausing to examine the growing role of the European Union (EU) in the making and implementing of transport policy at all levels (Chapter 4) we explore first the planning system for transport and the environment (Chapter 5) and then the impact within all these legal and institutional frameworks of the numerous non-governmental bodies which seek to influence transport policy at every level, from local and regional authorities through Whitehall to Brussels and Strasbourg (Chapter 6). In all these areas there has been considerable change since the first edition; the influence of the European Union on British transport policy has advanced considerably with the progressive development of a common transport policy, and within the United Kingdom much decision-making has been devolved to regional and local governments, albeit within frameworks of policy guidance and financial control that are designed to maintain strategic control at the centre.

As British transport policy faces the challenges of the twenty-first century, the nature of the relationship between the public sector and the private sector is of fundamental importance. Against the background of the institutional context described in earlier chapters, we explore (Chapter 7) the remarkable variety of arrangements under which the private sector has been engaged, within contractual frameworks devised by successive Conservative and Labour governments, to operate local bus services, mainline railway services, and the London Underground. The hope was that engaging the private sector in the provision of public transport would deliver better quality services on the back of increased investment, whilst reducing the volume of public expenditure, and Chapter 7 considers whether this goal is likely to be achieved. Building on the evidence of these three important case studies, Chapter 8 goes on to examine the private and public sector sources of finance for all transport infrastructure and services, as well as the arrangements governing the appraisal of transport projects for government funding. It explores the merits of both existing and potential new sources of finance, including bonds and tolls, non-domestic rates and road charging, which are likely to be critical to any future debate about transport policy and investment in transport infrastructure. The final chapter seeks to draw the threads together, identifying the strengths and weaknesses of the practical, political and organizational arrangements which will shape and govern the future development of transport policy in Britain.

Pragmatism has played a large part in the development of transport policy in Britain. Although transport developed in the private sector, the earliest roads legislation dates back to the sixteenth century, and governments found it necessary to begin regulating railway safety as early as 1840 and even tariffs (from 1844) in order to safeguard the public interest. In the latter part of the nineteenth century, and more particularly with the advent of the motor car, governments came under increasing pressure to fund the building of roads, which became the first transport network to be developed in the public sector. In two world wars, transport had to be managed in the national interest, and helped through the difficult economic conditions which followed. The role of government grew continuously in response to these pragmatic demands until almost every aspect of transport policy and operations was subject to some degree of government ownership or control. The process of disengagement also began slowly and pragmatically, but after 1979 the political impetus of a radical Conservative government accelerated the process of change. The Labour government which followed at the turn of the century endeavoured for a while to pursue an alternative vision; the elusive concept of an environmentally sustainable, integrated transport policy. But the ideologies of Left and Right stand or fall by their results. Transport has to work. The operation of a modern economy as well as the enjoyment of a modern lifestyle depend on the smooth functioning of an efficient system of transport, and this drives transport policy ultimately towards pragmatic solutions, however they may be dressed up.

The issues raised by transport policy are complex and inter-disciplinary, even if the results are familiar and accessible. Arguably it is precisely the openness of British transport policy to both political pressures and pragmatic solutions that makes it so interesting to anyone with an interest in politics, economics, government, geography or social science. This book draws on the collective familiarity of the authors with all these disciplines, as well as our experience of transport policy-making both inside government and in various advisory capacities, to explore the structures, institutions and policy communities which work together to shape a policy that merits more attention both politically and academically than it has generally received.

Transport policy may have slipped down the political agenda for a while, but the pressures which brought it into the centre of political debate have not diminished. Traffic continues to grow at least as fast and often faster than the national economy. As incomes rise, people are prepared to spend more on transport, which lends powerful support to those who insist that the demand should be met. However, there is increasing resistance to the social costs of other people's transport, not only the burden of increased taxation to pay for infrastructure built in the public sector, but also the reduced amenity. People object to the damage done to both urban and rural neighbourhoods, the increased pollution and associated health risks which arise from exhaust gases, as well as their contribution to global warming, not to mention the noise and the perpetual glow of lighted highways which have banished darkness and starlight as well as peace and quiet from broad strips of countryside along the major transport arteries. These pressures and the resentment they generate can be hidden for a while if controversial road and rail schemes are avoided and environmental protest denied a focus for the media to report, but eventually, as congestion becomes more and more widespread and journey times lengthen, the issues posed by our reluctance to face up to the consequences of increased wealth, increased leisure and increased mobility will finally have to be faced. The technical, economic and social questions raised by road charging, for example, cannot always be for another day. It is our hope that this book will contribute to the broadly based and well informed discussion which must eventually carry transport policy back into the mainstream of political debate.

STEPHEN GLAISTER
JUNE BURNHAM
HANDLEY STEVENS
TONY TRAVERS

Crown copyright material in Tables 5.1, 5.2 and 5.3 and Figures 2.2 and 2.3 is reproduced with the permission of the Controller of Her Majesty's Stationery Office under click licence CO1W0000276. Figure 4.1 is reproduced by permission of Palgrave Macmillan.

Chapter 1

The Historical Context

From canals and turnpikes to state-regulated private railways

The crowds which gathered in October 1829 to watch the Rainhill trials, which resulted in the choice of Stephenson's 'Rocket' for the Liverpool and Manchester railway when it opened a year later, would have been proud of the tremendous advances in transport that had been made within their lifetime. As children some might have watched the construction of the Bridgewater Canal in the 1760s, in the same transport corridor between Manchester and Liverpool, signalling the start of the great era of canal building that by the end of the century had linked the Mersey first with the Trent and then with the Thames and Severn in a network which laid down the essential transport infrastructure for Britain's Industrial Revolution. Over the past decade or so the appalling state of the roads had been much improved by John Loudon Macadam's better surfaces and Thomas Telford's engineering on the London–Holyhead road, which together had reduced coach journey times between London and Manchester from four-and-a-half days with the first 'Flying Coaches' in 1754 to a mere 18 hours and 18 minutes by the 'Manchester Telegraph' in 1830 (Savage, 1966: 30). The canals and turnpikes were transporting goods and passengers more speedily and efficiently than before, but their monopoly position enabled them to charge excessive prices.

The new railway between Manchester and Liverpool promised vigorous competition, reducing the transit time from 36 hours to only five or six and cutting charges by a third. It was a huge success for both goods and passenger traffic; it was soon carrying nearly half-a-million passengers in a year. However, far from stimulating competition, it would not be long before the traders who applauded Stephenson's 'Rocket' would find they had exchanged one monopoly for another. The economic advantages of railways over canals and turnpikes were so great that within 25 years the railway network had grown to nearly 10,000 miles and had very largely

1

overwhelmed any competition there might have been at first from the canal companies and the turnpike trusts.

Given the success of private enterprise in so radically improving transport provision by water, by road and now by rail, it is not at all surprising that the liberal politicians of the nineteenth century were content to 'leave it to the market' to choose how and where to invest in service provision whilst using state intervention to limit monopoly profits and protect rights to life, liberty and property. They thought these rights should be defended, where necessary, by state regulation against large or monopoly enterprises. Thus one of the earliest pieces of rail legislation was the Railway Regulation Act 1840 empowering the Board of Trade to appoint railway inspectors to check new passenger lines and receive information about rail accidents. The Whigs (or Liberals) were more willing to intervene in a 'utilitarian' search for efficiency, and to defend rail users, especially small businesses. The Tories (or Conservatives) were more protective of property-owners' rights. But all were 'free market' when contrasted with the Labour Party of the following century, which expected to plan and coordinate transport through centralization and nationalization (Morrison, 1933). With these principles in mind it is easier to understand the route transport policy took.

Once the steam locomotive was developed, high canal charges stimulated the rapid construction of commercial rail lines, though opposition from canal-owners and landowners demanding high compensation made the passage of private bills difficult (or at least expensive). Rail companies needed parliamentary approval to come into being, but Parliament took only limited interest in the 'network' which was being created, ad hoc, from local lines. In 1844, the growing pressure of private rail bills encouraged MPs to set up a select committee on railways, chaired by William Gladstone, then a 'Peelite' (liberal Tory) and President of the Board of Trade. The committee wanted the construction of lines to be more rational. It thought the duplication of lines would take trade from existing companies without necessarily keeping prices down. Gladstone set up a railways board within the Trade department to oversee railway promotion, but the railway interest groups opposed it. Peel abolished it in 1845 after Gladstone left the department, and between 1845 and 1847 Parliament approved 425 Acts covering more than 8,500 miles of railway.

The oligopolistic competition of the early 1840s soon gave way to a process of consolidation which progressively limited competition as moves towards the creation of a more coherent rail network were taken by the rail companies themselves. The Railway Clearing House had already been established voluntarily by companies to facilitate through-traffic across company boundaries when it was made statutory in 1846. The same year also saw the passage of 18 Acts sanctioning railway company amalgamations, including the London and North Western Railway, the major trunk route between London and Manchester/Liverpool via Birmingham. The taking over of weaker companies by successful ones from the 1840s improved coordination and efficiency without government having to act. From the mid-1850s until after the First World War the railways enjoyed an almost complete monopoly of inland passenger and freight transport. Few British canals remained prosperous after the 1840s and by 1850 stage coaches had been all but driven off the road. Parliament worried about the establishment of monopolies in certain regions, but in 1872 a select committee concluded that railway amalgamations were inevitable and perhaps desirable. Product emulation, such as the copying by all railways of Midland Railways' third-class carriages, had improved and standardized service quality. In 1909, following another wave of amalgamations, a Departmental Committee on Railway Agreements and Amalgamations concluded that some regulation of cooperation would be to the advantage of the public as well as the railway companies.

In these circumstances the main role of government, exercised through the Board of Trade, was to defend the trading community against the monopoly power of the railway companies. Gladstone's 1844 Railway Regulation Act gave the government the option of revising prices downwards if a company paid dividends of 10 per cent or more, and the right of compulsory purchase after 21 years, though these options were never exercised. The so-called 'Parliamentary' train, under the same Act, was an early instance of consumer protection. All companies were required to provide one return passenger train a day at a reasonable speed (at least 12 mph) and maximum fare (1d or 0.4p a mile). In 1854, under a coalition government, Parliament passed the Railway and Canal Traffic Act which required each railway company to take all trade offered (to be 'a common carrier'). They had to set and publish the same levels of fares and charges to all for any particular service (that is, not give 'undue preference'). Though the state did not intervene directly in rail provision, neither did it allow rail companies to set tariffs flexibly on strictly commercial criteria, or pick and choose between the types of traffic they would carry.

1555	Highways Act: parishes to maintain roads using their own labour and equipment.
1663	First Turnpike Trust established under private Act of Parliament. Creation of about 1,000 Trusts administering some 22,000 miles of road by 1830. Acts allowed companies to charge tolls to finance improvements and repairs.
1767	Bridgewater Canal opened, linking Manchester and Liverpool.
1791–4	Height of canal investment boom, with 81 canal bills in Parliament. Main network in place by about 1800.
1820	Macadam pioneered improved road surfaces. Telford improved road engineering (for example on London–Holyhead road).
1830	Opening of Liverpool and Manchester Railway.
1835	General Highway Act replaced statute labour for parish roads with power to levy a rate.
1840	Railway Regulation Act: Board of Trade could appoint railway inspectors.
1846	Rail gauge standardized at four feet eight-and-a-half inches. 219 private bills in Parliament at height of railways investment boom: mileage increased from 2,000 miles in 1843 to nearly 10,000 miles by 1854. Mileage reached 15,000 in 1870, 23,000 in 1910, falling back to 15,000 in 1960 and 10,000 today.
1854	Railway and Canal Traffic Act prohibited undue or unreasonable preference in setting fares and required the provision of convenient interchange.
1873	Railway Commission – from 1888 Railway and Canal Commission – established as regulator at arm's length from Board of Trade.
1894	Railway and Canal Traffic Act froze rail freight rates for a generation by giving traders a right of appeal to Railway and Canal Commission against any increase.
1910	Lloyd George introduced Road Fund and Road Board. All revenue from vehicle licences and fuel duty put into Road Fund. Raided for other purposes from 1926, subsumed into general budget from 1937.

FIGURE 1.1   *Transport policy 1555–1914: early development*

Even so, under the multitude of private Acts of Parliament the railway companies retained extensive scope to exploit their monopoly position, and as the process of railway amalgamations proceeded, the trading community, often powerless in the face of a monopoly carrier, became increasingly agitated. The Railway and Canal Traffic Act of 1873 compelled the publication of all rates in force, broken down into their component elements, and set up a Railway Commission to enforce the legislation requiring the railways to offer the same rate to all their customers, but the legal situation was complex and the Commission lacked teeth. Eventually the Railway and Canal Traffic Acts of 1888 and 1894 required companies to set maximum rates which could not be raised without the permission of the Railway and Canal Commission (a Board of Trade-appointed quango). This Act was to prove all too effective in constraining the commercial flexibility of the railway companies. They could not raise their rates without permission, which was hard to obtain, and they dared not lower them – even to attract new business – for fear that they would be unable to raise them again if the lower rate proved uneconomic. The combined effect of more than 50 years of monopoly domination of the transport market, together with a degree of government regulation that tended to stifle any commercial initiative which might have survived, left the railways ill-prepared to face effective competition from road transport when that began to emerge after the First World War (see Figure 1.1 for a summary of developments).

From local to national roads: the creation of the Road Board

Before the canals were built in the closing years of the eighteenth century, navigable waterways were used to bring goods as far inland as possible, and then they had to be carried by pack horses. Since 1555 road maintenance had been a parish responsibility, relying on local labour and equipment which had to be supplied gratis for up to six consecutive days in a year. It was not till 1835 that the statutory labour requirement was replaced by the right to levy a rate, and even then the control of the work was left in the often ill-qualified hands of locally appointed surveyors. The development of Turnpike Trusts after 1663, and especially in the second half of the eighteenth century, created about 20,000 miles of better roads, particularly once their administration and surfacing was improved after 1810 under the influence of Macadam. But even the improved road surfaces could not tolerate the heavy loads which might have been conveyed by steam-driven road vehicles, and the condition of the turnpikes deteriorated when they became uneconomic in the face of railway competition. The Trusts themselves were gradually abolished by Parliament between 1870 and 1890, the burden of maintenance being thrown back on the parish authorities who could not afford to maintain roads to suitable standards for faster, long-distance traffic, or did not see why they should do so. From 1876 they had some help from a government grant, and after 1878 there were contributions from county funds. But it was only with the Local Government Act of 1888 that the parishes were relieved of part of their ancient responsibility, the maintenance of main roads being transferred to the county councils with additional aid from the government Exchequer.

Part of the impetus for this important change seems to have come from the touring cyclists of the 1880s. In 1886 the Cyclists' Tourist Club and the National Cyclists' Union set up a joint body, the Road Improvement Association (RIA), to campaign to improve road surfaces. The transfer of highways maintenance to the new county councils and county boroughs created in 1888 was said to be as a result of RIA pressure (Hamer, 1987: 23). However, the roads were not much improved, and the RIA itself soon ran out of funds. When the (Royal) Automobile Club (RAC) was set up in 1897 as a 'gentlemen's club' for motorists it joined the RIA, whose honorary secretary from 1901 was William Rees Jeffreys, then a civil servant at the Board of Trade. The motorists revived the RIA. There was little opposition to motor vehicles from the railway lobby until the 1920s; it thought they would act as 'feeders' for rail, bringing goods and passengers to stations. The anti-motor lobby was made up of horsebreeders and residents of rural areas who worried about accidents; they thought motorists should pay for road maintenance. County magistrates imposed high speeding fines because until 1920 the money subsidized the rates (Plowden, 1971: 64).

In 1901 the RIA sent a delegation to the Local Government Board (LGB) proposing that a single-purpose, national body should be set up to control and develop the road system. The LGB recommended setting up county road boards, to be given grants in proportion to the class of road. The government appointed a Royal Commission to look at possible legislation on speed limits and roads finance. The Commission decided motorists, not ratepayers, should pay, probably through vehicle taxation. However, the LGB was unwilling to administer it. The RAC suggested a Road Fund, administered by a central highways department and financed by taxation on vehicles. But the government found it difficult to implement the Commission's report on road finance because the conflict over speed limits had not been settled (Plowden, 1971: 75–8).

Both the anti-motorist campaign and the roads lobby became increasingly active. In 1908 the Chancellor, David Lloyd George, told RAC members he wanted to increase revenue from vehicles through a tax on petrol; in return he would do what he could for roads. He argued that the amount raised would not justify a special roads board. However, the Treasury did not want money raised and spent from this special tax to form part of the general budget, because it might lead to further hypothecation (earmarking) of the budget (Plowden, 1971: 88–9). In the 1909 budget Lloyd George introduced the Road Fund, to be administered by a public body, the Road Board. The revenue from vehicle and fuel taxes would be spent on roads.

Rees Jeffreys was appointed secretary of the Road Board; it was chaired by a railway director. Plowden criticized the Road Board for building no new roads, allocating nearly all grants to small-scale improvements, and failing to spend its income. Rees Jeffreys blamed opposition from the Treasury, landowners and the railways, but a civil service inquiry found the board was badly administered and had insufficient technical expertise (Plowden, 1971: 101). During its short life, 1910–20, the Road Board received £16 million, committed £13 million and spent only £7 million (Savage, 1966: 149). But from 1914 the local authorities, because of wartime restrictions and increases in costs of labour and materials, were unable to take on the reconstruction or improvement of roads, even though vehicle use multiplied.

Road versus rail, 1919–39

In 1918–19 the government took a series of steps to remedy the problems of roads and road transport made apparent by the war. In 1919 the newly created Ministry of Transport took over the powers and functions of the Road Board, and the duties of the Local Government Board in regulating traffic, road design and road vehicles. The ministry co-financed the highways work of local authorities from the Road Fund, the grant depending on the class of road. It employed a divisional road engineer in nine regions in England and Wales from 1919 (the origin of its modern regional offices) to advise it on road funding priorities. Partly as a consequence of RIA pressure, the Local Government Act 1929 transferred most of the important roads from districts to counties (Hamer, 1987: 32). County boroughs, small in area but with a county's powers, remained responsible for all roads within their boundaries, in return for central government taking over their Poor Law (social welfare) duties in 1929; this arrangement's consequences still linger since main road improvements often halted at their boundaries until county boroughs were abolished in 1974. Under the Trunk

Roads Act 1936 the Ministry of Transport took over from counties full financial liability for 4,500 miles of roads of national importance. The Road Fund had been 'raided' by Churchill and other Chancellors from 1926, and was wound up in 1937 (though the name lingered on), vehicle receipts becoming part of general Exchequer funds.

During the First World War the railways had been controlled by the government and run by an executive committee of rail company managers. In 1919 a decision had to be made on how the railways should be returned to the private sector. Coordinating and pooling arrangements during the war had saved costs, suggesting there should not be a return to the pre-war network of more than 130 separate lines and 21 major companies (Savage, 1966: 98–9). Four regional groupings were created.

Thus the four 'historic' railway companies (LNER, LMS, Southern, and Great Western) were less the product of private enterprise than of the rationalizing efforts of government, Parliament and the Ministry of Transport, as promulgated in the Railways Act 1921. Brunner refers to the 'partial nationalization' of the railways because the charges set by these railways, each given a virtual monopoly, were in government hands (Brunner, 1929: 89). The Railway Rates Tribunal, whose members were appointed by the Minister of Transport, the President of the Board of Trade and the Lord Chancellor, replaced the Railway and Canal Commission. The Act gave little incentive for rail companies to increase efficiency or improve services. Rules on revenue and prices meant companies would retain only a small proportion of any economies made. Employees could not be given a worse post in a new company than they held in a pre-war company, which resulted in over-manning at senior levels compared with firms in other sectors, according to Brunner, who campaigned against the railways, 'the proud monopolists of the transport world' (1929: 48, 26). Though it proved easier than expected to get the approval of the Railway Rates Tribunal to increase charges, if only because the railways never reached the target revenues based on their 1913 results which they were not to exceed, the heavy hand of price regulation nevertheless seriously handicapped the rail companies in competing with road transport. Rates had to be published and were determined on a value-for-weight basis, which implied high charges for carrying valuable manufactured goods, and low charges for bulky and heavy commodities such as coal. The charges had to be the same right across the network and could not show undue preference to any particular customer over another. Customers could demand the disaggregation of the rate charged into its component elements (such as collection, transit and delivery) and choose which parts of the service they would take from the railway and which they would do themselves or offer to road freight carriers who were not subject to price or quantity regulation (until 1933) and who would take goods at any price that covered their costs (Savage, 1966: 141–6). Between 1919 and 1938 rail freight tonnage for general merchandise declined by a third (Gwilliam, 1964: 90). The regulatory arrangements, made on the assumption the rail industry was a monopolistic predator, made it difficult for rail to compete effectively with road transport.

By the end of the 1920s the railway's effective monopoly was reduced to 'very long-distance express passenger traffic, outer-suburban business traffic . . . coals and minerals, and the coarsest and lowest classes of goods traffic' (Brunner, 1929: 32). There had been an increase not only in road haulage contractors but in firms distributing their own goods. There were commercial advantages for companies in being able to ensure the delivery of goods on time and securely in vehicles that advertised the firm's name. Rail's advantages over road on freight were mainly in heavy, bulky goods and over long distances; but heavy industries were in decline and British industrial geography was relatively compact. In passenger transport, rail was already losing first-class fares in the late 1920s because that section of the population could afford cars. Rail had chosen to compete on speed of journey, but not on costs or quality of service; and it was nearly always at a disadvantage on ease of access compared with lorries, cars or buses. Whereas at the beginning of the century it had seemed that road and rail transport would be complementary (operating in different markets), they were now competing for the same goods or travellers.

Brunner argues that the demand for 'coordination' of road and rail in the 1920s came from the railway companies, worried about the trade they were losing to road traffic (1929: 88–9). The road transport lobby's suspicions were fuelled by the rail companies' campaign to run road services, culminating in the Railway (Road Transport) Act of 1928. Rail companies were seen as trying to change 'from railway companies to general operators of transport services' (1929: 71). Rail companies said their users, unlike road users, had to pay the full cost of transport, including track costs: a continuing and familiar complaint. Road transport interests said they were unfairly taxed. Figures produced by Christopher Savage

(1966: 174) show that motor taxation receipts (fuel tax, vehicle and licence duties) exceeded road expenditure (by local and central government) until 1932, but after that date the inverse was true. Social and environmental costs, from coal-fired engines as well as motor vehicles, did not at that time figure much in transport or any other calculations.

In response to such disputes, and concern about the large number of road accidents (killing about 3,000 pedestrians a year; see Hamer, 1987: 31), Baldwin's Conservative government in 1928 appointed a Royal Commission on Transport to consider road traffic control and safety, how best to review the deployment of transport resources 'to the greatest public advantage', and to propose how they should be better regulated and controlled in the public interest 'to promote their coordinated working and development' (Royal Commission on Transport, 1930: vii). The Commission's recommendations on the licensing of motor vehicles and drivers, and on the regulation of passenger services, were implemented in the Road Traffic Act 1930 introduced by Herbert Morrison, the transport minister in MacDonald's Labour minority government.

Until 1930 the licensing of buses and coaches was the responsibility of local authorities but not always taken seriously. During the Depression bus operators and owner-drivers were more likely to work long hours at low capacity and little profit. The Road Traffic Act 1930 put in place a series of Area Traffic Commissioners, appointed by the Minister of Transport, who worked as quasi-judicial bodies, examining applications for licences from bus and coach operators. They were expected to 'introduce stability into an industry where competition was resulting in chronic instability'. The Commissioners restricted entry to the road passenger industry by requiring applicants for licences to show the public need for the additional service. Existing operators on a route were protected from newer applicants. Local buses and regular train services were protected from long-distance coaches; long-distance coaches were protected from tour operators. Tramways were given some protection from buses. The Commissioners' work was somewhat contradictory in that one of their purposes was to weed out those operators working unprofitably, yet they also had to look at the overall needs of the area, including the provision of unremunerative services. Licence applicants felt they had to provide some services on unrewarding routes or at unrewarding hours as evidence of a 'public service' commitment. The Commissioners had powers to ensure fares were not 'unreasonable', and could fix them 'so as to prevent wasteful competition', yet their deliberate use of cross-subsidy as a condition of granting licences made it difficult for them to determine what was a reasonable fare. Stability was introduced 'in the public interest' by protecting existing operators from new enterprises and from the market discipline of route profitability, but such a policy was not necessarily in the public interest (Savage, 1966: 154–62).

Despite their terms of reference (see above), the Commission's 1930 Report said little on 'coordination'. The government therefore asked a conference of road and rail interests to find a fair regulatory system for road haulage. The result was the Road and Rail Traffic Act 1933, which required the Area Traffic Commissioners to regulate road haulage under a system of quantity licensing like that introduced for buses. Applicants for road freight licences had to prove a need for new licences, and incumbents, including the railways, could object. The principle used in granting licences was again that 'wasteful competition' was against the public interest. Licences were often refused on the grounds that new services would abstract revenues from the railways. The system caused distortions, leading to a few, over-large firms, though traders carrying their own goods were less severely constrained than hauliers carrying goods on contract. 'The effects of the Act of 1933 were therefore to check the growth of a highly competitive industry' (Savage, 1966: 171). Chester expressed the 'liberal' aims of the legislation in a classic formula. The 'legislation concerning railways and tramways . . . was designed to obtain some of the benefits of competition in an industry mainly monopolistic, whilst the [Road Traffic Act 1930] was introduced to secure the benefits of monopoly in an industry mainly competitive' (Chester, 1936: 198). Savage summed up in the 1960s the balance of advantages of a regulated passenger transport industry in terms that would be used again in the 1980s when deregulation became the transport policy in vogue. The 1930 system had produced safer, more reliable services; but protecting the 'little monopolies' by barring the entry to newcomers, and not relying on the normal economic criterion of profitability, had over-emphasized stability at the cost of enterprise (Savage, 1966: 162).

The most significant move towards transport coordination through structural integration before the Second World War was the creation of the London Passenger Transport Board (LPTB). It was expected to solve the particularly acute problems in the capital caused by the growth of traffic, road congestion and bus competition, especially through developing the Underground. The prime movers were Lord Ashfield, who chaired London Underground, and Herbert Morrison, Minister of Transport and former Labour leader of the London County Council. The private and municipal transport companies in the London area were transferred to the LPTB in 1933. Mainline railway companies were excluded but they and the LPTB were required to share receipts from services provided by joint lines and within the London area: Ashfield had organized a similar agreement on a voluntary basis since 1929. The London Passenger Transport Act 1933 made LPTB a monopoly provider of road passenger transport in London. The performance of the new system proved difficult to judge, partly because it had only six years to establish itself before the impact of the Second World War. Operating costs increased, for which growing traffic congestion – the very thing it was supposed to reduce – was held to blame (Savage, 1966: 164). However, its success in administering a coordinated transport service appeared to provide a good model for full-scale nationalization of transport services after the war.

Post-war nationalization and the switch to roads

During the Second World War the government took overall control of rail transport. Road transport was more difficult to organize because of the multiplicity of small operators, and in 1943 the government set up a fleet of lorries hired from their owners. For the post-war Labour government there was no question of returning the controlled enterprises to the private sector. The Transport Act 1947 created the British Transport Commission (BTC), operating through separate executives dealing with rail, canals, road transport, and London transport. The main exception was in road freight, since licensed short-distance hauliers were left out of the BTC, and firms could still transport their own goods.

Since the purpose of the BTC was to provide an integrated system, financial control was given to the BTC, not the separate executives. This arrangement perpetuated the accounting practices of the railway companies by allowing cross-subsidy between different parts of the operation, and between different financial years. It hid changes in rail use and allowed the postponement of difficult decisions. BTC's charges were regulated by a Transport Tribunal and ministerial directives, and both the Tribunal and ministers used their powers to limit BTC's proposed fare increases even where it would worsen deficits (Gwilliam, 1964: 96–8). Manufacturers

1914–18	First World War. Railways controlled by government.
1919	Creation of Ministry of Transport, which subsumes Road Board.
1921	Railways Act moved towards state control. Railways amalgamated into four regional groups; maximum rates under 1894 Act replaced from 1928 by standard rates, which could be varied to achieve net revenue equivalent to that earned in 1913.
1928	Royal Commission on Transport (Final Report 1930) established to improve regulation and control of the available means of transport and 'to promote their coordinated working and development'.
1930	Road Traffic Act established licensing system for bus services under Area Traffic Commissioners responsible for licensing both vehicles and services.
1933	Road and Rail Traffic Act established licensing system for goods vehicles, also under the Area Traffic Commissioners. Licences to be granted only on basis of proof of public need.
1933	London Passenger Transport Act established Board to own all Underground railways and bus companies serving London.
1936	Trunk Roads Act transferred responsibility for 4,500 miles of trunk roads to Ministry of Transport.
1939	Amalgamation of Imperial Airways and British Airways to form state corporation: granted monopoly of scheduled air services from 1946.
1939–45	Second World War. Most transport under government control.
1947	Transport Act nationalized railways, long-distance road haulage, parts of road passenger transport, London Transport, canals, all to be run by the British Transport Commission, charged with providing a 'properly integrated system of public inland transport'.

FIGURE 1.2   *Transport policy 1914–50: coordination and control*

exploited rail's value-based pricing structures and obligation to take all trade by sending 'expensive' loads in their own lorries, and 'difficult' loads by rail. Changes were in any case taking place in the relative popularity of the two modes of transport (Figure 1.2 summarizes developments to this point).

The changing preferences in transport from rail to road for both goods and people had been masked in the 1940s by wartime and post-war fuel rationing and by the need to increase vehicle exports. Savage (1966: 178–81) gives some comparative figures which show clearly the difficulties facing the rail executive. In 1963 there were almost four times as many motor vehicles as in 1939, and about two-and-a-half times as many as in 1951. The number of goods vehicles had risen by over 300 per cent between 1939 and 1963, and these vehicles were likely to be larger than before. The number of buses and coaches had risen from about 50,000 to about 80,000, though growth had ceased by the early 1960s as passenger journeys started to fall. Rail freight traffic increased enormously during the war but fell back to pre-war levels after 1948. Rail passenger traffic was fairly stable but was thought to have combined decline on some, especially rural, lines with increased demand on others. However, rail was not sharing in the general increase in people's expenditure in the same way car travel did. Between 1950 and 1960 expenditure on cars (including running costs) rose by 400 per cent; expenditure on travel by public transport was unchanged.

The growth of road traffic was seriously under-estimated by the Ministry of Transport in the 1950s and later decades, and indeed there is some doubt about the actual figures for road passenger transport and car mileage in the 1950s and 1960s (Savage, 1966: 180–2), a problem that was bound to affect the drawing-up of realistic policies for both rail and roads. The Ministry's permanent secretary in the early 1960s expressed his regret that British governments had not been able to improve run-down or inadequate infrastructure in the 1950s and 1960s.

> There was naturally considerable enthusiasm both at headquarters and among local authorities to get on with things, many of which had been planned in detail before the war started . . . When, then, decisions were taken which made it clear that nearly all schemes would have to go back into the pigeon hole the result was, to say the least of it, discouraging. (Dunnett, 1962: 259)

There is reason to believe the Treasury would not have entertained the idea of an increase in roads spending even had transport forecasts been more realistic: in 1952 the Treasury said it would be satisfied if the ministry continued its roads spending at about 70 per cent of the 1938 figure (Savage, 1966: 199–200). However, the debate about spending priorities might have been conducted in different terms if the growth in traffic had been recognized earlier.

Coordination and control

During the nineteenth century the public demand for coordination, articulated by Gladstone and others, had been largely met by voluntary cooperation among the railway companies themselves, within a framework of government oversight designed to control any abuse of their monopoly power. Coordination with other modes of transport was not an issue after 1850 because there was no other mode of transport which needed to be coordinated with rail in the public interest. Canal transport had been largely superseded. Coastal shipping remained important but was not in direct competition, and horse-drawn road services concentrated on local business which included feeder services to the railway. Each mode had its own clearly defined market and, so far as coordination was required, it was in the interests of both parties to cooperate in ensuring it.

The experience of transport coordination during the First World War, and thereafter the growth of competition between road and rail, prompted a more active approach to coordination. In 1919 the most urgent task of the new Ministry of Transport was to put the railways back on a commercial footing, but when financial problems persisted and seemed to be exacerbated by growing competition from commercial road transport, the response of the Royal Commission of 1928–30 and the government of the day, embodied in the Acts of 1930 and 1933, was to seek to manage the market through licensing and control, first of road passenger services and then of road freight haulage.

The Second World War again seemed to demonstrate what could be achieved in the national interest when all transport provision was centrally coordinated, and the British Transport Commission, established under the Transport Act 1947 (as seen above), was designed to provide 'an efficient, adequate, economical and properly integrated system of public inland transport'. This was the high water mark of government coordination and control of the transport industries. However, extensive government ownership failed to deliver the benefits which had been hoped for, and over the succeeding 50 years, especially after 1979, most of the transport industries were returned to private ownership with an emphasis on the benefits of commercial disciplines and competition. In the end the zeal with which this process was carried out, and the rough edges of competition which it exposed here and there, reawakened old concerns for coordination and tougher regulation in the public interest, enhanced by a new concern for the effect of transport on the environment; and in 1997 a government was once again elected with a commitment to establish and develop 'an effective and integrated transport policy at national, regional and local level that will

1953	Transport Act denationalized long-distance road haulage.
1960	Civil Aviation (Licensing) Act creates Air Transport Licensing Board with duty to 'foster the development of British civil aviation'.
1962	Transport Act abolishes British Transport Commission, but retains railways, docks, canals, London Transport in separate public ownership. Coordination is assigned to an advisory council for nationalized transport.
1963	Beeching Report on the Reshaping of British Railways recommends closure to passenger traffic of 2,000 stations and 5,000 miles of track.
1963	Buchanan Report on Traffic in Towns suggests more investment to separate vehicles from pedestrians.
1968	Transport Act endeavours to put railways on a more commercial footing. Road haulage released from capacity controls.
1969–72	Passenger Transport Authorities created in six major English metropolitan areas.
1971	Civil Aviation Act establishes Civil Aviation Authority leading to the gradual licensing of more competition.
1980	Transport Act deregulates long-distance coach services.
1982	Sale of National Freight Corporation completes the privatization of the road haulage industry.
1984	White Paper on Buses, implemented through Transport Act 1985, leads to deregulation of bus services, break-up and sale of National Bus Company.
1984	White Paper on Airline Competition opens domestic market to competition.
1985	White Paper on Airports leads to privatization of British Airports Authority.
1987	Privatization of British Airways.
1989	Dock Work Act abolishes dock labour scheme, opening market to competition.
1991	Ports Act enables trust ports to become private sector companies.
1993–7	Break-up and privatization of British Rail under Railways Act 1993.
1996	National Air Traffic Services becomes public limited company within the Civil Aviation Authority; converted to Public–Private Partnership in 2001.
2001	Public–Private Partnership established for London Underground.

FIGURE 1.3   *Transport policy after 1951: rediscovering competition*

provide genuine choice to meet people's transport needs' (Labour Party, 1997: 29). An 'integrated transport' White Paper (Department of the Environment, Transport and the Regions, or DETR, 1998) was followed by a 10 Year Plan under the same banner (DETR, 2000). In the last section of this chapter we examine the record of what has actually been done, but there has certainly been no return to the policies of central coordination and control which failed after 1947 (see Figure 1.3 for a summary).

Rediscovering competition

Although the liberalization of the transport industries was driven through most vigorously between 1979 and 1997, under the Conservative governments of Margaret Thatcher and John Major (which were imbued with a conviction that the public interest was best served by moving the transport industries into the private sector), the process had begun in the early 1950s under the first post-war Conservative governments, which privatized but did not deregulate the road haulage industry. It was carried forward by the Labour governments of 1964–70, particularly in respect of road haulage and civil aviation, and the last monuments to the old orthodoxy of public ownership and control were demolished by Labour after 1997, albeit in the form of Public–Private Partnerships (PPPs) for air traffic control and the London Underground.

Under the Labour governments of 1964–70 there was at first a return to policies favouring coordination through integration and public control, but when public expenditure had to be reined in after the devaluation crisis of 1967, the benefits of competition and a more commercial approach to the provision of transport services once again gained ground, particularly in respect of road haulage and civil aviation. Similarly, the Labour government after 1997 was strongly attracted to an integrated transport policy, but its actions, including the two PPPs as well as the steps it has taken to reassert public control over the hastily privatized rail network (see below), have been more pragmatic than ideological. David Starkie (1982: 145–8) remarked that the continuity in road policy-making from the Second World War to the 1980s showed little sign of party-political influence. The motorway building programme reflected a practical response from all sides to a growth in road traffic, at a time when concern for the environment was regarded as eccentric. Road-building was highly conflictual, but the conflict was mainly between policy-makers and local people who suffered the impact of the new construction. It was spurred on or held back by financial considerations, but not much by party ideology, and that has remained the case. It was convenient to advance environmental grounds for cutting the road-building programme after 1997, but construction resumed when public expenditure constraints became less acute.

In road haulage, liberalization began with the Conservative government's Transport Act 1953 which aimed to denationalize those parts of road haulage which Labour had nationalized. The attempt to privatize the whole of the British Road Service fleet was only abandoned when some vehicles found no buyers. However, the 1953 Act left in place the quantity licensing regime in force since 1933 under the Area Traffic Commissioners. The Geddes Committee, appointed by a Conservative government to inquire into the way licensing was working, recommended the abolition of all restrictions on the capacity of the road haulage industry. Its report, *Carrier Licensing* (1965), was received by a Labour government, which passed the Transport Act 1968 abolishing capacity controls on all vehicles under 16 tonnes, but tightened the safety regulations and proposed to maintain control on heavy lorries. In the event a Conservative government was returned before these latter provisions entered into effect, and capacity controls were abolished completely from December 1970.

As a 'quid pro quo' for road freight privatization in the 1953 Act the government simultaneously removed the requirement on the railways not 'to show undue preference' between traders, in order not to worsen rail's financial position relative to road haulage (Gwilliam, 1964: 100–1). The Railway Executive was replaced by six area boards, whose general managers were told to modernize and compete with other modes of transport. However, in 1960 a Select Committee inquiry showed modernization programmes had been embarked upon with no clear idea of their value, and that the debts incurred would not be balanced by increased traffic. The Committee's report also criticized governments over the years for muddling commercial criteria and social needs in their expectations of the BTC. In 1962 the government abolished the BTC, and reconstituted the British Railways Board, putting an outsider, Dr Beeching, in charge. The railway would no longer have to take all goods as 'a common carrier' or have its charges approved by the Transport Tribunal. While remaining within the public sector, it was promised more commercial freedom.

The reforms broke up what was left of the 'integrated transport' organization which the BTC had been supposed to bring about. Moreover, Beeching's investigations into the rail network broke it up financially so that for the first time the viability of each part became explicit. His report, *The Reshaping of British Railways*

(British Railways Board, 1963), was criticized for its narrow definition of costs (for example, not taking account of social or economic development needs, or of savings in urban congestion or environmental damage). His recommendations for widespread closures of loss-making stations and lines horrified many politicians, especially in the Labour government which had to implement his closure programme after winning the 1964 election, and some loss-making lines remained open into the 1990s. But the Beeching exercise was a necessary first step in 'transparency', relating public subsidy to specific lines and services so that decisions about whether to keep them open could be based on accurate information.

In those respects the Buchanan Report on roads, *Traffic in Towns* (1963), performed a similar service in making policy-makers and citizens consider the consequences for the physical and social environment of allowing urban traffic to grow unchecked, except by congestion. The alternative was high expenditure on reconstruction (opponents called it destruction), to accommodate traffic but separate it from residential and pedestrian areas. A different approach was offered by the Transport Act 1968, an important piece of Labour legislation, which made provision for government subsidy of unprofitable but socially-necessary public transport. The Act created 'Passenger Transport Authorities' (PTAs) in four of the conurbations outside London (two more were added under the Local Government Act 1972), whose remit was to develop and improve the coordination of services as the London Transport Board was seen to have done. In these areas the British Railways Board did not control rail services but supplied them on contract to the PTAs, who specified the terms and recovered any subsidies from the constituent local governments. They coordinated bus and rail services and fares across the modes of transport until the deregulation of bus services (outside London) in the 1985 Transport Act, but the abolition of the metropolitan county councils in 1986 and the privatization of rail services under the Railways Act 1993 changed the structure within which they worked twice in a decade.

The first steps towards the gradual relaxation of state control over civil aviation took place in 1960. Many of the companies which had pioneered air services in the 1930s, under licences issued by the Air Ministry, were small independent operators (though some were partly owned by the railways), but competition among them gave rise to a rather unstable pattern of services; in 1938, following the recommendations of the Maybury Committee in

1937, an Air Transport Licensing Authority was established. This was followed by the 1939 amalgamation of Imperial Airways and British Airways, and after the war the state corporation was granted a monopoly of all air services. From 1948 independent companies were allowed to operate complementary services under associate-ship agreements, but it was not until 1960 that the Air Transport Licensing Board (ATLB) was required to issue licences 'in such a manner as to further the development of British civil aviation' (Civil Aviation (Licensing) Act 1960). This half-open door proved unsatis-factory. The decisions of the ATLB were hard to predict, and in any case a dissatisfied party could appeal to the minister, who might take a different view. There was a gradual growth of scheduled services provided they did not compete too directly with the state corpora-tions (by now British European Airways and British Overseas Airways Corporation), but the private companies found more scope for their initiative and enterprise in the development of charter services for the growing market in inclusive tour holidays.

The Civil Aviation Act of 1971, which established the Civil Aviation Authority (CAA) in place of the ATLB and promoted the recently formed British Caledonian Airways as a second force inde-pendent airline, was passed under a Conservative government, but it was based on the recommendations of the Edwards Committee, set up by Labour. The CAA was itself a nationalized industry, but the guidance it received from government on the licensing of air services was published; fewer decisions were overturned by minis-ters on appeal; and gradually through the 1970s the CAA fostered the development of a competitive industry, albeit under policy guidelines which continued to give priority in scheduled service provision to British Airways and British Caledonian.

Privatization and deregulation

Under the Conservative governments of 1979 to 1997, policy was characterized by a much more radical commitment to privatization and deregulation. The government which came to power with Margaret Thatcher in 1979 was determined to remove barriers to competition, in order to foster the free market in the belief that this would encourage efficiency. Norman Fowler had written a pamphlet in 1977 arguing that there was no reason for the strict system of quantity regulation in the bus industry to be maintained. He became Secretary of State for Transport in 1979, and one of the new government's first pieces of legislation was the deregulation of long-distance bus services (discussed below). The prime aim was to reduce the involvement of the state to a minimum.

The Conservative government subsequently discovered additional motives for privatization. The sale of British Telecom demonstrated the substantial sums privatization could generate to meet the cost of public expenditure without having to raise taxes. Transport privatizations in the period 1982–84 (National Freight, British Rail Hotels and Sealink, Associated British Ports and Jaguar) yielded about £500 million. By contrast, transport privatizations in the years 1987–88 (British Airways, Rolls-Royce aero engines, British Airports and the National Bus Company) yielded about £4 billion (Banister, 1994: 73). It was thought too that privatization could be used to introduce the experience of share ownership to a much wider range of people, in the expectation they would continue to hold shares and thus perhaps become more sympathetic to the values espoused by the Conservative Party.

However, there may well be a conflict between the desire to promote competition and the desire to sell public utilities at a good price for the benefit of the Exchequer. For example, the sale of the British Airports Authority as a single entity handed it a virtual monopoly of airports in the London area. In the case of London Buses (see below and Chapter 7), Price Waterhouse was asked to have regard to both competition and proceeds in its advice to the Department of Transport. The number of companies was more or less determined by the existing structure, but there was debate over whether it would be better to sell companies off one-by-one, simultaneously or in a few groups to maximize the proceeds. Yet there was also serious consideration of the terms under which companies would be free to vary their services (for example, to compete with a neighbouring company). Ministers wanted them to have more freedom to innovate than had been allowed under LRT in the past, but there were fears that complete deregulation would cause chaos on the streets of central London, and would also reduce the potential proceeds of the sale. It was therefore decided that whilst deregulation should remain the long-term policy objective, London Transport Buses would retain a powerful role as regulator for the time being.

Aviation and shipping

The intention to privatize British Airways (BA) was announced in July 1979, within weeks of Mrs Thatcher's first government being elected, and the legislative framework was provided in the Civil Aviation Act 1980. However, the recession of the early 1980s delayed the privatization of BA until January 1987. The 1980 Act also required the CAA to give the interests of airline users equal standing in its licensing decisions with those of service providers. As a result British Midland was allowed to open services from London Heathrow to Belfast, Edinburgh and Glasgow in direct competition with BA, whilst Cathay Pacific and British Caledonian were both allowed to start services to Hong Kong, albeit from London Gatwick. In October 1984 another White Paper on Airline Competition encouraged the CAA to further relax its domestic licensing regime by allowing airlines to serve any routes within the UK, and removing the requirement for fares to be approved specifically. The White Paper also committed the government to a policy of liberalizing the bilateral and multilateral agreements under which international air services are operated, especially within the European Community, and this goal was very largely achieved between 1983 and 1992 (see Chapter 4).

Most major British airports have been privatized. In June 1985 the Airports Policy White Paper paved the way for the British Airports Authority to be privatized as a holding company (BAA plc) for its airports, including three around London and four in Scotland. Many other British airports are owned by local authorities (for example, Manchester, Birmingham, Luton) who are reluctant to privatize them, and the government has stopped short of requiring them to do so; but they have been encouraged to involve the private sector to the maximum extent possible, especially in the provision of capital facilities, such as the Eurohub air terminal at Birmingham which is owned by BA.

There was less need to liberalize and deregulate the shipping industry since the principal companies have never been in the public sector, and economic regulation has long been liberal. The only significant privatizations were the sale of British Rail's ferry operator, Sealink, and of the Scottish ferry operator, Caledonian MacBrayne. There was more need to open up the ports industry to market forces. The Dock Labour Scheme, which required the registration of dockworkers and the licensing of their employers, was abolished by the Dock Work Act 1989. It opened the labour market to competition, and provided substantial compensation to those dockers who were made redundant within three years: a high proportion of those registered. The Ports Act 1991 enabled the major trading trust ports, which are autonomous statutory corporations, to become private-sector companies, and several of the larger ports soon took advantage of this opportunity to move into the private sector. By 1993 well over half British national port capacity was owned or run by private-sector companies (Department of Transport, or DoT, 1993: 125), but plans to force the privatization of the remaining trust ports were shelved by the Labour government of 1997 (DETR, 1998: 102).

With the exception of a few local authority ports and airports, the aviation and shipping industries and their infrastructure are now very largely in private ownership. The result is an industry which is considerably more competitive than it was in the 1970s, and which provides a more responsive service to its customers.

Road freight

The deregulation of the road haulage sector predates the liberalizing agenda of Margaret Thatcher's post-1979 administration by more than a decade. The quantitative licensing regime which had restricted competition between road and rail since 1933 was swept away under the Transport Act 1968, which provided for licences to be issued freely to road haulage operators by the Traffic Commissioners provided that they could demonstrate professional competence, good repute and sound financial standing. The remainder of the state holding, the National Freight Consortium, was sold in a management buy-out in 1982, and has subsequently proved to be a profitable business. Having qualified for a licence, operators must also meet various regulations on vehicle safety and drivers' hours, including requirements agreed with other EU states, as shown in Chapter 4. Road haulage now has many of the classic characteristics of a free entry, competitive industry; that is, low profits, a substantial turnover of firms entering and leaving the industry, and widely varying firm sizes. A large proportion of output is produced by single-vehicle, owner-driver firms. Distance travelled per vehicle increased from 60,000 km to 75,000 km a year during the 1980s. Real operating costs decreased by an average of 2.5 per cent a year followed closely by haulage prices to users. There have been policy reviews of the sector but in recent years no strong arguments have been advanced for making further changes to the economic regulation of the system.

Long-distance (express) coaches

Norman Fowler's Transport Act of 1980, deregulating coach services, applied to long-distance 'express' coaches (as distinct from local services), which were previously defined as services with a minimum passenger journey length of 30 miles. In the legislation the criterion was adjusted to 15 miles, bringing more services into the deregulation provision. Most services were then being operated by the state-owned National Bus Company (NBC). Outside the major conurbations NBC also ran the majority of local services, under the supervision of the Traffic Commissioners in place since 1930, who restricted quantity and controlled fares. In the new legislation all quantity and price restrictions were removed; the residual regulations related, as in road freight, to relatively uncontroversial safety requirements. However, the NBC itself was not privatized at that time.

Initially there was large-scale competitive entry to the business. Fares fell markedly and the volume of services increased. Other attributes of service quality also changed: product differentiation emerged with the introduction of luxury vehicles with television screens and steward services on board. Nevertheless, the competition was fairly quickly defeated by the NBC who re-emerged as the dominant operator because of three factors: first, the NBC was a good, experienced bus operator which was able to respond to the spur of competition by improving its own efficiency; second, it was allowed to keep exclusive rights to the existing major coach terminals, Victoria in central London in particular, where 25 per cent of passengers transferred to other routes; third, it was alleged it used profits earned in some of its local businesses to cross-subsidize the long-distance business.

These last two features were clear failings of the deregulation process. The government did not recognize that if competitive forces are relied upon to police a market then it must ensure there are no substantial barriers to competition. The failings were corrected in the 1985 Transport Act: the NBC was broken into a large number of distinct companies and all hidden cross-subsidy was prevented. Equal access was granted to terminal facilities, and the Victoria coach station was transferred to London Transport. Since then the benefits of the deregulation of express coaching seem to have stabilized. Fares fell and service levels improved relative to the period just before deregulation, as shown by Thompson and Whitfield (in Bishop, Kay and Mayer, 1995a). As in the case of road freight, the success of deregulation and privatization of long-distance bus services can be attributed to the benefits of promoting competition both in the market for passengers and in the markets in which inputs are procured by the bus companies.

Bus deregulation

Although the government expressed hopes of increased patronage and lower fares, the prime motivation for the policy of bus deregulation was to change the way the industry worked in order to meet the overall goal of reducing subsidy whilst minimizing the damage done to passengers by increases in fares and reductions in service. The policy was laid out in Nicholas Ridley's White Paper, *Buses* (DoT, 1984), which contained three main proposals:

1   *Privatization.* The nationalized National Bus Company was to be broken up into a large number of smaller entities and sold to the private sector. The remaining publicly-owned operators, in the metropolitan counties and other municipal enterprises, were to be made into regular, 'arm's-length' companies, owned by the local authorities but with normal company accounts.
2   *Deregulation.* Safety regulation would remain essentially unchanged, but the controls over service provision would be swept away. Instead of having to apply for a road-service licence specifying the services to be operated, the bus companies would simply be required to register the routes and timings of their services, and give notice of their intention to commence or withdraw a service, or to make significant changes.
3   *Subsidies.* Companies were to register only those routes and services they were willing to operate on a commercial basis, without subsidy. It would then be for the local authority to secure any additional, subsidized, routes or services they considered necessary through a competitive tendering process which gave equal access to any operator who cared to bid.

The government believed the publicly-owned bus companies (including the National Bus Company), protected from competition and subsidized by local authorities, had become inefficient, and that free competition among private companies was the way to drive down costs, and in consequence the volume of subsidy provided through public expenditure. On the basis of investigations of bus operators' costs and the level of earnings in the industry by comparison with other similar industries such as road haulage, the White Paper concluded that 'the potential exists for cost reductions of up to 30 per cent of total costs of public operators' (DoT, 1984: para. 4.10).

In the public debate that followed, many of those involved in the industry advocated an alternative approach based on some system of requiring authorities to put routes out to tender, but disallowing free competition on the road. This option, which was later adopted in London, became summarized as competition *for* the route rather than competition *on* the route. Gwilliam, Nash and Mackie give good contemporary statements of the arguments (1985 and 1985a). Their argument was that tendering would avoid the risks perceived from deregulation, such as bad behaviour on the road in the attempt to win passengers; and that it would allow local authorities to keep control of fares and to plan an integrated set of services with cross-subsidy, perhaps optimally adjusted according to the principles of the second best familiar to economists. At the same time competition for tenders would provide the required pressure on costs. Glaister (1985) and Beesley (1985) gave counter-arguments and responses.

The government went ahead with its proposals in the Transport Act 1985. All the former NBC companies were sold within a couple of years and the new deregulated regime took effect, after a short transitional period, on 1 January 1987. The consequences for competition are discussed in Chapter 7; it is sufficient to note here that a far higher proportion of routes was registered as commercial than anyone had predicted – over 80 per cent – and the cost to public expenditure fell dramatically. Although some municipal bus companies have remained under local authority ownership, a considerable number were sold, so that by the mid-1990s the industry was substantially in private hands.

Railways

Consideration of the options for rail privatization began under Margaret Thatcher, but the debate was inconclusive until John Major included it in his manifesto for the 1992 election. In July proposals were outlined in a White Paper, *New Opportunities for the Railways* (DoT, 1992a), and legislation was rushed through Parliament in the next session, allowing very little time for informed debate either in public or in Parliament. The main thrust of the policy was to break up the monopoly, which was perceived as showing 'too little responsiveness to customers' needs, whether passenger or freight; no real competition; and too little diversity and innovation' (John MacGregor, Secretary of State for Transport, *HC Debates*, 2 February 1993: 124). This was to be achieved by fragmenting the railway into a large number of private businesses, linked to one another by a network of service contracts. The Railways Act reached the statute book in November 1993, ushering in three-and-a-half years of intensive activity as some 80 separate companies were formed, and train services were franchised out to 25 operating companies (see Chapter 2 for a description of the resulting structure). The organizational changes proceeded more smoothly than opponents had expected, and almost immediately, with the sale of Railtrack, went further than envisaged, so that the whole process was completed just before the general election of May 1997. After 18 years of Conservative governments, the only transport industries left in the public sector were air traffic control and the London Underground, and these would soon follow, even under a Labour government.

Transport and the environment

Transport projects are controversial and arouse strong passions in their advocates and their opponents. In the past people have sat down in the street to demand much-needed bypasses, and new transport ministers are always surprised by the constant stream of delegations led by constituency MPs who come to make the case for particular new roads or road improvements. But the same schemes may well prompt others to climb into trees and barricade themselves into houses and even tunnels under the ground to protest against the destruction of the urban and the rural environment. The physical obstruction of road-building activity became larger in scale during the 1990s and the techniques used more sophisticated, winning more media coverage and increasing the cost to the authorities and therefore to the taxpayer. But such scenes were not new; they were only the latest in a long line of protests which have focused public attention on the cost to local communities of new structures cutting a swathe through city neighbourhoods or attractive countryside. The history of such protests dates back to the Westway extension of the A40 through North Kensington in the 1960s or the Third London Airport proposals in the 1970s, and even to the objections which were raised to the building of the railways in the nineteenth century.

As recently as the early 1980s it was possible to dismiss most such objectors as belonging to the 'not in my back yard' tendency, but the increasing importance which needed to be attached to the environmental implications of transport policy came to the fore as a national concern following publication of the White Paper, *Roads for Prosperity* (DoT, 1989). Responding to the rapidly-worsening road congestion which accompanied the economic boom of the late 1980s – traffic increased by 7 per cent in 1989 alone – and a new national road traffic forecast which predicted further increases of between 87 per cent and 142 per cent by 2025, *Roads for Prosperity* proposed a substantial increase in the road building programme to keep traffic moving. The new programme was welcomed by the Freight Transport Association (FTA) and the Confederation of British Industry (CBI), which pointed to the heavy economic costs associated with congestion, but the climate of public opinion was changing. New doubts were beginning to be expressed by those who argued that providing for increased road transport on the scale proposed would do unacceptable damage to the environment.

Such views had been heard before, and ignored, but when the Green Party won 15 per cent of the votes in the 1989 elections for the European Parliament, all the major political parties were obliged to review their policies and give themselves a greener image. The Department of the Environment published *This Common Inheritance* (DoE, 1990), which was followed in July 1991 by the Department of Transport's own report, *Transport and the Environment* (DoT, 1991). The DoT report acknowledged the importance of environmental concerns, and explained what the department was already doing to address them, but it also drew attention to the requirements of a growing economy, making the point that 'we must accept that preserving the environment has a cost and be prepared to bear it' (1991: 3). Treasury ministers were not slow to spot the opportunity presented. The pre-election budget of November 1991 had been generous to transport but, a year later, following the Earth Summit at Rio de Janeiro with its high-profile focus on climate change and global warming, the Chancellor of the Exchequer (who by then urgently wanted to redress the balance between taxation and public expenditure), found it irresistibly convenient to increase fuel duty immediately by 10 per cent, and to announce a commitment to further annual increases of a minimum of 5 per cent above the rate of inflation, which he could justify as being required to encourage consumers to demand, and manufacturers to design, cars whose emissions would cause less of the pollution believed to contribute so much to global warming.

Raising fuel duties was a significant practical move, but it was only one aspect of the commitment to 'sustainable development' which was the central feature of the Earth Summit. Sustainable development had been defined by the 1987 World Commission on Environment and Development as 'development which meets the needs of the present without compromising the ability of future generations to meet their own needs'. In 1994, as a direct response to its Earth Summit commitments, the government published a White Paper setting out a wide-ranging strategy for sustainable development (DoE, 1994). The transport chapter of that document (ch. 26), stronger on analysis than on prescription, noted the commitment to annual fuel duty increases as the main means of reducing transport emissions of carbon dioxide, and EU plans to tighten up on other standards governing exhaust emissions. It drew attention to the forthcoming planning guidance (PPG13) as a longer-term means of reducing the demand for transport, but it also included a justification of the road building programme on the grounds that a smooth flow of traffic causes less pollution than stop-start conditions on heavily congested roads. Looking to a future in which it might be 'no longer acceptable to build some roads', in which case 'prices and physical management measures would be the best way to ration the limited resource', the White Paper confirmed the government's intention, already announced in 1993 (DoT, 1993a), 'of introducing electronic tolling on the motorway network when the technology is available. Motorway charging will help to address congestion from rising demands for road capacity as the economy grows. It will improve the competitive position of rail and other forms of transport' (DoE, 1994: paras 26.33–4).

Further work has followed from the 1994 White Paper. The Department of the Environment and the Government Statistical Services (1996) published a set of some 120 indicators of sustainable development for the UK. The indicators for energy use and for transport use since 1970 showed that, whereas there had been dramatic increases in the fuel efficiency of the industrial and commercial sectors, there had been little change in the fuel efficiency of road transport. Passenger mileage by car had doubled while rail mileage had remained about the same, and bus mileage had fallen by a quarter. As a result transport was burning twice as much fuel in 1995 as it had done 25 years before, with obvious consequences not only for the depletion of energy reserves but for the volume of exhaust emission gases.

Meanwhile, the Royal Commission on Environmental Pollution (1994) had published a major report on *Transport and the Environment* (known as the Houghton Report), which advocated a wide range of policies to reduce the impact of transport on the environment, and proposed demanding targets for the reduction of transport-related sources of pollution to be backed up by severe measures to achieve them. Shortly afterwards the Standing Advisory Committee on Trunk Road Assessment (SACTRA, 1994) published evidence that new roads intended to alleviate congestion may themselves be responsible for generating significant volumes of additional traffic. For 30 years traffic generation had been ignored in the economic appraisal of road schemes because it was harder to evaluate than the benefits to existing traffic, and not regarded as significant for decision-making – if it occurred it was probably a bonus, suggesting that the new road link had increased economic activity – but, following SACTRA's 1994 report, the government accepted that the likely significance of traffic generation should in future be assessed in the case of every scheme in the national roads programme (DoT, 1996: paras 11.54–5).

Faced with this growing body of weighty advice calling into question many of the fundamental tenets of transport policy, the then Secretary of State, Dr Brian Mawhinney, used a series of speeches in 1995 to air the many issues which needed to be addressed in what he called a national debate on transport policy. His speeches, published as a consultation document (DoT, 1995) covered all the main issues: a competitive economy, impact on the environment, the special features of freight transport and of urban transport, and not least the thorny issues associated with freedom and personal choice. Echoing the position which Malcolm Rifkind had taken five years earlier in his foreword to *Transport and the Environment*, Dr Mawhinney concluded his speech on transport choices with these words:

> We must be realistic in our debate. It is not the role of Government – certainly not a Conservative Government – to limit people's choices unnecessarily. Our instinct is to extend choice and to allow individuals to make decisions that best suit them. By the same token, people must not feel that there is little that they can do as individuals. On the contrary, there is a great deal they can do. I would like those who put forward calls for great national strategies to recognise this. (DoT, 1995: 51)

More than 260 organizations and individuals set out their views in response to the invitation to participate, and in April 1996 the government published its response, *Transport: The Way Forward*

(DoT, 1996), taking the same opportunity to respond formally to the 1994 Houghton Report. After such an extensive and serious re-examination of transport policy over several years, culminating in more than a year of a national debate, there were hopes that this new statement would attempt to answer the many important questions which had been raised. In the event, the Green Paper was little more than a skilful restatement of the problem with some limited development of current policies, such as the constructive suggestion that national trunk road planning might be adjusted to take more account of regional priorities and local needs (1996: ch. 11 and Annex 1), as the newspapers were quick to recognize (*Guardian*, 26 April 1996: 'Transport policy going nowhere'; and *Independent*, the same day: 'Transport paper opts for the easy route').

The numerous targets proposed by the Houghton Report were largely dismissed on the grounds that no one knew what measures might be needed to attain them or what such measures might cost. The government preferred to wait and see how local authorities got on with achieving the targets some of them had set. Comparisons with other countries (particularly those which suggested that the UK could aim for a higher proportion of passengers and freight to be carried by public transport) were dismissed on the grounds that circumstances in other countries are different, which is no doubt true but scarcely a sufficient response. Although the government seemed to have come close to recognizing in the course of the debate that restraining traffic would require some combination of the stick and the carrot, the only carrot on offer was the expectation that privatized public transport would be more attractive than it was in the public sector.

Transport: The Way Forward shied away from using regulation or charging to discourage further growth in the use of the car, and the Annexes contained much detail about the difficulties surrounding any evaluation of the environmental costs which the motorist ought to be asked to bear (DoT, 1996: paras 8.16, 9.3 and Annexes 4 and 5). There were plans to start trials 'to explore whether it is technologically feasible to introduce electronic tolling on motorways', but any positive commitment to charging was limited to the use of the existing economic instruments, namely vehicle excise duty and fuel duty. Progress has been slow since November 1993 when the government first announced its intention to introduce motorway tolling when the technology was available.

The indecision which characterized the Conservative government's response to the transport debate was perhaps no more than could be expected of an end-of-term government, reluctant to make policy commitments which could threaten an already fragile parliamentary majority. Whatever the cause, the Green Paper took refuge in worthy generalities, insisting that transport policy must reconcile the desire for a healthy, sustainable environment with the aim for a prosperous, competitive economy under conditions of careful control over public spending. The summary concluded, with becoming modesty, that:

> It is not a prescription for all time. Public attitudes on what measures are acceptable is bound to continue to evolve [*sic*]. But we need to change the way we think about transport; and this paper is intended as an important milestone on the way ahead. (DoT, 1996: 12, 14)

The rise and fall of an integrated transport policy

In May 1996, within weeks of the Conservative government's Green Paper, the Labour Party issued its own document, *Consensus for Change*. It declared that a consensus had now emerged to the effect that we 'should not try to build roads to keep up with projected traffic growth' and 'we need better public transport in order to keep the roads moving'. Within this new consensus Labour looked forward to working with Public–Private Partnerships (the Labour successor to the Private Finance Initiative: see Chapter 8) and local–national partnerships 'to create the long-term thinking, combined with urgent action, that our transport needs require'. In contrast to the fragmentation and lack of direction which was perceived as characteristic of Conservative transport policy, *Consensus for Change* advocated an integrated transport policy – integration between different areas of policy, different levels of government, different areas of the country and different transport modes and operators – and this was duly reflected in the Labour Party's election manifesto.

The Labour government which took office in May 1997 took an immediate first step towards a more integrated policy when it created a large Department of the Environment, Transport and the Regions. This arrangement brought together policies for transport, planning and the environment under a senior Secretary of State: indeed, John Prescott was additionally Deputy Prime Minister (see Chapter 2). On 5 June 1997, in a speech to mark World

Environment Day, he nailed his colours to the mast, inviting his audience and the general public to judge him against the promise he made that 'within five years, more people will be using public transport and driving their cars less' (*Independent,* 6 June 1997). He accepted that some policies needed to protect the environment would be unpopular with voters, and promised to lead the battle to win over public opinion, but he seems to have under-estimated the scale of the challenge he faced, and the strength of the opposition he would provoke from the motoring lobby. Roads spending was cut forthwith, and in July 1998 the White Paper *A New Deal for Transport* (DETR, 1998), reflecting 'the Government's commitment to giving transport the highest possible priority', set out policies for sustainable and integrated transport, with a Commission for Integrated Transport being established to provide ongoing advice. The hope was that better public transport could persuade more people to use it, leaving their cars in the garage. Building more roads was not the answer, though there was scope to improve the management of the existing network, and new powers would be needed to impose congestion charging in cities, to tax workplace parking, and to introduce road charging. The new approach would cut pollution and enable Britain to meet its obligations on climate change. The White Paper was followed by a succession of seven more detailed daughter documents on different aspects of transport policy, and finally, in July 2000, by *Transport 2010: The 10 Year Plan* (DETR, 2000).

Rarely if ever can transport policy have had such a clear sense of direction, or such comprehensive plans for delivery; but, in retrospect, the 10 Year Plan turned out to be the high water mark of New Labour's commitment to an integrated and sustainable transport policy. The government's enthusiasm for an environmentally-sustainable transport policy had created the impression that they were anti-car, and the Conservative opposition was quick to exploit this. Moreover, with public expenditure severely constrained, public transport was not getting any better. By the summer of 1999 a *Guardian*/ICM poll identified transport as Labour's least successful policy. The Prime Minister will not have been pleased when he was forced to defend in Parliament his own use of the empty bus lane on the M4 between Heathrow Airport and central London, when his official car had got caught in the traffic jam caused – or at least exacerbated – by the new restriction (*HC Debates*, 23 June 1999: 1,167). It was presumably not the car John Prescott had in mind when he declared that he wanted buses in cities to go faster than cars (*Guardian*, 6 June 1997). Even before the launch of the Commission for Integrated Transport, a separate Motorists Forum and a Road Haulage Forum had been set up to head off some of the criticism which was building up, and in the 1999 summer reshuffle Lord (Gus) Macdonald, a tough Glaswegian media magnate, was sent in to sort the Department out, and in particular to oversee preparation of the 10 Year Plan. This Plan provided for £180 billion to be shared more or less equally between roads, rail and public transport. Nearly half of the new investment (£56 billion out of £120 billion) was to come from the private sector, and although rail investment (£49 billion) was expected to be three times the investment in strategic roads (£16 billion), the difference was almost entirely accounted for by the forecasts for private investment (rail: £34.3 billion, roads: £2.6 billion). Alongside all the assertions about more and better public transport provision, 100 new bypasses were promised, and 360 miles of motorway and trunk road were to be widened. Despite this evidence that the government was not anti-car, the allegations still would not go away.

Scarcely was the ink dry on the 10 Year Plan when rising fuel prices triggered protest movements all over Europe. There is a strong tradition of direct action in France, which rarely spreads to other European countries, but on this occasion when the blockades of ports mounted by French fishermen and road hauliers succeeded in extracting fuel tax concessions, a spark was carried across the Channel which ignited an almost spontaneous protest movement. Farmers for Action UK, a loose association led by an angry group of Welsh farmers and hauliers, set out to blockade major refineries and oil depots, and in mid-September came close to shutting off the supply of fuel to industry and petrol stations. For the first time since 1997, Labour fell behind the Conservatives in the opinion polls. The government refused to make any immediate concession, but ministers were sufficiently shaken by the scale of popular support for the farmers and hauliers to promise a review of vehicle taxation in the next budget. The outcome, trailed in Gordon Brown's pre-budget report on 8 November but not implemented until the budget itself in the following March, was a major cut in the tax on heavy vehicles, bringing British taxes more in line with the rest of Europe, and the abandonment of the automatic higher-than-inflation increases in fuel tax, which had been applied by successive Chancellors since 1992. This measure had done more than anything else to restrict traffic growth, and its abandonment, contributing to increases in traffic, congestion and associated carbon dioxide emissions, raises serious questions about the depth of New Labour's commitment to sustainable transport policies.

From autumn 2000 the DETR, continually represented in the Press as 'beleaguered' or 'embattled', fought a losing public relations battle in defence of its transport policy. Addressing the CBI Conference on 7 November, the day before the Chancellor announced reduced fuel taxes, Lord Macdonald made the most of the 10 Year Plan's roads programme, which had delighted the business community in the summer. But he was clearly on the defensive:

> We are pro-car and want better, safer, less congested roads. The car will remain the only realistic option for many journeys, especially in rural areas. A car must be affordable to those single parents and the shift workers juggling complicated lives. A car can help get people back to work and reduce social exclusion. So the 10 Year Plan will deliver as much for roads as for any other mode – £59 billion in total investment. Pro-car but anti-pollution, anti-congestion.

But the media and the public were not listening. By the time this speech and the Chancellor's concessions were being made, the sense of disarray, which had begun to overtake the Department's road transport policy with the fuel price protests in September, had also engulfed its public transport policies. The immediate cause was a railway accident at Hatfield on 17 October, caused by a broken rail, which threw a sharp spotlight onto Railtrack's poor maintenance of the railway infrastructure (Wolmar, 2001). In November, dividend payments to Railtrack's shareholders went ahead as planned, but the travelling public had to put up with a massive programme of speed restrictions, delays and cancellations. These in turn led to reduced payments from the train operating companies to Railtrack, helping to precipitate a financial crisis in a company already wrestling with the consequences of massive over-expenditure on the rebuilding of the West Coast Main Line. As the crisis at Railtrack deepened, it cast doubt on the capacity of John Prescott's department to deliver the improved public transport system which was critical to his ambition to reduce dependence on the car. Politically, the DETR's management and presentation of an integrated transport strategy had been a disaster. The department was perceived as both anti-car and as having failed in its responsibility to make provision for a safe and reliable system of public transport.

Following the election of May 2001, the Prime Minister took the opportunity to dismember the DETR. Environment was separated from transport immediately, and planning was unhooked a year later when a further reshuffle was precipitated by the resignation of Stephen Byers, whose tenure as Secretary of State had been punctuated by crises over his management of the department's relations with the media, as well as the controversial manner in which he finally pushed Railtrack into administration. His successor, Alistair Darling, was probably under instructions to keep transport out of the news altogether by following less controversial policies. The political risk inherent in the introduction of congestion charging was successfully carried by the Mayor of London. Mr Darling proved a persuasive advocate of road charging, but not till 2014; and the road charging scheme for lorries, expected to be introduced earlier, was postponed indefinitely. The road-building programme, severely cut back in 1997 and partially restored by the 10 Year Plan, was further boosted in December 2002 and again in July 2003 in the face of the inexorable growth in car use and associated congestion. Another step difficult to reconcile with sustainable transport policies was taken in December 2003, when an aviation White Paper (Department for Transport, or DfT, 2003), similarly reverting to old habits of 'predict and provide', made provision for a major expansion of airports capacity at 20 airports throughout the country, including a new runway at London Stansted by 2012, and another at either Heathrow or Gatwick by 2020. The Commission for Integrated Transport, whose Chair commented that a large road building programme without road pricing 'is as ludicrous as giving a heroin addict a last fix' (*The Economist*, 14 December 2002), has been largely side-lined with the establishment of an influential transport policy unit within the Prime Minister's office, and in July 2004 a further White Paper, *The Future of Transport* (DfT, 2004) gave formal expression to the balanced, pragmatic policies which were once more in favour. Faced with popular demand for affordable motoring, more roads and cheap flights, the most striking feature of New Labour's transport policy since 2000 has been its growing resemblance to the Conservative policies of the 1980s and 1990s. If there has been a consensus, it does not appear to have been the consensus for change so confidently proclaimed by New Labour in the foreword to the 1998 White Paper, which launched the integrated transport policy. On the contrary, the major actions of the Labour government suggest a consensus for continuity rather than the radical programme of change which was promised. Whilst road building was first cut and then restored, the last of the transport industries were being moved out into the private sector.

Privatization of National Air Traffic Services

The Civil Aviation Authority remains the regulator, but its other functions have been further reduced. In 1996, in preparation for the eventual privatization of air traffic control services, National Air Traffic Services (NATS) was established as a public limited company within the CAA. The Labour government of 1997 was torn between reluctance to privatize a safety-related public service on the one hand, and the requirement to raise large sums of money for investment in new en-route air traffic control centres. The urgent need for investment carried the day and, since this could not be funded from public expenditure, negotiations with the interested parties led in July 2001 to a Public–Private Partnership, under which a consortium of British airlines paid £750 million for a 46 per cent stake in the company, and the staff received 5 per cent to overcome their opposition to privatization and give them a continuing stake in the company's success. The government retained 49 per cent, but with NATS ownership predominantly in the private sector, its investment would no longer count as public expenditure. As the regulator for the aviation industry the CAA's remaining functions are now mainly safety-related, though it also retains economic functions (for example, in advising the government on the need for airport expansion, licensing airlines for specific international routes and approving international fares) where these functions are required by international agreements.

Privatization of the London Underground

When the New Labour government was elected in 1997, the only remaining transport business of any size still owned and operated by central government as a nationalized industry was the London Underground. John Major had identified London Underground Limited (LUL) as a candidate for privatization at the Conservative Party conference in October 1996, but it was known to have an investment backlog of £1.2 billion, which was more than the likely proceeds of sale, so the formal announcement in February 1997, which promised reinvestment of the proceeds, amounted to a giveaway offer. The Labour opposition immediately countered with an undertaking to keep LUL in public control, and when this undertaking had to be squared after the election with the urgent need to remove LUL capital investment from hard-pressed government expenditure, John Prescott proposed a PPP, under which private consortia would bid to take over the infrastructure, and maintain and renew it for 30 years under contract to LUL, whilst services would continue to be run by LUL within the public sector. The attraction of this scheme was that it would take all infrastructure investment into the private sector, whilst honouring the undertaking to keep the services themselves in public control.

The intention was to complete the process before May 2000, the date set for the election of a London Mayor, and one year before the earliest likely date of a general election, but this plan ran into serious difficulties, both practical and political. The contracts which had to be agreed before bids could be invited for the infrastructure companies were highly complex, but the greater difficulty arose from the determined opposition of Ken Livingstone who, as candidate for Mayor, denounced the proposal as a partial privatization, and said that he would keep a unified underground railway in public ownership, raising money by means of a bond issue (the approach followed in the United States). Following his election he commissioned an independent review by Will Hutton, Chief Executive of the Industrial Society, which also favoured bonds, and raised doubts about the proposals, including their safety implications (*Guardian*, 25 September 2000). He further strengthened his position, and set himself on a collision course with the government, by appointing Bob Kiley, who had run the New York Subway, to be his Commissioner for Transport; and he resisted transfer of responsibility to Transport for London (TfL) unless and until his concerns were met. In the early months of 2001, as the PPP negotiations approached completion, the Health and Safety Executive, whose approval would be required by law, found 69 significant issues in the proposed contract which needed to be addressed; the National Audit Office said the case for franchising the infrastructure remained 'unproven'; and Parliament's Transport Select Committee joined the chorus, describing the PPP as a 'convoluted compromise'. Kiley was briefly appointed Chair of London Transport to lead the negotiations, and although he was sacked after ten weeks when about to publicize another report critical of the PPP, the final contracts strengthened substantially his control as TfL's Commissioner for Transport, and that of the London Underground as service operator, over the companies taking on the ownership, maintenance and renewal of the infrastructure. Moreover, permission was subsequently given by the government for TfL to raise additional money for investment by issuing bonds.

Railway privatization revisited

Meanwhile the government's relations with the privatized railway industry were running into ever greater difficulty. The government's supporters among the railway unions had always been opposed to privatization, as an article of political faith no doubt, but also because the fragmentation of the industry diminished their own power; and the government itself, having opposed privatization in opposition, was distinctly ambivalent about the arrangements it had inherited. Having accepted their predecessors' limits on public expenditure for the first two years, they could not afford to buy the railway back into the public sector even if they might have wished to do so. However, as we shall see in Chapter 7, the complex new structure was subject to intense strains and stresses, and as these came under the spotlight of critical opinion in the wake of a series of accidents, the government had the opportunity to modify both the regulatory arrangements and the structure of companies.

They began by establishing a Strategic Rail Authority, a toothless body at first, but one which eventually grew to absorb the Office of Passenger Rail Franchising, as well as some consumer protection functions previously carried out by the Office of Rail Regulation. A major opportunity to reverse the privatization process occurred in October 2001, when Railtrack's share price collapsed as a result of the surging expenditure on track maintenance, authorized in the wake of the accident at Hatfield in October 2000 (see above). The government took Railtrack into administration and restructured it as Network Rail, a not-for-profit company answerable to a 115-member public interest board, but the new company was still classified as falling outside the public sector for public expenditure purposes. By the summer of 2004 Network Rail had taken back under its own management the contracted-out track maintenance work which had contributed to the accidents at Hatfield and at Potters Bar (May 2002), and in April 2005 a new Railways Act abolished the Strategic Rail Authority, taking its functions back into the Department for Transport. The balance between private and public sector control has certainly shifted back towards the public sector, but it is arguable that the strategy behind these changes has had more to do with the control of public expenditure than with any intention to reverse the process of privatization. The current structure, as well as the original fully-privatized structure, are both described in Chapter 2.

Conclusion

The brief survey in this chapter has traced the evolution of transport policy from its origins in the regulation of privately-owned providers of transport services in the interests of safety and the public interest, through a brief period in the middle of the twentieth century when, as a result of two world wars, the government assumed direct responsibility for the operation of most transport services within the public sector, to the progressive re-creation of a pattern of service provision mainly within the private sector under government regulation. There was a clear ideological basis for such policies under the Conservative administrations of Margaret Thatcher and John Major, but very similar policies have been carried forward since 1997 by a government which set out, under John Prescott's over-arching Department of the Environment, Transport and the Regions, with quite different ambitions for an environmentally-sustainable, integrated transport policy. Since 2001, policy has reverted to more familiar patterns of 'predict and provide', as more pragmatic ministers have tried to steer a course determined by political expediency and the need to raise as much money as possible from the private sector.

Yet we are not back to where we started, for several reasons:

1   The volumes of passengers and freight carried are very much greater, leaving much more room for viable competition between operators and between modes of transport.
2   Regulation, which has long been required on safety grounds, and to protect the public interest in the face of dominant service providers, is now also required in order to protect the environment.
3   Government supervision, which always had to strike a balance between local and central government powers, now also has to take account of the European dimension.

British transport policy may have been nudged over the years by politicians from either end of the political spectrum, now towards more competition, now towards a stronger emphasis on coordination and integration, but the ever-changing, kaleidoscopic pattern has always been influenced by a powerful streak of British pragmatism. Whether by accident or design, successive British governments have created a wide range of different structures for the involvement of private and public sector partners in the operation of transport services. The result may be an organic policy riddled with inconsistencies, but it does constitute a fascinating mixture of public and private sector influences which merits study, both for its own sake and for the lessons which may be derived from it.

Chapter 2

The Role of Central Government

One of the strengths of the British system of governance is the collective responsibility of ministers for all aspects of the government's policy; but this collective strength carries with it the consequence that the minister responsible for transport is by no means a free agent. Other ministers, especially the Chancellor of the Exchequer and the Chief Secretary (Treasury), as well as the ministers responsible for planning and local government, for environmental protection and for industrial competitiveness, all have a major impact on the shaping of transport policies. Implementation is in the hands of a wide range of agents in both the public and the private sector, and although the Department for Transport controls some of them directly, its ability to influence others is more limited. Since 1997 Labour's commitment to an 'integrated transport policy' has led to the creation or re-creation of structures designed to facilitate greater coordination and more intrusive regulation, particularly of the railways, than they inherited from their Tory predecessors, but the partial privatization of air traffic control and of the London Underground has dismantled the last remaining vestiges of nationalization. On balance, in the first decade of the twenty-first century it would probably be true to say that the transport industries have more freedom from direct government control than at any time since at least 1930, and possibly since before the First World War.

The Department for Transport carries the primary responsibility for shaping transport policy in Britain, but that responsibility is constrained in a number of ways. First, all policy must be devised and exercised with due respect for Parliament and the law. Second, it must be consistent with Britain's international obligations, including particularly those which arise from membership of the European Union (Chapter 4). Third, although the DfT carries the central responsibility for transport policy, it has to work with other departments of central government, a wide range of executive and regulatory agencies, and the institutions of local government which have a significant role in implementing the policies laid down at the centre (Chapter 3). Finally, central government cannot afford to ignore the large number of stakeholders and their representatives, whose influence is discussed in Chapter 6. Meanwhile this chapter explains how the different institutions of central government relate to one another and to the transport industries.

Central government departments

The organization of central government is subject to continual change as roles and titles are shaped and reshaped around the personalities and policy priorities of the day, but there is also a considerable measure of stability and continuity about the major elements of the structure, however much they may be rearranged.

The Department for Transport

There has been a Department for Transport since 1919 (see Chapter 1) although it was called the Ministry of Transport until 1970, and since then it has twice been absorbed within larger departments for a few years (see below). The difficulty which such changes of name or structure might otherwise cause for the legal powers of the department is avoided by the convention that all such powers vested in ministers by legislation are invariably attributed to 'The Secretary of State'. He or she carries the primary responsibility for proposing and implementing transport policy, whether it is carried out directly by the department (for example, through the Highways Agency), by a non-departmental public body sponsored by the department (for example, the Office of Rail Regulation), or by local government. Some responsibilities are exercised for the United Kingdom of Great Britain and Northern Ireland, some for Great Britain, and others for England alone (see Table 2.1). There is a concordat between the DfT and the Scottish Executive, and another with the Welsh Assembly setting out the basis on which the department cooperates with them. For the most up-to-date description of each department's structure and functions readers should consult the current annual edition of the *Civil Service Yearbook* (published by the Cabinet Office), the annual reports of the various departments (for example, DfT, 2005), or their web-sites.

The Secretary of State is assisted by a variable number of other

TABLE 2.1   *Allocation of governmental responsibilities*

Policy	Tier of government			
	UK	GB	Sub-state government	Local authorities
International (all modes)	✔			
Strategic (all modes)	✔			
Air and sea services	✔			
Ports and airports				
• strategy	✔			
• land-use planning			✔	
Sea, air and rail safety	✔			
Public transport				
• rail services		✔	✔ (services wholly within region)	
• bus services			✔	✔
Road construction				
• motorways, trunk roads			✔	
• other roads			✔ (grants)	✔
Vehicle licensing and testing	✔			

Note: The sub-state authority in Scotland is the Scottish Executive, in Wales the Welsh Assembly, in England the Secretary of State for Transport and/or the Environment, and in Northern Ireland the Department of Environment.

transport ministers whose responsibilities depend on the volume of legislation and other political business to be managed; one of the ministers is usually a peer, who can deal with all the department's business in the House of Lords, but when this is not the case another peer can speak for the department there. At official level, the constant elements within the organization include policy directorates dealing with railways, roads, urban and public transport, road and vehicle safety, freight and logistics, aviation and shipping, ports and airports; a range of executive agencies to administer such services as the testing and licensing of both drivers and vehicles, the construction and maintenance of national roads, maritime safety and the coastguards; a network of regional offices which bring together staff from transport, environment, trade, education and employment departments; and central services such as finance, personnel, statistics, legal services and information. Figure 2.1 gives the structure at April 2005.

The policy directorates are subject to continual reorganization, partly in response to changing political priorities, which can have a dramatic effect on workloads and consequently on the staff and organization required (for instance, the successive reorganizations of the rail industry since 1994), and partly in response to the continual pressure to economize in the use of staff and resources. These changes also reflect a constant search for the ideal structure. Transport is a set of interlocking networks, and the interfaces between them present problems to which answers may sometimes be found by bringing the relevant policy divisions together. For example, it seemed sensible in the mid-1980s for the department to link its oversight of British Rail's London rail services with those of London Regional Transport (LRT) in order to facilitate the search for joint solutions to meet complaints about the lack of a coherent transport policy for London; later, when British Rail was being privatized but LRT retained in public ownership, the two groups were separated again. In recent years maritime affairs, traditionally linked with aviation, have been part of a larger grouping concerned with freight transport generally.

The benefits claimed for such reorganizations are debatable. As well as signalling a political intention, they may prompt the development of a fresh perspective in policy-making by bringing together topics which had previously been kept apart, but they may also separate other topics which had usefully been held together. Fortunately, their main impact is on senior managers who are accustomed to adjusting quickly to changing circumstances and priorities. Much of the department's more routine work continues more or less undisturbed, but the constant upheaval in response to the latest pressure could well contribute to the culture of the short-term political fix, which some commentators find to be characteristic of British policy-making, and not only in regard to transport.

Although the structure of the department's policy directorates is predominantly modal, there are some important exceptions. One of the most significant of these is the analysis and strategy directorate. The small transport policy unit which Conservative ministers inherited from their Labour predecessors in 1979 was abolished in the early 1980s, and although useful work continued to be done under the aegis of the department's chief economist until this post was also cut, a policy unit was not re-established until a decade later to work

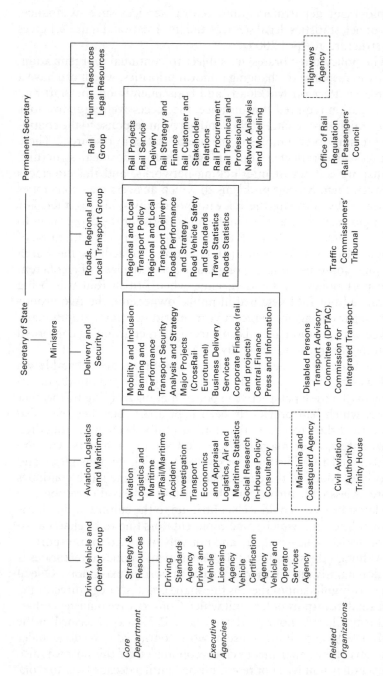

FIGURE 2.1 *The structure of the Department for Transport, 2005*

with the DoE on a joint submission to the Royal Commission on Environmental Pollution (DoE and DoT, 1992), to provide support to ministers for 'the Great Debate' in 1994–95 (DoT, 1995), and to prepare the White Paper, *Transport: The Way Forward*, which set out their response (DoT, 1996). Raised to the status of a full directorate in 1997, it occupied a key position within the united DETR, dealing with a range of inter-modal issues, including safety, transport and the environment, transport taxation, and the preparation of successive White Papers related to the concept of an environmentally-sustainable integrated transport policy.

Another small division with cross-modal responsibilities is the Mobility and Inclusion Unit, which considers the impact of all traffic and transport polices on disabled people and on others who may have particular transport needs, such as elderly people, women travelling alone or passengers with young children. Other groups with cross-modal responsibilities include the directorate dealing with transport security, and the directorate which acts as a coordinating point for the department's relations with the European Union (see Chapter 4). In addition, the directorates handling communications, finance, human resources and legal services are provided as common services to the whole department.

Transport executive agencies

About 90 per cent of the department's staff work in six executive agencies (see Figure 2.1) including the Driver and Vehicle Licensing Agency which has been classified as a non-departmental public body since 1 April 2004. The Department of Transport was in the forefront of the Next Steps administrative reform programme, the Vehicle Inspectorate – now part of the Vehicle and Operator Services Agency – being the first executive agency to be set up by any department in 1988. Executive agencies remain part of the department. Their financial and policy objectives are set by the Secretary of State and monitored by the department, but the agencies' chief executives are given day-to-day managerial freedom in how they achieve those objectives. For example, the Driving Standards Agency operates within the commercial disciplines of a trading fund regime, which is more flexible but no less demanding than the Treasury control of running costs (a rigid limit) which applies to government departments. The Driver and Vehicle Licensing Agency also operates under the discipline of a trading fund.

Relations between departments and their agencies work best where they are able to reflect a clear distinction between the formulation of policy and the delivery of a service. Difficulties arise where the delivery of a service is itself so sensitive and controversial that ministers cannot or will not refrain from intervening personally in the day-to-day operations of the agency. This consideration was important in deciding which sections of the department would form the Highways Agency. The agency has been given responsibility for the operational side of motorway and trunk road construction and maintenance, but ministers remain responsible for the politically sensitive decisions about which schemes should go ahead.

Another agency, the Transport Research Laboratory (TRL), was privatized in 1996. Privatization was a natural evolution of the customer–contractor relationship which had been established for several years. There was a risk that resources might be squeezed further and expertise lost in those areas where paying customers could not be found, but the department has continued to sponsor research under contracts with TRL, and the disciplines associated with financial provision are expected to ensure that research is more effectively and economically focused on topics to which the department attaches priority.

Environment and local government

Land-use planning, supervision and support of the construction industry, housing, local authority spending and environmental controls (for example, for noise or for air pollution) are all issues that link Transport with Environment or Local Government, or both. Indeed the departments responsible for transport, environment and local government have twice been combined into super-departments, first under Peter Walker (Conservative) in 1970, and more recently under John Prescott (Labour) in 1997. Many of the policies in these areas, including the provision and maintenance of local roads and public transport services, although subject to central guidance, are locally administered and in part financed by local taxation. Large departments are theoretically attractive because they bring together so many related topics, but they are also for that very reason difficult for one Secretary of State to manage. The first experiment lasted six years, the second for only four before it began to be broken up, and five before transport emerged again as a fully separate department. From 1976 until 1989 the staff of the separated departments of transport and the environment enjoyed 'common citizenship' and inhabited the same headquarters building, which encouraged the maintenance of good working relations; but no such arrangements have persisted since the break-up of the second united department in 2001 and the demolition of the Marsham Street towers.

In 2001, policy for the environment found new partners in a Department for Environment, Food and Rural Affairs (DEFRA). From 2002 to 2006, policies for housing, land-use planning, local and regional government were overseen by the Office of the Deputy Prime Minister (John Prescott, who had previously covered environment and transport as well). In 2006, when Prescott lost his executive role, the ministry was renamed the Department for Communities and Local Government. Transport provision can play an important part in major development programmes. For example, the route of the Channel Tunnel Rail Link, and especially the decision to have an international station at Stratford in East London, was an important factor in Michael Heseltine's plans for the development of the East Thames corridor, later known as the Thames Gateway area, when he was Secretary of State for the Environment. Equally the availability of good public transport links, or the potential to expand them, may be a factor in determining where major urban growth should be allowed to take place in order to meet the demand for more housing (for example, Stevenage, Aylesbury). Road schemes have required the approval of both Transport and Planning ministers since the departments were first united in 1970, and nowadays such decisions routinely entail the consideration of public transport alternatives. Planning decisions for large out-of-town shopping developments, frequently referred to the Secretary of State on appeal, are also matters which clearly have implications for both transport and land-use planning.

Spending by local authorities on highways and transport is heavily influenced by decisions on local government finance (see Chapter 3 and Chapter 8). The department responsible for relations with local government determines standard spending assessments by service (central government's estimate of how much each local authority should spend), including on highway maintenance and capital financing. It pays transport-specific grants to highway authorities for capital projects, but all local authorities use part of the non-hypothecated revenue support grant allocated by central government, or their own resources within limits set by ministers, to pay for road maintenance or to subsidize transport services. Under the Local Government Act 2003 local authorities can raise additional capital by issuing bonds up to the borrowing limit they judge affordable, but the Secretary of State retains the power to set a lower limit. In recent years strenuous efforts have been made to delegate as many decisions as possible to local and regional levels of government, but such delegation has often been accompanied by increased guidance, and the direction of resources towards projects favoured by central government. A recent example is the Transport Innovation Fund (DfT, 2004: 102), which is planned to increase from small beginnings to reach £2 billion a year by 2014–15.

Department of Trade and Industry

Sponsorship of the vehicle manufacturing industry lies with the Department of Trade and Industry (DTI), which has an automotive unit to keep in touch with the main manufacturers of vehicle and components, as well as such representative bodies as the Society of Motor Manufacturers and Traders (SMMT). The inclusion since 1992 of the Department of Energy within this department was expected to result in the integration of vehicles and energy policies. However, the implications of vehicle design for safety, environmental pollution and taxation revenue (including value added tax, or VAT) give DfT, DEFRA and HM Revenue & Customs a greater interest than the DTI in measures affecting engine size, fuel consumption or emissions. Transport takes the lead in negotiating and implementing in UK law most of the relevant EU legislation which now governs vehicle design, and any improvement in the fuel efficiency of vehicles is probably due to the adoption of European Directives and associated industry standards, particularly since Sweden, Finland and Austria joined the EU in 1995. The DTI's intervention in transport focuses more on the provision of support to the vehicle manufacturing industry and to construction companies building transport infrastructure both at home and overseas. UK Trade and Investment, the government's overseas trade organization reporting to DTI and the Foreign and Commonwealth Office, supports companies in the development of export opportunities and in the attraction of inward investment.

The Office of Fair Trading (OFT), which is attached to DTI, plays an important part in trying to ensure fair competition in the transport market and especially in those parts which are not otherwise subject to economic regulation, notably the deregulated bus industry. The OFT has concurrent jurisdiction with the Office of Rail Regulation over competition issues in the privatized rail industry.

The OFT also determines whether mergers in the privatized transport industries should be allowed to go ahead. For example, P&O was not allowed to merge with Stena Sealink, the other major ferry company at Dover, until the OFT was satisfied that Le Shuttle rail services would provide effective competition via the Channel Tunnel. Where there is concern that companies might operate against the public interest, mergers can be referred to the Competition Commission.

The Home Office

In the Home Office, 'road traffic' is grouped with public order, firearms and other offensive weapons in a division of the police department. If the police could be persuaded to put more resources into controlling illegal parking in bus lanes, or checking overloaded freight lorries or the parking on pavements which causes most of the structural damage to roads and pavements, costs would be saved and there might even be some effect on the balance between road and rail use, and between public and private transport. Because the Home Office and the Metropolitan Police were unable to find the resources needed to keep bus routes in London unobstructed, the DoT introduced a measure in the Road Traffic Act 1991 allowing local government officials to control street parking in London (Burnham, Jones and Travers, 1992: 14–17). Similar considerations have led to the extension of local authority powers to deal with minor moving traffic offences (for example, at box junctions and where left or right turns are prohibited), first under the London Local Authorities and Transport for London Act 2003, and then nationally under the Traffic Management Act 2004, which also makes provision for a Traffic Management Service within the Highways Agency to employ some 1,200 traffic officers to keep the traffic moving on the motorway network (DfT, 2004a: 9).

For the Home Office these questions are peripheral to its main concerns. The White Paper, *A New Deal for Transport*, noted that road policing was not one of the Home Secretary's key objectives, though his letter to chief police officers did note that he would 'expect traffic policing to play a full part in achieving my overall objectives for the Police Service, particularly in relation to community safety and crime reduction and in achieving a safer environment on the roads' (DETR, 1998: 131). This half-hearted expression of support led the DETR to conclude its comments on the role of the police with this unusually barbed remark: 'We will continue to consider ways to promote effective road policing.' The Department thought it had found part of the answer in the use of speed cameras, but the fierce opposition of the motoring lobby led ministers to insist that all such cameras must be clearly identified, presumably so that motorists would know when they had to slow down.

HM Treasury

The Treasury is more important than any other Whitehall department because it controls both economic and fiscal policies, and public expenditure. Transport is important to the Treasury as both a significant source of revenue and a major area of public expenditure. In common with the practice followed by all departments, the government's expenditure plans for transport have long been presented to Parliament by the Secretary of State for Transport and the Chief Secretary, but since 1998 the annual report, as this is now called, has also included a Public Service Agreement (see below) which sets quantified and/or timetabled targets for most areas of the department's work. The requirement for joint sponsorship of these important documents gives the Treasury a very powerful influence at a strategic level over every aspect of the department's work.

The Chief Secretary, who oversees all public expenditure, which includes budgetary provision for the Department for Transport as well as the terms of Public–Private Partnerships which are such an important supplementary source of transport finance (see Chapter 8), has his own seat in Cabinet as the most important of the team of Ministers supporting the Chancellor of the Exchequer. The Economic Secretary, whose remit concerns the efficient functioning of the economy, oversees the Treasury's work on policies for competition and regulation, as well as environmental issues including transport taxation and road user charging, whilst the Paymaster-General oversees the tax-raising activity of HM Revenue & Customs, a semi-autonomous Treasury department created in April 2005 from the merger of the Inland Revenue and Customs & Excise, as recommended in the O'Donnell Review (HM Treasury, 2004). HM Revenue & Customs collects both fuel taxes and VAT on fuel and cars, and administers the rules governing the taxation of company cars, but road vehicle taxes are collected by the Driver and Vehicle Licensing Agency. The new Revenue and Customs Department advises the Treasury on policy maintenance and delivery, but the

Treasury is firmly in the lead on all matters of policy development (including, for example, the development of road user charging).

These distinctive strands of involvement in transport policy are also reflected in Treasury organization at official level. According to the Treasury web-site (www.hm-treasury.gov.uk, April 2005), public expenditure on transport falls within the public services directorate, but corporate and private finance for the transport industries, together with issues of competition and economic regulation, are dealt with under the directorate for finance, regulation and industry, whilst policy on transport-related taxation, together with its implications for the environment, comes under the directorate for the budget and public finances.

Treasury influence over transport policy, as over the policies of all other departments, finds its chief focus in the Chancellor's annual budget, which deals with fiscal and economic management (including all changes in direct and indirect taxation), and in the spending review, which used to take place annually but has been moved onto a two-year cycle since 1998. The Chancellor's budget report for 2005 (HM Treasury, 2005: paras 7.33–54) demonstrates the extent of Treasury influence over the main levers of transport policy. The report dealt with:

(a)   changes in fuel duty (linked to the rate of inflation and postponed by five months), balancing the need to stimulate the economy and avoid upsetting the powerful motorists' lobby with the need to reduce emissions of carbon dioxide;

(b)   proposals to encourage the use of alternative fuels;

(c)   changes in company car taxation;

(d)   changes in vehicle excise duty;

(e)   plans for the introduction of road user charges for lorries from 2007–08 (later abandoned), and confirmation of the policy on national road user charging;

(f)   confirmation of the policy on the taxation of aviation fuel, or rather support for its inclusion in the EU's emissions trading scheme from 2008.

We note in Chapter 8 the scale of resources generated by transport taxation. Since the government has almost invariably resisted proposals for linking the revenue from any particular tax to any particular purpose, there is no direct link between the revenue generated by transport taxes and the volume of transport spending. The point here is rather the impact which taxation has on transport policy. The Chancellor's decision in 1992 to increase fuel duty by 5 per cent more than inflation held back the growth in travel and congestion, an effect which was reversed when the linkage was abandoned following the fuel tax protests which swept through Europe in September 2000. Decisions on the nature of any national road user charging scheme and on the scale of charges could have a huge impact on the volume and distribution of traffic, as has been demonstrated by the success of the London congestion charge, but these are decisions which the Chancellor takes under conditions of budget secrecy which seriously restrict the final stages of the policy debate which ought to take place.

Although the privatization of the railways, the negotiation of PPPs for the London Underground, and the intention of an integrated transport policy to reduce the demand for road building by getting people out of their cars were all expected to reduce the DfT's requirement for public expenditure, the level of spending, which fell from £6.6 billion in 1992–93 to £4.4 billion in 1998–99, rose to £11.7 billion in 2005–06, and is expected to rise further to £17.7 billion by 2014–15 under the government's long-term funding guideline (DfT, 2004: Annex A). Transport remains heavily dependent on public finance, controlled by the Treasury under spending reviews which are now carried out in every second year.

The planning and control of public expenditure has itself been the object of a major programme of reform since 1998, when the annual spending review gave way to a biennial cycle. Each spending review sets out expenditure limits for three years, with the third year becoming the first year of the next cycle. (The Treasury generally resists re-opening budgets for the 'new' first year.) In the case of transport, the expenditure planning horizon extends to ten years in recognition of the need for longer-term planning and a greater degree of financial stability in an area where PPPs and franchise agreements with private sector companies may commonly entail commitments extending over periods ranging from seven to as long as 30 years. Moreover, a major transport project may take a decade or longer to carry through from planning to completion. But the department's *10 Year Plan*, published in 2000, was revised in connection with the Spending Review 2004, and a distinction is drawn in the Spending Review between the allocations made for the first three years and the 'long term funding guideline'. This relates to the remaining seven years of the plan, and amounts to a reasonable expectation of resources rather than a guaranteed commitment. Another major change, implemented in two stages over the

2000 and 2002 spending reviews, is the move from simple cash accounting, which had been applied to government accounts since the nineteenth century, to resource budgeting, which reflects the full economic cost of departmental activity (including charges for depreciation and the cost of capital on their assets). This has a major impact on the Department of Transport, whose assets include a network of motorways and other major roads worth about £60 billion in 2005. As a result of these changes, annual departmental resource accounts have much more in common with the accounts of a large company or corporate group than they did in the past.

Another major reform is the distinction which has been drawn between expenditure which a department can be expected to plan and control over a three-year period under strict Departmental Expenditure Limits (DELs), and Annually Managed Expenditure (AME) which comprises those costs which a department has less ability to plan and control. Across government spending as a whole, the largest block of AME spending consists of welfare payments, the scale of which reflect changes in the economy rather than just decisions by individual departments. For transport spending, the cost of capital charge for the strategic road network is in AME, reflecting the volatility in the level of charge resulting from changes in the index-based valuation of the network.

With so much at stake in the biennial spending review, the negotiation of each review is a major focus of official and ministerial attention in both departments. The process begins in the summer almost two years before the start of the review period – in July 2004 for the 2006 spending round covering the years 2006–07 to 2008–09 – with a Treasury paper indicating the themes which will be the focus of special attention (for example, expenditure which will enhance service delivery). Over the course of the summer and autumn the department reviews its own programmes in the light of this guidance and any long-term plans which may have been agreed with the Treasury. Most major transport expenditure is covered by the *10 Year Plan* which was first published in 2000, then reviewed and extended to 2014–15 in 2004. During the autumn and winter bilateral discussions will take place between officials, and between ministers if necessary, either bilaterally or collectively within the Cabinet committee on public expenditure, both about the terms of the Public Service Agreement (PSA) which sets targeted objectives for the department, and about the resources required to deliver these objectives and to carry out other work not specifically covered by them. In the light of these discussions with all departments the

Chancellor sets out the formal parameters for the spending round in his budget speech, and this leads to the formal submissions (or bids) and a final round or rounds of negotiation to fix the expenditure plans which can then be published during the summer, well in advance of the first year to which they apply.

These reforms have gone some way towards addressing the criticisms which were commonly levelled against the Treasury in 1994 when interviews were conducted for the first edition of this book. Since that time, many of the rules which militated against good value for money in an annual cash accounting regime have been sensibly relaxed in the context of biennial reviews and an acceptance of the case for longer-term transport planning. The department now has a ten year plan, and the 'use it or lose it' rule, which used to create an incentive to spend before the end of the financial year without being too fussy about value-for-money considerations, has been relaxed by the application of much wider end-year flexibility, allowing departments to carry forward unspent resources into future years. On the other hand, these sensible reforms have been accompanied by even tighter Treasury control over departments through the integration of Public Service Agreements into the public expenditure round.

The Treasury's reluctance to engage in full and open consultation, particularly in respect of matters which affect taxation, is less likely to have changed. Neither the Department of Transport nor the Department of the Environment was consulted before the Chancellor in his 1993 budget announced his intention to increase fuel duties every year by 5 per cent more than the rate of inflation in order to encourage the faster adoption of technologies leading to lower carbon dioxide emissions (Potter, 1993: 42), and there was no consultation before the margin was raised to 6 per cent in 1997 either. There is an annual round robin seeking proposals for changes in advance of each year's budget, but it suits the Treasury well enough to spread the cloak of budget secrecy over all the key decisions on both spending and taxation. This obliges the Chancellor to take many important decisions within a very small circle of Treasury officials. Such an absence of fully informed debate, even behind closed doors, would be a matter of concern in any circumstances. It is particularly serious when prices (heavily influenced by taxation) are a key component of transport strategy, yet the Chancellor's decisions are taken in a context where the implications for the national economy are his first priority, whilst the consequences for transport policy and for the environment, if indeed they are properly understood, are a secondary consideration and are used as additional arguments for the budget speech, to be adduced where convenient, ignored if they do not fit the case which needs to be made, or even dismissed if they add to administrative costs in HM Revenue & Customs. It is difficult to assess the validity of such criticism. A transport official, focusing on the needs of the particular policy area or organization for which he or she is responsible, is likely to feel some frustration when faced by a department with broader concerns and more clout. There are advantages for sound policy-making in having a Treasury which is neutral between service departments and powerful enough to be impervious to special pleading, but there remains a risk, given the extent of Treasury control over the key components of transport policy, that decisions may be taken which are, if not irrational, then at least sub-optimal from a transport policy perspective.

Central government and the transport industries

Whilst local authorities have an important part to play in implementing the government's transport policies, it is central government that establishes the regulatory and financial framework within which each of the transport industries operates. Since 1960, one industry after another has been set free from direct control, but the public still holds the government responsible for the safe and efficient functioning of the transport system, particularly any form of public transport, and this is reflected in the Public Service Agreements which now accompany DfT's biennial public expenditure settlements. The department runs no trains or buses, but under the terms of its 2004 Public Service Agreement (DfT, 2004: Annex B) it is still expected 'by 2010, [to] increase the use of public transport (bus and light rail) by more than 12 per cent in England compared with 2000 levels' and to 'improve punctuality and reliability of rail services to at least 85 per cent by 2006, with further improvements by 2008'. It also has performance targets relating to enhanced safety and less damage to the environment, as well as improved cost-effectiveness, robust cost control and clear appraisal of transport investment choices across different modes and locations. A nationalized industry could be given directions, and ultimately, if the management failed to deliver what the government required, the Chair and Board members could be sacked. Such intervention is not possible with a private company. Instead, the government has to accomplish its purposes through the regulatory regime, which may include the contracts under which services are provided.

In setting the regulatory framework for the transport industries to safeguard the public interest, the government has to balance four major requirements:

- safety
- competitive markets for transport services
- value for money, particularly where public expenditure is concerned
- protection of the environment

The diversity of these requirements has led to the creation of a wide range of regulatory agencies responsible for different aspects of regulation in the different industries (see Table 2.2).

Standards for safety and for environmental protection are often agreed internationally, and implemented under UK law or EU regulations which have the force of law throughout the European Union (see Chapter 4). No one questions the principle of safety regulation, but the requirements can have a significant bearing on costs (for example, automatic train protection), or on working practices (for example, tachographs to monitor the working hours of coach and lorry drivers), and they may suddenly become the focus of impassioned debate in the wake of a serious accident. The department's Railways, Marine and Air Accident Investigation branches are staffed by highly-regarded professionals, and all three branches are now institutionally separated from the safety regulation authorities, as well as the transport service providers whose actions they may need to criticize. In the case of the most serious accidents, the Transport Secretary may further reinforce the standing and independence of the investigation by setting up an inquiry headed by a senior judge, such as Sheen (sinking of the *Herald of Free Enterprise*, 1987), or Fennell (fire at King's Cross Underground station, 1987).

There may be some debate about the extent and terms of regulation for safety or the environment, but it is relatively narrow by comparison with the debate which surrounds economic regulation, and it is in this area that British governments have experienced the greatest difficulty over the past 20 years or so whilst moving transport industries into the private sector. Where there is room for competing services to operate, competition may be

TABLE 2.2 *Regulation of the transport industries*

Mode	Safety regulation	Environment	Economic regulation
Bus services	EU and UK laws apply. Buses licensed by Vehicle Inspectorate. Operators licensed by Traffic Commissioners. Bus drivers tested by DSA and licensed by DVLA.	EU and UK Law	Outside London, services registered by Traffic Commissioners. Fair Competition policed by Competition Commission. Within London, competition for contracts awarded by TfL.
Road freight	EU and UK laws apply. Trucks licensed by DVLA. Operators licensed by Traffic Commissioners. Drivers tested by DSA and licensed by DVLA.	EU and UK Law	Liberal access to markets within UK and EU.
Railways	EU and UK laws apply. Infrastructure and train operating companies licensed and inspected by Railways Inspectorate.	EU and UK Law	DfT and Ofice of Rail Regulation; see Figure 2.3.
Aviation	ICAO rules apply. EU and UK laws apply Aircraft licensed and inspected by CAA. Airlines licensed and inspected by CAA.	ICAO rules EU and UK Law	Liberal access to markets within UK and EU. Access to destinations outside EU governed by bilateral agreements. CAA regulates charges by NATS and designated airports.
Marine	IMO rules apply. EU and UK laws apply. Inspection by Marine Safety Agency.	IMO agreements EU and UK Law	Freedom of the seas. Anti-competitive practices policed by EU.

DSA = Driving Standards Agency
DVLA = Driver and Vehicle Licensing Agency
ICAO = International Civil Aviation Organization
IMO = International Maritime Organization

largely self-regulating within the laws governing fair competition generally, but such conditions may not be feasible on busy city streets, on heavily used railway lines, or in congested bus or railway stations. Moreover, the conditions will vary across the country, so that the same arrangements may not be necessary or appropriate everywhere. For example, whereas it was thought right to allow direct competition between bus services outside London, the alternative of franchising, where competition is confined to the bidding process, was preferred within the capital (see Chapter 7).

The most difficult and contentious issues of all have arisen in relation to the regulatory framework applying to main line railway services (see below). The 30-year contracts signed by London Underground (before its transfer to Transport for London) and the two companies that maintain the Tube infrastructure are also coming under pressure, with Transport for London expressing its 'concern about the progress made by the companies' (TfL, *Annual Report 2004–05*: 5); but no government likes to undo its own handiwork, and the situation has not yet reached the point at which the complex contractual relationship must unravel.

Regulating the privatized railway

We discuss in Chapter 7 some of the issues that have arisen in the regulation of the privatized railway. Here we set out the structures within which the railway has been managed and regulated, charting their evolution over the first decade since privatization. The original post-privatization structure is set out in Figure 2.2.

Under these arrangements *Railtrack* owned the signalling and fixed infrastructure, including the land and stations. Railtrack recovered its costs through charging users for access to its facilities, except that the Secretary of State retained the power to give direct capital grants for freight facilities if justified on public interest grounds. Railtrack 'bought in' most of its services – such as track maintenance engineering – through competitive tender. It was responsible for central timetabling and coordination of all train movements and signalling, planning investment in infrastructure and ensuring it was carried out. It was responsible for safe operation of the network under the supervision of the Health and Safety Executive. Railtrack's property portfolio included stations, railway land, buildings, installations and light maintenance depots, many of which were leased to train operators. However, 14 large mainline stations remained under Railtrack's direct control.

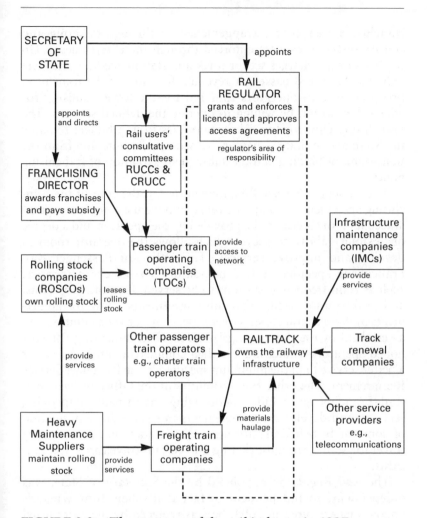

FIGURE 2.2   *The structure of the rail industry in 1997*
Source: Reproduced from Office of the Rail Regulator, *Annual Report 1996/97*.

The *Franchising Director* headed the Office of Passenger Rail Franchising (OPRAF). Financial support to the railway passed through the Franchising Director with the exception of certain freight grants and any capital grants. The Franchising Director's function was to define rail passenger franchises and sell them to train operating companies using a competitive tendering procedure. He defined passenger service groups that would be offered as 25 franchise agreements. Arrangements for through-ticketing and concessionary fares were enforced through these agreements. On the basis of the charges set for track and station access, costs were expected to exceed passenger revenues for most of the franchises; prospective train operators thus bid for the lowest subsidy for which they would be willing to operate the defined services. The Franchising Director funded the subsidies from a budget fixed by the Secretary of State. Chapter 7 discusses the outcome from the first round of bidding and the subsequent evolution of franchising policy.

The Passenger Service Requirement lies at the core of the franchising agreement. It comprises two components: a minimum guaranteed level of services to be provided by the operator, and a degree of flexibility above this level which allows the operator room to develop and improve services. The Office of Passenger Rail Franchising specified certain mandatory service characteristics, such as train frequency, stations to be served, first and last trains, and peak train capacity. Franchise agreements allow for adjustments of these characteristics over time, subject to consultation and a veto held by the Franchising Director. The Franchising Director hoped operators would find it in their commercial interests to offer a better service than the minimum specified in the Passenger Service Requirement. The other responsibilities of the Office of Passenger Rail Franchising include encouraging investment, improving services, and developing arrangements to ensure the continuation of some of British Rail's former services, such as concessionary travel for staff, through-ticketing and certain travelcards and railcards.

The *Rail Regulator*, appointed by the Secretary of State, was independent; so independent in fact that when Tom Winsor's appointment expired in 2004, he was replaced by the more usual regulatory structure of an Office of Rail Regulation run by a Chair and a small Board (see below). The Regulator's approval was required for all access agreements between Railtrack and passenger and freight train operators. Railtrack had a network licence administered by the Regulator. Any train operator requires an operator licence. Operators include: franchised passenger service operators; independent, non-franchised (that is, 'open access') passenger service operators; and freight train operators. The Regulator had statutory functions in four main areas: the granting, monitoring and enforcement of licences to operate railway assets; the approval of access agreements between facility owners and users of railway facilities; the enforcement of domestic competition law; and approval of railway line closures.

The Regulator's duties were to protect the interests of both providers and users of rail services, to promote competition together with efficiency and economy, to promote the development and use of the network, to safeguard through-ticketing for the benefit of the public, and to ensure that Railtrack did not find it unduly difficult to finance its activities. In fulfilling those duties, the Regulator must take into account the financial position of the Franchising Director, whose budget was decided separately by the government. The Regulator could vary licences by agreement: if the licence-holder did not agree, the matter could be referred to the Competition Commission. The Regulator was charged with ensuring that arrangements for allocating train paths and settling timetable disputes were fair and reasonable. In relation to the monopoly supply of railway services, the Regulator had concurrent jurisdiction with the Director General of Fair Trading.

A significant difference between privatized rail and other British regulated utilities is the role Parliament has assigned the Regulator over the commercial contracts which give infrastructure users permission to operate. In other industries, the regulator's role is based primarily on the licences the industry players hold. In the case of the railway industry, however, much of the important economic regulation – particularly the control of prices charged for the use of railway assets – is based on access agreements not licences, and the Regulator's approval of every access agreement is required. If it is not approved, it is void. The Regulator has considerable powers. However, there are many things over which he has no power, most of them stemming from the railway's complicated regulatory structure. That structure, in turn, ultimately derives from the fact that the railway receives a substantial subsidy from central government. Many contracts are not regulated, such as the terms of leases for rolling stock and for stations, and the contracts between Railtrack and providers of engineering services (the greater part of Railtrack expenditure). Most important, and most surprising to the general public, the Regulator has no power to regulate passenger fares. This power was given to the Franchising Director through the contracts offered for passenger franchises, presumably on the grounds that fares regulation has direct implications for subsidy and therefore for government expenditure.

Over the past decade these arrangements have been continuously tested and contested, not least under the pressure of events, but also as a result of continuing tensions within the Labour Party. It had opposed privatization before it was elected, and found itself in government saddled with the distasteful task of overseeing a privatized railway which it was nevertheless reluctant to buy back into the public sector. These pressures, taken together, have resulted in the progressive assertion of more direct control by the government over the railway industry, and some simplification of its structures, but these have been evolutionary rather than revolutionary, and the structure in Figure 2.3 is not so very different from the earlier model.

The main changes which have taken place are as set out below:

1 *Railtrack* ran into severe financial difficulties following the response it made to the Hatfield accident (2000) and its poor handling of the major contract for the renewal and upgrading of the West Coast Main Line. Since these difficulties coincided with the Rail Regulator's periodic review of the access charges through which Railtrack was financed, this presented the Secretary of State with the opportunity to push Railtrack into Railway Administration (see Chapter 7) and replace it with *Network Rail,* a new not-for-dividend company answerable to a Board of 115 stakeholders drawn from the train operating companies, and representatives of passengers and the public sector. Network Rail has subsequently taken back under its own control the infrastructure maintenance work whose contracting-out to a range of private companies had failed to deliver good value for money, and was thought to have contributed to the accidents at both Hatfield and Potters Bar.

2 The *Franchising Director,* who plays a key role in specifying the services to be delivered, was brought under the control of the Strategic Rail Authority (SRA) from 2001, coming under the direct control of the department when the SRA was in its turn abolished under the Railways Act 2005. The nature of the franchise agreements is little changed but, as the original franchises fell due, the opportunity has been taken to reduce their number, and in some cases to offer them for much longer periods than the seven years which was the normal length of the first franchises, in order to allow the companies more time to make a return on their investments.

3 The independent role of the *Rail Regulator* has been absorbed into an enhanced *Office of Rail Regulation* (ORR), which has been established to oversee safety as well as reliability, efficiency

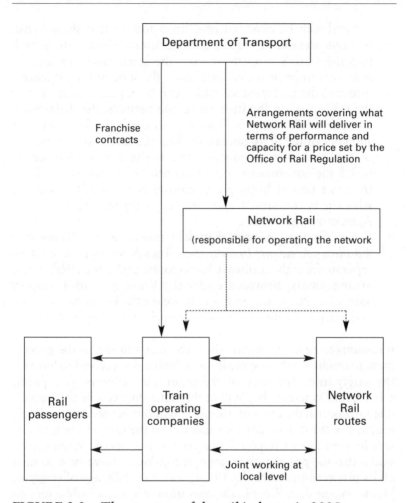

FIGURE 2.3 *The structure of the rail industry in 2005*

Source: Reproduced from Department for Transport, *The Future of Rail* (TSO, 2004e), p. 62.

and cost. Under the Railways Act 2005 the former responsibility of the Health and Safety Executive (HSE) for safety regulation, as well as the Railways Inspectorate which was part of HSE, will be transferred to the ORR. The hope is that this arrangement will enable the government to maintain through the ORR, which sets the access charges on which Network Rail depends, a more effective control than hitherto over what the network can be expected to deliver, and what it should cost, without prejudice to safety considerations which will be built into the ORR's assessment from the start. Since the level of resources to be provided, and hence the state of the infrastructure and the performance which can be expected of it, will be the subject of an iterative procedure between the department and the ORR (with the Treasury no doubt looking over the shoulder of the department), leading ultimately to a 'statement of reasonable requirements', this is the key mechanism by which the government hopes to control expenditure, whilst at the same time delivering the improvements in rail services to which it is committed under the department's Public Service Agreement (see above).

4   One addition to the regulatory structure is the establishment of a *Railway Accidents Investigation Branch* within DfT, and thus separate from the Railways Inspectorate under the ORR. These arrangements, provided under the Railways and Transport Safety Act 2003, are similar to those for the investigation of air and marine accidents. This new branch was set up in 2005.

It remains to be seen whether these changes will enable the government to discharge the responsibility which it is perceived to have for the safety and efficiency of the main line railways as a public service, and whether they will at the same time enable the government to control the costs of provision without becoming too deeply engaged in the day-to-day management of the railway industry. As will be seen from Chapter 7, we are not convinced. What can be said is that the present government is continuing to wrestle, as have all its predecessors since the 1950s, with the challenge of engaging private-sector disciplines in the operation of a major public service. This is a journey which may never reach its destination.

Coordination and control

An account that sets out public responsibilities for transport department-by-department, and in its separate arm's-length relationships with each of the transport industries, inevitably emphasizes its fragmentation; it would be unbalanced if it failed to acknowledge the forces for integration. Several mechanisms exist for coordinating the work of departments, bringing them together at central and local levels or, more often, bringing together officials, local authorities and other interests to debate a particular issue. They are not easy to describe; some of the structures and responsibilities of ministerial committees have been made public, but much remains confidential and the work of informal gatherings is extensive, ever-changing and difficult to pin down. However, they have been encouraged and developed since 1997 under the umbrella of an integrated transport policy.

Whilst every Secretary of State must focus primarily on his or her own responsibilities, the government as a whole must also act coherently. The doctrine of collective responsibility has always depended on the leadership of the Prime Minister and the support of the Cabinet. Much can be achieved by good coordination at every level, and in the past this was how most prime ministers exercised their leadership role, acting through the weekly meeting of the Cabinet on Thursday morning, under-pinned by an extensive network of formal and informal structures centred around the Cabinet Office under the supervision of the Secretary to the Cabinet. Though the Prime Minister might consult a 'kitchen cabinet' of close friends and political associates, his own staff consisted of little more than a Private Office which was only slightly larger than that of a busy departmental minister. However, since about 1980, prime ministers – notably Margaret Thatcher and Tony Blair – have wanted to exercise closer control over the direction and presentation of policy than these traditional arrangements allowed. The number of political advisers and civil servants attached to the Prime Minister's Office has grown substantially, allowing him or her to engage with departmental ministers and their advisers on much more equal terms.

The Prime Minister

Even so, it remains rare for a prime minister to take much interest in transport policy. Margaret Thatcher's appointment of Nicholas Ridley in 1987 to drive through a programme of privatization and deregulation was something of an exception. John Prescott's relatively high profile as Deputy Prime Minister and Secretary of State for the Environment, Transport and the Regions (1997–2001) became a liability when his commitment to an integrated transport policy with a strong emphasis on public transport began to stir up resentment among the motoring public. By and large transport is regarded as a rather unglamorous technical portfolio to be given to someone at the far end of the Cabinet table, a 'safe pair of hands' who will keep transport off the front page of the newspapers. When Alistair Darling was voted the most boring politician in 2003 and again in 2004 (*Guardian*, 5 January 2004), he probably received – or at least deserved – a note of congratulation from the Prime Minister. Transport Secretaries who appear too often in the news, sometimes through no fault of their own (for example, when there has been a succession of railway accidents) are liable to be sacrificed to the ensuing hue and cry (Paul Channon, 1987–89; Stephen Byers, 2001–02). Under an increasingly presidential style of government, when the department's integrated transport policy was seen to be in difficulties, the Prime Minister turned not to his Secretary of State to devise a new strategy but rather to Lord Birt overseeing a small unit within his own office (*Guardian*, 8 January 2002).

The Cabinet Office

The main function of the Cabinet Office is to support the Cabinet and the Prime Minister in maintaining collective responsibility for government policy. It acts as the clearing house and secretariat for the committees which ensure that the government maintains a coherent policy, determining priorities and resolving differences among departments as necessary. Since April 1992 the existence of Cabinet committees, together with their names, membership and general area of concern, have been made public. The actual topics of discussion are made known only through leaks of information from participants. The general working principle is for them to handle any inter-departmental issue which cannot be settled by correspondence or meetings at official or ministerial level among the parties most directly concerned. The committees refer on upwards for discussion by full Cabinet items of high political significance only, or those unable to be unresolved at committee level; otherwise, Cabinet is merely informed. There is a supporting structure of committees at official level which may resolve some issues and clarify others for discussion among ministers.

Some Cabinet committees have particular relevance for transport policy. The Cabinet committee on the environment handles major cross-departmental issues on the environment, which would include controversial transport infrastructure projects. It is a large committee of more than a dozen ministers including senior ministers responsible for Environment, Transport, Trade and Industry, Agriculture, Scotland, Wales and Northern Ireland, together with the Chancellor of the Exchequer and the Chief Secretary. The

Minister for Transport is also a member of the Cabinet committee on local government, which discusses local government financial issues, including transport finance. The Cabinet committee on public expenditure, set up in 1992 so that Cabinet ministers could consider collectively the government's annual expenditure programme, is probably more important than all these committees combined, just as the Treasury is more important to transport than any other department. This committee has the last word in the biennial review of transport spending (see above), subject only to final endorsement by the full Cabinet.

The Cabinet Office may also be entrusted with more specific functions, particularly where these cut across departmental responsibilities. In recent years such functions have included the Deregulation Unit and the Competitiveness Unit which coordinated and spurred on the relevant programmes in all government departments. These policies were of crucial importance in the privatization of the transport industries. In addition, within the Office of Public Service (itself part of the Cabinet Office), the Next Steps Unit drove forward the reforms which led to the creation of the Department of Transport's Executive Agencies, and the Efficiency Unit worked tirelessly for the application within the public service of management practices adopted and adapted from the private sector. The tendency of such units to outlive the political initiative which gave rise to them has led some commentators to refer to the Cabinet Office as the rest home for the pet projects of past prime ministers. That would be unkind and a little unfair, but the growth of the Prime Minister's own office has perhaps reduced the relative importance of the Cabinet Office as the primary focus of coordination within government.

Other coordinating mechanisms

Coordination between departments takes place not only in committees preparing the ground for ministers to take decisions in Cabinet committees, but in dozens of other inter-departmental groups, formal and informal, for which no public list exists. To these should be added many advisory committees bringing together officials, experts, members of interest groups and professional organizations and a wide range of other bodies with nationwide remits on highways and transport, such as the Standing Advisory Committee on Trunk Road Assessment and the Royal Commission on Environmental Pollution. Coordination among the departments most closely concerned with transport policy takes place whether they are separate or united, though it can be more fully integrated when they are together than when they are apart. Coordination between officials responsible for transport and planning is closest within the nine regional offices which were established in 1971 under the first united department. When the DoT and DoE separated again in 1976 the shared regional offices were retained (except in London), and both Secretaries of State had to approve recommendations for road schemes. In 1994 creation of the Highways Agency removed from regional offices their responsibility for supervision of road maintenance, but they continued to work closely with regional and local authorities on their development plans, including both road construction and public transport.

In 1993 the regional offices were given additional responsibilities for the coordination of urban regeneration programmes, and extended accordingly to include the regional staff of the then Department of Employment (now Work and Pensions) and the Department of Trade and Industry, and one representative each from the Home Office and Education. Government Offices for the Regions, working first with regional planning conferences of local authorities, and now with the regional assemblies and the Greater London Authority who have formal planning responsibility (see Chapter 5), remain the key focus for the coordination of land-use planning and transport at the regional level. They link policies and priorities for housing, transport, the environment and economic regeneration under the broad umbrella of Regional Spatial Strategies. At local level central guidance on the preparation of local transport plans requires local authorities and the regional assemblies to coordinate decisions on transport and land-use planning as they address such issues as accessibility, road safety and air quality as well as congestion (DfT, 2004: 99–100).

At the headquarters of the Departments of Transport and the Environment there was less emphasis on the coordination of national policies during the 1980s. Environment ministers were preoccupied with sales of council houses and the reform of local government finance, whilst Transport ministers were busy privatizing and deregulating the transport industries. However, coordination gradually strengthened during the 1990s as it became increasingly urgent to reconcile policies for transport and the environment, bearing fruit particularly in joint planning guidance to local authorities. This process reached its peak in the emphasis on coordinated planning arrangements at central, regional and local levels which informed the government's White Paper on Integrated Transport, *A New Deal for Transport* (DETR, 1998). Since many of the procedures were institutionalized within the arrangements for the supervision of regional and local government, they have largely survived the break-up of the integrated Department of the Environment, Transport and the Regions.

The department's *Annual Report for 2003–04* (DfT, 2004b: 18–19) emphasizes the extent to which the department depends on coordination with others for the achievement of its own objectives, identifying in particular:

(a) DEFRA on air quality, climate change, sustainability;
(b) the Office of the Deputy Prime Minister (ODPM) on the development of sustainable communities, and particularly the role of transport in reducing social exclusion;
(c) the Department of Health on issues concerning the welfare of air passengers;
(d) the Treasury, DEFRA and DTI on powering future vehicles;
(e) the Department for Education and Skills and the Department of Health on issues affecting child road safety and health, including the need to reverse the rapid rise in the number of children travelling to school by car;
(f) the Home Office on vehicle-related criminal and anti-social behaviour.

Some of these linkages are formally recognized in joint inter-departmental objectives set out in each department's Public Service Agreements. For example, in 2004 DfT shared air quality targets with DEFRA, and greenhouse gas emission targets with DEFRA and DTI.

There cannot be coherent government without coordination, but the mechanisms required for coordination can also be used to exercise central control. At all levels of government there is a certain tension between control which is imposed from above and coordination which is less hierarchical. This tension manifests itself in the relationship between the Prime Minister and his Secretaries of State, as it does in the relationship between the Treasury and spending ministers. It is present again in the relationship between central government and local authorities, which we explore in more detail in Chapter 3 and Chapter 5. Central government wants local authorities to take responsibility for their own decisions, particularly those which might be politically controversial (for example, congestion charging, road user charging), but it also knows what it would like local authorities to do, so it seeks to exercise control by means of guidance and financial incentives.

The dual-state thesis, as developed by Cawson and Saunders (1983), asserts that central government and its bureaucrats, relatively insulated from a wide range of interest groups and public debate, keeps for itself control over investment decisions in infrastructure important to private-sector producers. It allows local authorities and local pluralist competition for the less critical social consumption goods or social welfare services. The DfT's payment of Transport Supplementary Grant and the efforts by some local authorities to build their own light rail systems do not negate the validity of the theory since their spending and borrowing is very much determined by central government.

More significant, however, is the 'public choice' theory of Niskanen, not because it is necessarily valid, but because it was promoted by New Right think-tanks and believed by Mrs Thatcher as Prime Minister and Nicholas Ridley as Secretary of State for the Environment. By defining public bureaucracies as intrinsically wasteful and self-serving, Niskanen's work reinforced the determination of Conservative leaders to reduce public spending, particularly by those not closely under their control. Nevertheless, it would be a mistake to suppose that central government 'rolled back the (local) state' only under Mrs Thatcher. Jerry White (1993: 20) has shown there was a continuous transfer of power and functions from local government throughout the twentieth century, the period of greatest centralization being under a Labour government between 1946 and 1948. Without a written, codified constitution, British local government is always at the mercy of central government.

After John Major became prime minister, there was some repairing of the relationships between central and local governments, particularly in relation to transport policy. Moreover, local authorities and their regional associations have much to teach central government departments on how to cooperate in the strategic planning of land-use and transport (see Chapter 5). Central government for its part has begun to recognize the importance of cooperation among local authorities in neighbouring areas which form a coherent unit for transport purposes, and has encouraged this through the emphasis placed on the 'package approach' since 1993 as the preferred basis on which to bid for resources in the annual round of transport policies and programme submissions (TPPs). Within an agreed package of transport works and measures designed to achieve locally agreed objectives, which may well include safety, enhanced modal interchange, cycling and walking as well as traditional road and public transport schemes, the cooperating local authorities had the benefit of flexibility in the allocation of the approved expenditure.

This process has been carried forward under Labour governments since 1997. Integration of transport planning was central to the White Paper, *A New Deal for Transport* (DETR, 1998). TPPs were replaced from 1999/2000 by Local Transport Plans (LTPs), whose aim was to deliver integrated transport at the local level, but these in turn were to be prepared within the context of regional transport strategies, and in some circumstances local authorities would be encouraged to produce joint LTPs. The tension between coordination of devolved responsibility and central control is apparent in the offer of increased resources, later subsumed in the Transport Innovation Fund, to those local authorities showing the political courage to use their new powers to introduce local road charging or workplace parking levies.

Informal contacts between officials on transport issues are impossible to chart. Some of them are mentioned here and there in this book. The working methods and personnel management of the civil service are designed to overcome some of the deficiencies of Whitehall's departmental structure. Examples include: the Cabinet Office's use of departmental officials on two-year secondments to staff the Cabinet Secretariat; the telephone networks of civil servants in ministers' private offices and at all levels in departments; the secondment of officials from their 'home' department to other service departments or the Treasury, and from the Treasury to other departments (nearly all top civil servants have served in the Treasury or the Cabinet Office or both), absorbing a common culture. The advantage is that every senior official has a personal acquaintance of other departments and a set of easy contacts around the Whitehall community. The disadvantage of such regular movement is sometimes thought to be a lack of continuity and depth of knowledge, which risks being altogether absent from policy-making within government if it is not supplied by officials, since ministers seldom spend more than two or three years in the same department. Over the 50 years from 1947 to 1997 the average for transport ministers was two years, and since four of them lasted between four and six years, the remaining 21 averaged only 16 months each (Paxman, 2002: 209).

Parliament, the law and the media

This chapter has been concerned with the many different pressures which affect the formulation of transport policy within the British system of government, and its application to the transport industries. Once policy has been decided and announced, the British government is usually in a position to pass the necessary legislation and to command the necessary resources for its implementation. The government resigns if it no longer has a majority in the House of Commons, and the Commons can over-rule the House of Lords. This puts the executive in a very powerful position, particularly when it has a large majority, as is usually the case under the first-past-the-post electoral system which is very sensitive to relatively small swings in public opinion. Even so, a powerful government can be driven off course by the opposition it faces in Parliament, the law and the media, as well as the lobbying organizations whose role is discussed in Chapter 6.

Every department is shadowed by a Parliamentary Select Committee, which has the right to summon witnesses, and make reports and recommendations. The government does not have to accept the recommendations, but it does have to reply to them, so that the process of critical inquiry is very open. The Transport Select Committee published nine reports in the parliamentary year 2002–03, 18 in 2003–04, and another 10 in 2004–05. Some are routine examinations of the ongoing work of the Department and its Agencies, but most are sharply focused on matters of current political interest. The government has a majority in all the select committees, and can usually arrange for it to be chaired by a compliant MP. However, Mrs Gwyneth Dunwoody, who chaired the Select Committee dealing with transport in 1997 and was reappointed in 2001 and 2005, has been fearless and trenchant in criticizing the government's policies throughout that period (so much so indeed that the government made strenuous but unavailing efforts to get her unseated in 2001).

Ministers must avoid falling foul of the law. Here again the government is in a very powerful position, since it can change the law if it needs to do so, but ministers and officials have to be very careful not to ride roughshod over the law as it stands since their actions can be overturned on judicial review if they have overstepped their powers or failed to follow the correct procedures. Another very significant source of opposition is the media, which played a considerable part in forcing the resignation of Stephen Byers as Transport Secretary in 2002, after he had failed to dismiss

Jo Moore, his political adviser, when she was crass enough to send an e-mail to the department's Press Office on 11 September 2001 (the day the World Trade Center was attacked), suggesting that this was a good day to bury bad news. That episode seriously damaged the credibility of Byers's handling and presentation of policy, and when other disasters overtook the department, notably the Hatfield rail crash and the subsequent controversy over Railtrack, his word could never be accepted at face value. He finally had to resign after misleading Parliament over the circumstances surrounding the departure of his own Press Officer. More serious, since it had a direct effect on policy, was the support found in the media for the notion that the department's policy was anti-car, a campaign opportunistically supported by the Conservative opposition and their friends in the media, which allowed the fuel price protesters to feel assured of popular support and played a significant part in forcing the government to abandon important aspects of what it had been trying to do in support of a sustainable transport policy (see Chapter 1).

Conclusion

This chapter has described a very fragmented system for conceiving and delivering a national transport policy. For historic, and probably inevitable reasons, transport policy-making and implementation was already split between central government, public corporations and local government, between departments and divisions of departments, even before the New Right governments of the 1980s came into office. Those governments, searching for efficiency and a more effective public service, deliberately fragmented the system further, dividing the administration into separate agencies and the service-deliverers between a multitude of public- and private-sector bodies. Although the Labour governments since 1997 have adopted the rhetoric of an integrated transport policy, and have taken steps to reduce the fragmentation of the railway system, they have also extended the process of privatization to embrace both the National Air Traffic Services and the London Underground, the last significant transport operations remaining within the public sector when they took office.

The ideological drive towards a greater use of market mechanisms and privatization in air, rail and bus services in the 1980s and 1990s removed some large enterprises and large numbers of employees from the public sector, but the changes did not imply government had lost all power to direct and control the transport industries. Contracts are finite, and the powers of the Secretary of State to set objectives for regulators and public corporations could be used almost as easily to facilitate government intervention as to reinforce market disciplines. The reassertion of government control over strategic policy-making for the railway industry, under the Railways Act 2005, is the clearest demonstration of this principle. The positive features of the current, fragmented system are first, an increased 'transparency', deriving from a clarity of objectives, budgets and relationships which, because they had to be set out in documents, made ministers, officials and advisers think more carefully than before about what they required the system and its separate parts to deliver. Second, those documents often provide a means for ministers to exercise a far closer control over the system than the market rhetoric makes it appear. They can change the orientation of the system by changing the directions and objectives given to their appointees, directors and agency chief executives. Third, there has been a growing recognition of the value of cooperation among government authorities in tackling transport-related issues at the local level. The actions of central government are being more effectively coordinated through the enhanced regional offices set up to manage urban regeneration budgets. Since 1993, the guidance relating to the preparation of transport and policy programmes, now local transport programmes, has encouraged neighbouring local authorities, especially in urban areas, to cooperate more closely in dealing with transport issues.

These are some of the foundations on which an integrated transport policy was already beginning to be constructed at local levels and potentially at a regional level under the Major government. At the level of national policy, however, new structures and organizations were still being created – notably under railway privatization – or proposed (as, for example, the privatization of the London Underground) to facilitate and entrench competition and individual choice. Labour's bringing together of the Transport, Environment and Local Government departments in 1997 was a clear signal of their intention not merely to reconcile and integrate these policies within central government, but to pursue integrated transport, environment and planning policies at all levels. To the extent that such policies were institutionalized and built into the structures of government while the two departments were together, they may survive, at least for a while, the separation which has again taken place, but over time the new structures are likely to lead to new divisions.

Chapter 3

Local Government and Urban Transport

This chapter outlines local government's role in providing and planning public transport and local roads in Britain. It also considers the particular arrangements for the governance of transport by metropolitan authorities in the largest urban areas. There are many detailed guides to local government structures, finance and their many functions (see, for example, Wilson and Game, 2002; Carmichael and Midwinter, 2003); the following paragraphs are chiefly concerned with the way in which British local government is involved in the governance of transport.

Local government structures and responsibilities

Local government in Britain originated from the efforts of parishes, towns, cities and counties to make public provision in their area. Highways, drainage, markets, poor relief and early law and order arrangements were among the services most commonly provided. The Poor Law of 1601 gave parishes the right to levy a property tax to raise resources to fund poor relief. Turnpike trusts constructed roads and then charged for their use in a way that resembles today's toll motorways. The first local authority in Britain to be given firm legal status was the Corporation of London, which received a royal charter in the thirteenth century. Thereafter, other areas applied to Parliament from time to time for the right to make service provision of various kinds. However, it was the Industrial Revolution and the growth of large towns and cities that provided the greatest stimulus for the development of the modern system of local government. As cities such as Birmingham, Manchester and Leeds developed, their leading citizens applied to Parliament for legislative power to provide services and levy property taxes. The great corporations of major cities provided roads, lighting, tramways and other transport-related services. By the end of the nineteenth century, local government in Britain had been rationalized by Acts of Parliament that produced a broadly consistent pattern throughout the country.

As this short history indicates, the local government system in Britain is determined by legislation. Britain does not have a codified Constitution that might protect the rights of local authorities. The most important constitutional principle, that of parliamentary sovereignty, gives Parliament (or in practice the government that controls it) the power to alter at any time the laws governing the structure, functions and financial arrangements of local authorities. No country in the world reorganizes local and regional government so frequently. This flexibility enabled central government in the 1960s and 1970s to modify local authority structures to take account of new 'travel-to-work' patterns, setting up the Greater London Council in 1965, six metropolitan county councils in England in 1974 and Strathclyde Regional Council in 1975. Central government then removed these councils and some other county councils in the 1980s and 1990s (partly for political reasons, partly to clarify responsibilities). Today there is a single tier of local councils throughout Scotland, Wales and Greater London (plus a regional or sub-national tier as explained in the following section). In the rest of England, there is a tier of unitary councils (that is, all-purpose authorities) in most larger cities and towns, though also in some more rural areas. In most rural areas there is a two-tier system of county and district councils.

The functions of local authorities change too. Since 1945 a number of significant services (for example, health, public utilities and parts of higher education), have been removed from local government control and transferred to central government. At different times transport responsibilities passed from the private sector to not-for-profit trusts or companies and/or to the control of public corporations; some moved back to private control. Today, most roads, planning and local transport remain within local government. In the areas once covered by Strathclyde Regional Council and the English metropolitan county councils, the unitary councils are transport and planning authorities. However, the public transport functions that Strathclyde and the metropolitan county councils carried out as 'passenger transport authorities', were transferred to joint boards of councillors from the unitary councils, and they continue to assure the delivery of service through professional Passenger Transport Executives (PTEs). The public transport functions of the Greater London Council passed in 1984 to a public corporation, London Regional Transport, and in 1986 its highways and traffic functions were devolved to the boroughs, except for some important through-routes which were taken over by the DfT. Since the constitution of the Greater London Authority (GLA) in 2000 (see below), a new public corporation, Transport for London, has managed the planning and delivery of nearly all main road and public transport functions in Greater London, under the direction of the Mayor.

The various sources of funding available to local government that could potentially be spent on transport are strongly controlled by central government. This question is discussed in more detail below but, in summary, the financing of all local government services has become more centrally-determined since the introduction of expenditure capping in 1985. In 2005–06, local taxation, through the council tax, funded only 26 per cent of revenue (day-to-day) expenditure. The remaining 74 per cent was derived from government grants and business property taxes that government redistributes to councils. Local authorities also raise a limited amount of money from charges for services, including fare income to bodies such as TfL and the PTAs.

Regional government

Unlike Germany, which has had powerful regions since 1947, or France, Italy and Spain, which have had regional governments for some decades, Britain does not have a tier of elected regional government. Both the Conservative Party and the Labour Party usually argued strongly against regional government. However, the Labour government that took office in 1997 passed legislation to create a Scottish Parliament, a Welsh Assembly and a Greater London Authority. The Parliament and government of Northern Ireland, established in 1922, was suspended in 1972. In 1998 a new Assembly with a power-sharing executive was elected but suspended in 2002; and though new elections were held in 2003, it had not yet established an executive two years later. Nevertheless, by the mid-2000s, four different forms of elected regional government were in being. In Scotland legislative power over local government has transferred to the new Parliament. Thus, many transport responsibilities which previously rested with the UK government (concerning legislation and the supervision of local authorities) moved from London to Edinburgh. For Wales, transport and other legislation is still made by Westminster but the Welsh Assembly government is responsible for local implementation and more power is continually being devolved, such as in the Railways Act 2005 that gave the Assembly greater control over train services.

The Greater London Authority consists of a directly-elected mayor, overseen by a separately-elected London Assembly, and was an important political and constitutional innovation. The Mayor of London was given unusually concentrated powers, especially in the transport domain, where he or she decides the strategy, sets the budget and appoints the board of TfL (including its chief executive, the Transport Commissioner). Outside London, eight regional assemblies have been created in England. The 1997 Labour manifesto had proposed to create 'regional chambers to coordinate transport, planning, economic development, bids for European funding and land use planning'. John Prescott, as the first Secretary of State for DETR (including local government and the regions), was personally enthused by the idea and continued to pursue the idea through three different ministerial posts (Peele, 2003: 206–7). He set up regional assemblies in the English regions, appointing mainly councillors but also people from the CBI, Trades Union Congress (TUC), National Health Service (NHS), education, rural and green groups. From 2004 they were given the role of developing regional spatial and transport strategies (see below and Chapter 5). The intention of Prescott and the regionalists was for these assemblies to be directly elected; however, a referendum held in November 2004 in north-east England, where interest had been strongest, rejected the possibility of creating an elected regional government for the area.

Local government's spatial and transport planning

Land-use planning and transport are key local responsibilities. They have increasingly been integrated because of the focus on the environment by the Conservative government in its final years of office, and on accessibility by the Labour government after 1997. Both parties when in power required local authorities to utilize their land-use planning decisions to reduce traffic and change patterns of travel, even though local authorities lack the tools that only central government can provide (on bus regulation, for example), and most of them are reduced to the status of interest groups when it comes to major ports and airports and other infrastructure decided in the end by the Transport Secretary (see Chapter 5).

Local spatial planning

The Planning and Compulsory Purchase Act 2004, with its aim of 'sustainable development', changed the procedures for local planning in England and Wales that were described in the first edition of this book (see Glaister *et al.*, 1998: ch. 6). The characteristics of the reform at national and regional level are outlined in Chapter 5 of this edition. This section summarizes the new process at local level.

The metropolitan district councils, the London boroughs and other unitary authorities (including in Wales and Scotland) continue to be the local planning authorities for their areas. In England the county councils will no longer produce structure plans to guide non-metropolitan district councils; these councils will have the same planning duties as unitary councils. In England the unitary and district authorities must draw up local plans within the context of regional spatial and transport strategies prepared by the regional assembly (or the Mayor of London), and approved by the Secretary of State. In Wales the 2004 Act left the unitary council structure plans in place but, in conformity with the wishes of the Welsh Assembly, councils must fit their plans into the Welsh Spatial Plan. The Scottish Executive had already adopted a National Planning Framework on sustainable development as a context for council structure plans. This means that all parts of Britain now have planning systems based on local plans set within long-term regional or national strategies intended to promote sustainable development.

In England, the abolition of the county structure plans produced the loudest dissent to the 2004 Act (Transport Committee, 2002: para. 5). Opponents argued, first, that county councils were elected whereas regional assemblies were appointed, even if two-thirds of assembly members were also local councillors; second, that county councils had a duty to produce Local Transport Plans that ought to be integrated into land-use planning; and, third, that there was too big a 'planning gap' between the regional strategy and local plans. However the government insisted that, rather than 'perpetuate a separate tier of sub-regional planning outside the metropolitan areas', sub-regional strategies should be decided at regional level. Nevertheless it accepted that county councils should lead the development of these strategies (ODPM, 2002: paras 18, 20). Within the South West region, for example, five county councils are each leading a sub-regional strategy covering one or more urban areas, as are four unitary councils. Counties remain transport authorities with responsibility for producing Local Transport Plans.

One aim of the new planning system is to involve local business and residents from the start; however they and the planners have first to grapple with the new terminology. Councils must produce a *local development framework*, which is a folder of *local development documents*. Some development documents are compulsory, especially the *core strategy* which sets out the long-term spatial strategy that has been decided by the council in consultation with the local community. The strategy must conform to the regional spatial and transport strategies and address the council's objectives for economic development, housing, leisure and retail, essential public services and transport infrastructure (this last to be illustrated in rough diagrammatic form). It must take account of numerous other strategies (such as education and health), including notably the Local Transport Plans of the county council and/or neighbouring councils. Other documents develop the detail of the core strategy. Councils must include a *local development scheme*, which lists the compulsory and optional documents the council has decided to produce and its production schedule. All councils had submitted a scheme to the government by March 2005, with timetables for the following three years.

Three procedures are obligatory in the planning process: the consultation of local communities and other stakeholders (to be confirmed by a *statement of community involvement*), a *sustainability appraisal* of the framework, including any supplementary strategies (in conformity with the 2004 Act and the requirements of the EU's Strategic Environment Assessment Directive 2001/42/EC), and an *annual monitoring report*, showing central government how far the council has met its targets in relation to its timetable and the planning objectives.

According to the government (ODPM, 2004:1), the key aims of the new system are as set out below:

1   '*Flexibility*': by separating the plan into individual components, and removing the need for county and district plans, 'local planning authorities can respond to changing local circumstances and ensure that spatial plans are prepared and reviewed more quickly'.
2   '*Strengthening community and stakeholder involvement*': the local authority should consult from the start not only ministries, utilities and transport authorities but also consider a list of another 60 bodies, such as the Disabled Persons Transport Advisory Committee, Friends of the Earth, the Royal

Society for the Protection of Birds, the Freight Transport Association and Road Haulage Association (see Chapter 6).

3 '*Front loading*': by requiring councils to consult and take 'key decisions' early in the process, the government hoped to speed up plan-making by avoiding 'late changes being made' as the result of objections.

4 A '*sustainability appraisal*' was also to be conducted early on to guide decisions on options that would contribute most to the achievement of sustainable development.

5 '*Programme management*': the efficient management of the planning process.

6 '*Soundness*': local development documents must be soundly based in terms of their content and the process by which they are produced, giving greater certainty to developers about the type of development that might be permitted.

Despite the emphasis on 'community involvement', local councils are severely constrained by central government's instructions, set out in Regulations or in two dozen Planning Policy Statements about the approach they are to take to housing, retail development, nature conservation and so on. Most Planning Policy Statements are revised versions of the Planning Policy Guidance notes issued under the previous regime. *Planning Policy Guidance 13: Transport* (DETR, 2001), itself little changed from the *Planning Policy Guidance 13: Transport* (DoE and DoT, 1994) that figured strongly in the first edition of this book, will be the last to be revised because of its up-to-date nature in 1994, when it reflected the environmental concerns of the time. The advice given to local authorities in PPG13, summed up in Table 3.1, shows the potential for them to promote 'more sustainable transport choices for both people and moving freight' through spatial planning (DoE and DoT, 1994: para. 4), even if more could be achieved through national policies not within local control.

Local transport planning

Counties and unitary authorities are both highways and passenger transport authorities, with the ability to integrate traffic and transport policies within the legislative and regulatory limits determined by central government. They work alongside bus and rail companies to improve local public transport networks. They can give financial support to 'socially-necessary' bus services that make a

TABLE 3.1   Delivering sustainable development

Planning issue	Transport Planning Strategy
Urban growth	Shape to make full use of public transport
Shops, schools	Site near users in local centres to make accessible by walking or cycling
Housing	Site within existing urban areas, at greater density, accessible by public transport, walking or cycling
Mixed development	Provide choice of access by public transport, offices, housing, shops – walking or cycling
Rural areas	Locate most new offices, housing, shops, leisure in local service centres
Transport investment	Link to development plan allocations of activity
Parking policies	Use to reduce reliance on the car for work journeys
Mixed-use land areas	Prioritize people over improving traffic flow; provide more road space for pedestrians, cyclists, public transport
Disabled people	Ensure that their needs as pedestrians, public transport users and motorists are taken into account
Route protection	Safeguard sites likely to be critical in the future for widening choice for passenger and freight movement

Source: Compiled from information in DETR, *Planning Policy Guidance PPG13* (TSO, 2001), para. 6.

commercial loss. Districts, London boroughs and unitary authorities have responsibilities for a range of provision from highways, traffic regulation and the regulation of residential car parking to road safety and the provision of concessionary bus passes; they are also involved in providing cycle-ways and improving footpaths and rights-of-way. More than nine out of ten local authorities with a responsibility for transport have developed, or are in the process of developing, 'safe routes to school' for pupils in their area to allow them to walk or cycle to school safely. Local roads make up 96 per cent of total road length in Britain, though this figure under-states the role played by the Highways Agency, whose trunk roads carry 34 per cent of all traffic and 67 per cent of freight (DETR, 2000:

50). Central government oversees local authorities' executive responsibilities for roads as it does for public transport. The centre lays down advisory standards which apply to highway marking, traffic signs and signals, traffic calming works and other details.

The Transport Act 2000 gave local transport authorities a statutory duty to produce Local Transport Plans that follow guidance issued by central government. These five-year plans replace the Transport Policies and Programmes that figured in the first edition of this book, under which local authorities submitted annual bids for individual capital schemes, indirectly laying the stress in local policies on road schemes rather than public transport, cycling and walking. The first LTPs covered the five-year period up to 2005/06; a second set was then prepared for the period from 2006/07 to 2010/11. For the second set, authorities were expected to engage with the public in drawing up the plans but to prioritize four transport-related issues agreed between the DfT and the Local Government Association (the organization bringing together all local councils): congestion; air quality; accessibility; and road safety. Whitehall guidance (DfT, 2004c: 5–6) for the second round of LTPs emphasized four key themes that derived from the experience of the first round:

1 '*Setting transport in a wider context*': LTPs are expected to take account of the new regional economic and spatial strategies and of other local plans set for the area; and vice versa. Many 2000–05 LTPs had given rise to unrealistic expectations about transport improvements and the regeneration and housing development plans they would support. LTPs should also show how the authority intends to use central government resources, a requirement easier to fulfil because the DfT published guideline transport capital allocations to 2011 at the same time as its LTP guidance of December 2004. The LTP should demonstrate how the council intends to work across local authority boundaries; for example, metropolitan districts are expected to show how they will make a full input as highways authorities to PTE bus priority schemes. Other local 'stakeholders' must be involved in the planning process.

2 '*Locally relevant targets*': such targets include sustainable economic growth, new housing, social inclusion and the protection of the environment. The DfT felt that the first-round LTPs had set targets related to predetermined transport investment plans rather than transport targets whose achievement would

fulfil the purpose of the transport provision. Targets should relate to outcomes rather than inputs or outputs, and should focus on priorities such as congestion, accessibility, safety, air quality, and the quality of public transport. Local targets must take account of nationally-set ones. They should be, to use the government's word, 'challenging'.

3   '*Identifying the best value for money solutions*': LTPs should demonstrate how the best possible outcomes can be delivered for the available funding. Demand management should be attempted, while infrastructure should be used as productively as possible. Wherever possible, LTPs should avoid focusing on capital investment at the expense of other options. Local authorities should consider 'the new opportunities for supporting strategies to tackle congestion in towns and cities contained in *The Future of Transport*' (DfT, 2004).

4   '*Indicators and trajectories*': authorities are expected to set key targets that reflect the planned implementation of policies and programmes. There should be targets for outcomes and intermediate outcomes. Trajectories (the direction of change in relation to targets) are to be used in determining performance-related funding.

Local authorities were also invited to use their draft LTPs to apply for a 'pump-priming' grant that would fund more detailed applications for the *Transport Innovation Fund* (TIF), expected to offer £10 billion over 2008–11. This Fund was announced as an incentive to introduce measures such as road pricing, modal shift and better bus services. The government's guidance on LTPs suggested that preferred projects would put all three together, tackling congestion through improved local bus services and demand measures such as urban road pricing (DfT, 2004c: 7), following the lead given by the Mayor in central London (see below). By the end of 2005 a few dozen authorities had put in bids for these 'pump-priming' grants, proposing a wide range of schemes.

Local authorities must provide Annual Progress Reports (APRs) on implementing their LTPs, unless they have been judged 'excellent' by the Audit Commission's Comprehensive Performance Assessment (CPA) of local authorities (the reward for an 'excellent' CPA is supposed to be a lighter-touch form of central regulation). The DfT uses APRs, alongside other information requested from 'excellent' authorities who have not submitted a full APR, to make funding decisions on local schemes (the annual Local Transport

Capital Settlement). In the early years of the CPA, all 'excellent' authorities submitted APRs. 'Excellent' authorities need not submit a full LTP for the 2006–11 period. However, first, they must still submit a set of annual target figures for congestion, air quality, accessibility and road safety, if they are to receive their share of the 'integrated transport block' funds for small schemes (£0.7 billion in 2004/05), the share being calculated according to a pre-set formula which applies to all authorities. Second, because the DfT decided to reserve about a quarter of this 'integrated transport' funding for 'the best' LTPs, 'excellent' councils that wanted to benefit from this part of the funding had still to submit a full LTP. It seems that even councils whose performance is assessed as 'excellent' by the government's own inspection body cannot be trusted to spend taxpayers' money wisely.

Local government finance: a key limitation

Local government finance in Britain is a key limitation on transport authorities' freedom. Since 1974 it has often been a topic of high political drama. Successive governments have sought – unsuccessfully – to find a new local tax. In 1990 (1989 in Scotland) a deeply unpopular poll tax briefly replaced the former rating system. From 1993 the poll tax was itself replaced by the council tax, which restored a link with property values. In 1997 the Labour government inherited a local government finance system in which over three-quarters of local government's revenue funding came from central support; council tax accounted for the remaining quarter. One of the longer-term consequences of the Conservatives' local taxation nightmare, 1989–93, was that they had had to increase grants and other central funding to almost 80 per cent of councils' income. Because of the heavy dependence on central support, local authorities were in the position where a 1 per cent increase in spending led to a 4 per cent rise in local taxation. This phenomenon, known as 'gearing', put councils under immense – and unpopular – pressure.

A series of consultative documents outlined Labour's modest proposals to examine and possibly reform elements of the local government finance system. In the first year of the Labour government, 1997–98, John Prescott, Deputy Prime Minister and the Cabinet minister responsible for local government, announced an end to 'crude and universal capping'.

Council tax

Following its introduction in 1993, council tax proved remarkably successful. Like domestic rates it was easy to collect and did not produce an unacceptably adverse public response. In the years after 1993, successive governments set the local government finance system in such a way that council taxes rose, on average, by 6 or 7 per cent a year (ODPM, 2003). Expenditure was allowed to increase more rapidly than central support, which led the local tax to rise in real terms each year. The average proportion of council spending funded from local taxation inched up from 21 per cent to 26 per cent in the years after 1993. There were frequent complaints about increases in local tax bills, the visibility of the tax and the lack of a relationship between local tax bills and ability to pay. By the early 2000s the Liberal Democrats were committed to replacing the council tax with a local income tax. Labour set up two separate official inquiries (in 2003 and again in 2004) to review the funding problems faced by local authorities.

The National Non-Domestic Rate

The non-domestic (or business) rate, which had been nationalized by the Conservatives as part of the 1990 poll tax reforms, continued to be the subject of local authority concern. The Local Government Association was committed to the return of the national non-domestic rate (NDDR) to local control. Such a change would, at a stroke, have increased the proportion of funding raised locally from 26 per cent to over 50 per cent. But Labour resisted all arguments for a return to a locally-set non-domestic rate. All the major business representative organizations were opposed to such a change and the government did not want its pro-business credentials threatened.

For urban transport in particular the failure to return the non-domestic rate to local government control is of profound importance. Because of historical residential and commuting patterns around larger city centres, there is a close parallel between, on the one hand, the density of road use and public transport provision and, on the other, concentrations of the non-domestic tax base. This local taxation capacity would – in the past – have been used to fund local transport infrastructure and services. Unless and until greater freedom is restored to local and/or regional government to determine and retain the national non-domestic rate (NNDR) yield locally, the link between economic activity and taxable capacity within cities will be broken. This problem explains the need for major British cities to lobby government for every pound needed to provide new transport services and infrastructure.

During 2002 and 2003, however, modest reforms to the NNDR were proposed. First, the government proposed that powers would be provided to create Business Improvement Districts (BIDs). This idea, imported from the United States (Travers and Weimar, 1996), would allow local businesses to create a district within which a small additional non-domestic rate (NDR) could be levied in order to pay for additional street cleaning, improvement and warden services. Second, the ODPM announced a scheme to allow local authorities to keep part of the tax income yielded by rises in the local non-domestic rate base (ODPM, 2003a). This scheme was designed in such a way as to give incentives to authorities to increase the size of the local NDR base – or to slow its decline – above the recent trend of change. Although these changes undoubtedly constituted a move in the direction of increased local discretion, they were marginal in the great scale of public finance. Against a backdrop of local government expenditure in the UK of over £100 billion, the two new NDR-related sources might, over time, raise up to £1 billion of additional local income. The principle of a nationally-set and distributed NNDR was retained.

Grants

The redistribution of Revenue Support Grant remained a live issue throughout Labour's early years in office. Every council in the country received an allocation of grant and NNDR which, together and on average, made up three-quarters of their income. Marginal changes in grant affected local expenditure and taxation far more than the decisions of councillors. A massive and expensive annual round of research, negotiations and computer-aided exemplifications took place each year, involving the Office of the Deputy Prime Minister (or its predecessor departments), the Local Government Association and a number of other participants. This process embraced technical matters such as data changes and also more controversial issues, notably proposals to alter the grant formula. Since the 1970s local government and its associations have realized that marginal changes in the grant formula – or data – could have significant redistributive impacts on authorities' grant receipts.

Transport and roads receive support in a number of ways

through the Revenue Support Grant system. One element in calculating the grant formula is a 'formula spending share' (FSS) for highways maintenance. Another FSS covers 'Environmental, Protection and Cultural' services which, despite their name, embrace concessionary fares, street cleaning and a number of other transport functions. A capital finance FSS provides support for council debt payments, including those for transport.

In addition to this general funding of local authorities' revenue expenditure on highways and other aspects of transport, the government pays an array of revenue and capital grants in support of a wide range of services and priorities. Transport support is often included in regeneration schemes funded by the local government ministry. Schools' transport funding is handled by the Department for Education and Skills. Similar arrangements in Scotland are operated by Scottish ministers. Some of this financial contribution towards transport services delivered by local councils is in the form of revenue support from which spending is more or less at the council's discretion (for example, the £1 billion that councils spend supporting socially-necessary bus services). Some spending is probably more sensibly allocated by the DfT because the burden is concentrated in time and location (for example, bids for local road schemes costing over £5 million or light rail schemes), or linked to national taxation (fuel subsidy to bus operators amounting to £340 million in 2003/04). However, the proliferation of small, project-related grants, for most of which local authorities must compete inefficiently (because of the cost of preparing bids), is easily characterized as micro-management, and further illustrates the weak financial autonomy of local authorities in Britain. A fuller description of the following annual budgets can be found in the DfT's *Annual Report 2004* (2004b):

- Rural Bus Subsidy Grant (£50 million)
- Rural Bus Challenge (£20 million) to support rural bus networks
- Urban Bus Challenge (£20 million) to support bus services in deprived urban areas
- Transport Direct (£20 million) to install real-time information indicators
- funding for three guided busways (£90 million)
- Cycling Projects Fund (£5 million)
- projects to encourage 'sustainable' transport in towns (£2 million)

- Home Zones Challenge Fund (£30 million over 4 years for 59 schemes)
- School Travel Plans (£50 million over 2 years)

Capital finance

In one aspect of local authority finance the Blair government made genuine efforts to reduce financial control over local authorities. The 1997 government had inherited a cumbersome system of capital controls that had been put in place by the Conservatives in 1989. This system gave Whitehall control or detailed influence over borrowing, capital receipts, debt repayment and service-by-service expenditure. Indeed, control over borrowing extended to all forms of credit, including leasing and even barter deals. The belt-and-braces nature of the post-1989 system resulted from the government's efforts to stop councils using 'creative accounting' to thwart spending controls.

Labour proposed moving to a 'single pot' capital spending allocation within which authorities would be given a single spending maximum for investment in all services. This figure would still take account of individual authorities' capacity to sell assets and the need to plan effectively, but would then allow them considerable freedom in the determination of priorities and projects. Unfortunately, the Home Office and the Department for Education and Skills proved unwilling to allow all the services for which they were responsible to be subsumed within the single pot system. The DfT also retained much of its capital funding programme outside the single pot arrangements. Thus the liberation proposed by the reform of capital control extended largely to services within the remit of the ODPM.

The government's intentions had been signalled, however. A second reform was then proposed that would produce a significant shift of power to local government. The Local Government Act 2003 introduced a new system of capital controls based on the so-called 'prudential rules'. In future, authorities would be free to spend on capital – and to borrow where necessary – so long as they kept within pre-determined limits concerning overall indebtedness, their capacity to make repayments and maximum year-on-year increases. The prudential rules system would potentially give authorities far greater freedom to plan their capital spending predictably and consistently. It will take experience of the new arrangements over a number of years fully to test how effective they prove to be. The 2003 legislation also included fall-back powers that would allow the government to re-impose, authority-by-authority, capital spending limits if national economic circumstances were felt to require them. However, TfL took full advantage of the new prudential rules system, and in late 2004 issued a bond-financed programme of investments, including a major extension to the Docklands Light Railway, new tramways and a Thames Gateway Bridge. It was not, though, able to prevent the government deciding to renovate and renew the London Underground through a Public–Private Partnership (this will be examined in more detail in Chapter 8). The Mayor of London, Ken Livingstone, fought a long battle to stop the £16 billion PPP deal being imposed (Wolmar, 2002), but he failed and ministers ensured that the concession contracts with the private sector consortia were signed before the Mayor and TfL were given control of the Tube network.

Transport in major urban areas

The government and funding of transport in major urban areas vary significantly from the arrangements for other parts of the country. Superimposed on the tier of local councils, as noted earlier in this chapter, are passenger transport authorities covering the metropolitan areas surrounding London, Birmingham, Manchester, Liverpool, Sheffield, Leeds, Newcastle-upon-Tyne and Glasgow. These authorities have responsibilities for the organization and financial support of public transport.

It is impossible to understand the evolution of the local rail networks around Britain's major cities without understanding the growth of these cities as a result of the Industrial Revolution. Railways themselves were a product of engineering and technological advances that occurred during the first half of the nineteenth century. As industrialization encouraged workers to leave the land and move into rapidly-growing towns and cities, so transport systems evolved within the newly-created urban centres. Horse-drawn buses, trams and, relatively soon, railways were introduced. By the 1850s, London and Glasgow had even started the construction of underground railways. Private companies developed railways around the major cities of Scotland, the North and the Midlands. In London the world's largest network of urban railways was built. Councils proudly opened tramways and trolleybus systems. By the early years of the twentieth century, Britain's cities enjoyed – by international standards – good public transport provision. The London Passenger Transport Board was widely considered the world's leading transport utility.

During the long period between 1939 and today there was a profound change in the British economy and living patterns. The industrialization and urbanization of the nineteenth century has been followed by a significant reversal of both trends. It is common to describe the British economy as 'post-industrial': there has been a large shift away from manufacturing and towards service industries. In parallel with this change – and doubtless linked to it – there has been a steep decline in the populations and densities of older cities. Although such changes are by no means unique to Britain, the intensity, speed and scale of de-industrialization were probably more pronounced than in any other country in western Europe. The rise of the automobile has also affected cities. Public transport use has declined and roads have become badly congested. The arrangements for running transport in Britain's major cities have thus evolved during a period of significant political and social change. They have had to take account of the need to facilitate movement across large conurbations at times of sharp economic decline (during the 1960s, 1970s and 1980s) and, more recently (the 1990s and 2000s), during a period when massive government efforts were being devoted to regenerating British cities.

Passenger Transport Authorities

In the seven largest cities outside London, the instrument created under legislation passed in 1968 for the purpose of running public transport in urban areas was the Passenger Transport Authority. The 1968 legislation recognized the need for special-purpose strategic bodies to be established in the major conurbations to overcome the perceived inadequacies of the existing local authorities for dealing with conurbation-wide public transport provision, while maintaining the principle of local government accountability. The 1968 Act made provision for PTAs to take over responsibility for municipal transport undertakings in their areas, and to enter into agreements with the nationalized transport operators and British Railways. The PTEs were created as separate legal entities from PTAs, though a PTE is subject to appointment, direction and budget approval by the Authority and to the latter's general policies. The 1968 Act placed a corresponding duty upon the then British Railways Board and the nationalized bus operators to cooperate in each PTE area with each other and the PTE.

The ability of the PTA/PTE mechanism to deliver effective public transport policies was further enhanced in 1974 and 1975 when the English metropolitan counties and the Strathclyde Regional Council in Scotland were created as a tier of multi-purpose strategic authorities for the conurbations. These became the PTAs for their areas. They combined the exercise of these PTA powers with their responsibilities for roads, strategic land-use planning, transport, concessionary fares, and economic development. Since the abolition of the English metropolitan authorities the PTAs have been joint boards of councillors from the metropolitan districts. An analogous reform took place in Scotland in 1996. While the PTE continues under the political direction of the PTA, it none the less has independent statutory responsibilities of its own. Most PTAs have recently adopted 'brand names' (such as Centro in the West Midlands) for corporate purposes. A summary of the composition and characteristics of each PTA/PTE and, for comparison, TfL, is given in Table 3.2.

The 1985 Transport Act adopted a completely new approach to the organization of public transport based on privatization, deregulation and competition. The duty of PTAs to integrate public passenger transport was removed and they lost direct control over bus undertakings. In addition, PTAs were placed under a duty not to exercise their powers in a way which inhibited competition. The obligation to cooperate with bodies such as British Railways was also removed. The PTAs generally used their residual powers in respect of non-commercial bus services and subsidized parts of the rail network to maintain some degree of involvement in public transport. Many PTEs argued that difficulties emerged as a consequence of the unregulated operations of the commercial bus sector and because of a lack of capacity to link together different forms of local transport provision. Financial constraints emerged because the post-1986 PTAs relied on pooled funding from their constituent districts (they did not have their own power to set a local tax precept). When privatization was extended to the railways in the mid-1990s, a regulatory regime was applied both to railway infrastructure provision and to passenger train operators. Licence conditions imposed on operators ensured the continuance of obligations in respect of the provision of passenger information and inter-operator fares which had not been imposed on the bus industry. In addition, the role of PTEs in determining service levels and fares for rail operators was entrenched in the Railways Act 1993 and reinforced by a series of ministerial statements. The PTEs became joint franchisers (along

TABLE 3.2   *Metropolitan transport authorities*

PTA/PTE	Population in millions	Constituent authorities	Budget 2003–4 £m.
Strathclyde SPT	2.21	Argyll & Bute, East Ayrshire, East Dumbartonshire, East Renfrewshire, Glasgow, Inverclyde, North Ayrshire, North Lanarkshire, Renfrewshire, South Ayrshire, South Lanarkshire, West Dumbartonshire	105
Tyne & Wear Nexus	1.08	Gateshead, Newcastle, North Tyneside, South Tyneside, Sunderland	64
West Yorkshire Metro	2.10	Bradford, Calderdale, Kirklees, Leeds, Wakefield	131
South Yorkshire SYPTE	1.27	Barnsley, Doncaster, Rotherham, Sheffield	65
Merseyside Merseytravel	1.36	Knowsley, Liverpool, Sefton, St Helens, Wirral	270
Greater Manchester GMPTE	2.53	Bolton, Bury, Manchester, Oldham, Rochdale, Salford, Stockport,Tameside, Trafford, Wigan	192
West Midlands Centro	2.58	Birmingham, Coventry, Dudley, Sandwell, Solihull, Walsall, Wolverhampton	150
Greater London TfL	7.40	None, though TfL provides services within the area covered by all 32 London boroughs and the City of London	2,400

Sources: Data from Passenger Transport Executive Group, *PTEG: Delivering Public Transport Solutions* (undated); *Annual Reports* or *Annual Accounts* of each PTE (2003–04); Department for Transport, *Transport Statistics Bulletin: Regional Transport Statistics* (DfT, 2005a).

with a government agency) of the train operations which provided local services in their areas.

Since 2000, PTAs in all English metropolitan areas (as with every other local authority in England with responsibility for local transport) have been required to develop, agree with government, and adopt five-year Local Transport Plans as described earlier in this chapter. The functions of the plan are to set out a longer-term transport strategy for the area (in this case for the city and the larger metropolitan area) and to link it to the wider purpose of urban regeneration.

Table 3.2 suggests that most metropolitan transport authorities have budgets of a broadly similar scale, though Merseyside stands out – particularly given its relatively small population – for having a significantly larger budget, which is explained by the substantial subsidy given to local rail services within the area. London is bigger than any of the other conurbations, in terms both of its population and its budget. Indeed TfL's net budget (£2.4 billion) is more than twice the size of all the other PTEs added together. TfL's gross budget (that is, including spending funded from fares and certain grants) exceeds £5 billion.

The current duties of PTAs/PTEs include:

(a)   producing strategies for developing local public transport networks;
(b)   planning and funding socially-necessary bus services;
(c)   working with bus operators to improve bus services;
(d)   managing and planning local rail services (with central government or its agencies);
(e)   providing information about local transport services;
(f)   providing assistance for people with disabilities;
(g)   running concessionary fares schemes;
(h)   providing investment to refurbish and modernize all aspects of the transport system, such as rail and bus stations, bus stops and light rail systems;
(i)   acting as a leader and coordinator of local public transport provision, including securing joint working between regional and local institutions.

The pattern of transport use varies significantly from region to region and from city to city. Outside London, reliance on cars for journeys to work is greatest in Wales and the East of England (80 per cent in 2003) and least in Merseyside (69 per cent); buses are used most in Tyne & Wear (15 per cent) and least in east, south-east and south-west England (4 per cent); but more people cycle in the south and east (also 4 per cent). Rail is not much used for commuting anywhere outside London (5 per cent at most). Predictably, London is different: only 42 per cent of journeys to work are by car

TABLE 3.3   *Rail passenger journeys, 2003–04*

	Passenger journeys (millions)	Percentage change 1993–4 to 2003–4
National rail	1014	37
London		
Underground	948	29
Docklands Light Railway	49	484
Croydon Tramlink	20	n.a.
Tyne & Wear Metro	38	–2
Blackpool Trams	4	–33
Sheffield Supertram	12	n.a.
Manchester Metrolink	19	67
Centro West Midland Metro	5	n.a.
Nottingham Tram	0.4	n.a.

n.a. = not applicable (service started after 1993)
Source: Data from Department for Transport, *Transport Statistics Bulletin: A Bulletin of Public Transport Statistics Great Britain* (DfT, 2004d).

(only 12 per cent in central London); 13 per cent use the bus and 31 per cent the train (DfT, 2004d: Table 1.5b). The use of rail and light rail nationally, in London and in some other cities has increased during the past decade, as Table 3.3 shows. However, there was a small decline in the use of the Tyne & Wear Metro and a rather larger fall in Blackpool Trams even if new tram systems in Sheffield, Manchester, the West Midlands (Birmingham) and Nottingham show increases from a low or zero base.

Urban transport authorities have long sought to increase the proportion of people using public transport to travel to work, and to reduce car dependency. National government targets encourage a move from car to public transport or walking. Through agreements with the national rail system, PTAs have retained control over fares and ticketing on locally-supported rail services. In Glasgow the Underground is owned, managed and operated by Strathclyde. In Tyne & Wear the metro is operated by the PTE. In English PTA areas where there are tram systems, the authority has general responsibility for setting the overall framework within which the system operates (though the systems themselves are privately operated). However, PTAs/PTEs have no control over most bus provision and can only influence those bus services which are subsidized.

In contrast, the Greater London Authority (in the person of the

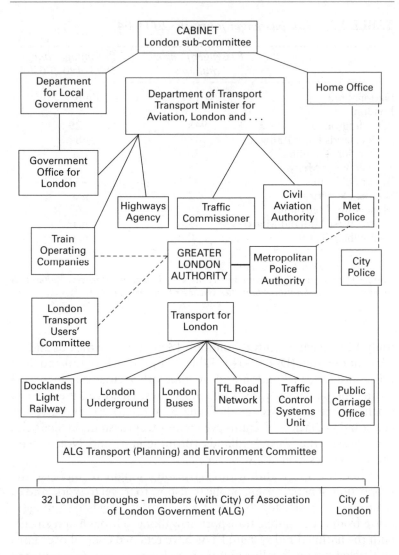

FIGURE 3.1   *Organization of transport in London in 2006*

Mayor of London) has, in TfL, a 'PTE' which operates directly, or through contracts it specifies, a wide range of passenger transport services (the London Underground, Docklands Light Railway, Croydon Tramlink, buses and river-buses), and can agree enhancements to commuter rail services with train operators. In contrast to the deregulation and privatization of bus services in the PTA areas, London's bus routes were not deregulated after 1985 but contracted to bus companies by competitive tender (see Chapter 7 for the details), giving TfL, unlike the metropolitan PTEs, the power to specify routes, levels of service and fares. Figure 3.1 illustrates the mayor's capacity to control through TfL both local transport, including taxis, and the main traffic flows. However, while the Greater London Authority is in a similar position to that of PTAs with regard to railways, traffic policing services, and government departments or agencies, it does not have the organic link with the boroughs that the joint boards of the PTAs have with their constituent authorities. The Mayor therefore still has to work hard if he wants the boroughs to cooperate (for example, on bus priority lanes) because they are the highway authorities for much of the bus network. Yet, overall, the organizational arrangements for Greater London after 2000 put the capital in a privileged position as far as the coordination of transport strategy and operation is concerned. In practice TfL, with the backing of the Mayor, has fulfilled the expectations of those who argued during the 1990s for a stronger coordination of transport in London, the Audit Commission in 2004 giving it a performance rating of 'excellent'.

The London congestion charge experiment

The special conditions that apply to London mentioned throughout this chapter (its own variant of regional government that gives strategic transport powers to a Mayor; a special-purpose transport authority, TfL, under the Mayor's control; London's extensive rail and Underground network; the high proportion of commuters using public transport; and serious road traffic congestion) made it a likely candidate for the first experiment with large-scale congestion charging in Britain. The introduction of the charge also needed the legal powers given by the new Labour government (Greater London Authority Act 1999, Schedule 23), and the election as first Mayor of Ken Livingstone. He had previous experience as leader of the Greater London Council in introducing ambitious public transport policies (even if critics questioned their good foundation), and was politically courageous. Livingstone and TfL had to withstand many apocalyptic warnings, including from ministers (the technological impossibilities; unimaginable overcrowding on the Tube; gridlock and possibly mayhem in the streets).

The scheme was launched in legal terms in 2001 with the Road User Charging (Charges and Penalty Charges) (London) Regulations, and put into action on 17 February 2003. Within a few days, over 100,000 people were paying the daily charge (£5, or £12 if paid late the same day). In the first months about 36 per cent paid in petrol stations or other shops, 28 per cent by telephoning the call-centre, 16 per cent by the Internet, 12 per cent by text-messaging (Short Message Service, SMS), 4 per cent by inter-active telephone, and 1 per cent by letter. Capita, the private company running the system, had usefully suggested SMS to TfL, but the firm's administrative problems (slow responses to telephone calls, inaccurate vehicle identification, and generally poor quality control) drew much criticism. Performance improved after TfL negotiated a supplementary contract with targets (TfL 2004: 29; 2005: 150).

Opposition was relatively muted partly because many vehicles were exempt or mainly-exempt from the charge (110,000 vehicles). The categories include disabled people, taxis, doctors, emergency services, buses and minibuses, two-wheelers and vehicles using alternative fuels. The 20,000 residents of the zone are entitled to a 90 per cent reduction. There was a debate about whether motorcyclists should pay, but they are a powerful interest group, and there are technical problems 'reading' their number plates. These exemptions are reasonable; and the Mayor resisted pressure from other groups (including post and parcel-deliverers, and market traders). However, the size of the computer database of exempt vehicles to be checked against entries and payments restricted the size of the congestion zone. Not only did the exemptions reduce the income from the scheme but so did the reduction of traffic and falling number of fines: net receipts were about £70 million in the first year instead of the £200 million mentioned in the Mayor's Transport Strategy (GLA, 2001); the Mayor did not have the funding for transport infrastructure projects he had envisaged, and which had encouraged Londoners to support the policy. In 2004/5 only £97 million was generated, of which 80 per cent was spent on bus services. In 2005 the charge was raised to £8 in the hope of generating about £120 million a year.

Errors made in charging fines are the most criticized aspect of the congestion charge. The registration numbers recorded at entries to the charging zone are checked by computer against the databases of charges paid and exempt vehicles. The list of vehicles which appear not to have paid is sent to the DVLA which subtracts the motorcycles and identifies the type and colour of the vehicle. Capita staff compare these details on a screen against photographs of the vehicle and its number, and if they match send a penalty notice to the registered owner. If aggrieved drivers are not satisfied with Capita's explanation they can appeal to a commission run by the London Government Association, under contract to TfL. About 2 per cent of drivers take their appeal that far, of which just under half succeed; the main disputes now concern leased vehicles, and new regulations are intended to reduce that problem.

The Audit Commission (2004: 19) judged that the scheme 'has operated smoothly with minimal disruption to traffic and no significant delays on roads on the periphery of the zone'. After two years of operation, Tfl's (2005) survey covered several points:

1   Traffic flows more smoothly in the zone, which is about 7 kilometres in diameter. Congestion has been reduced by about 30 per cent (in 2002, daytime journeys in the zone typically took 2.3 minutes per kilometre longer than a similar night-time journey, whereas in 2004 the average daytime delay amounted to only about 1.6 minutes per kilometre). Around the zone, congestion initially fell by about 10–20 per cent, but then returned to its pre-charging state. The Mayor's new powers eased the inauguration of a new London Traffic Control Centre in which road traffic managers, police and bus controllers work together in front of their monitoring screens to respond to incidents quickly and keep traffic flowing (TfL, 2003: 10).

2   De-congestion is mainly in the form of reduced waiting time at junctions rather than increases in vehicle speeds between junctions and therefore road accidents have not increased: indeed, there has been a reduction of over 40 per cent in accidents within the zone, and no measurable change in accident severity near the zone. For similar reasons emissions within the zone have decreased by about 12 per cent for both nitrogen oxides and carbon particles; there has been little change in air pollution around the zone.

3   Levels of traffic are 18 per cent lower, remaining at levels seen soon after the scheme came into operation, when roads inside the zone looked more like a Sunday than a weekday. Transport 2000 advised the Mayor to fill the empty tarmac with cycle lanes quickly, before it filled up with cars again. There is a little more traffic on the boundary road, though congestion has not increased, but 'no evidence of detrimental traffic effects on

roads outside of the charging zone resulting from diverting traffic'. TfL had taken care to improve traffic management to ease diversion (for instance, at cross-roads), before the introduction of the charge.

4   Bus delays were immediately halved; buses had to wait at bus stops in order to keep to their schedules, before these were revised to take account of this unusual phenomenon. Buses have continued to become more reliable, probably because operational arrangements have also improved.

5   Buses and the Underground did not become over-crowded as many feared: or rather, on the Underground it was no worse than before. The Mayor provided an additional 300 bus journeys, which accommodated satisfactorily 40 per cent more bus passengers in 2003; about half as a consequence of the congestion charge, and about half in response to improved services. It had been calculated that if 10 per cent of former car-drivers took the Tube, it would add only one passenger to each carriage, because a large majority of people travelling into central London were already coming by public transport. Probably because of a slight economic decline, fewer Underground trips were made in 2003 than in 2002: levels in 2004 were still lower than when the charge was introduced.

6   Travel behaviour has changed: of the car drivers who previously came into the zone, about a quarter were going straight through and chose to divert round it or go somewhere else after the introduction of the charge; just over half the former drivers still came into the zone but by bus or Tube (mostly bus); and another 10 per cent by other means (walking, two-wheelers, taxi). About 5 per cent still drive into the zone but outside charging hours; only about 5 per cent were drivers with a destination in central London who chose to drive somewhere else or come into London less frequently; this last figure gives one indication of the overall impact on retail and leisure activity in London.

The possible economic impacts have been a significant factor for other cities considering introducing a charge, and indeed for Londoners when considering an extension to the existing zone. In the case of London they are difficult to establish because the charge was only one factor among others at the time of the introduction of the charge, including the Iraq war (fewer tourists, avoidance of city centres), the closure of the Central Line during February–March

2003, and a general economic downturn. Putting together econometric analyses, case studies and business surveys, it seems that some sectors or activities benefit marginally while others lose marginally. A TfL survey of 700 firms of different types showed that shops and the leisure industry had lost about 2 per cent of turnover (but 6 per cent for newsagents and food shops), whereas the financial and business sector had gained from the reduction in delays between meetings. The Freight Transport Association said 70 per cent of firms in its own survey found that journeys were no quicker than before; 90 per cent had not been able to slot additional journeys into the day; only 37 per cent had been able to pass on the charge cost to customers; and 80 per cent thought the advantages did not outweigh the disadvantages. None the less, it accepted its members would have to live with the system (www.fta.co.uk). On the whole, restaurants and cafés are against the charge; other parts of the leisure industry, hotels and the financial sector remain in favour; while the retail and distribution sectors are ambivalent. In response, the Mayor has modified the scheme, by ending the charging hours earlier to help the leisure trade, increasing the time available to pay the charge, and making it administratively easier and cheaper for businesses with fleets of vehicles to pay the charges.

The Mayor and TfL soon started thinking of extending charging into west London. Although residents and especially businesses in the extension zone do not support the scheme, and it is not clear that the extension will raise additional revenues (because residents in the new zone will be entitled to concessionary access to the original zone), the Mayor has said he will go ahead in 2007. TfL was also studying a much larger extension to the whole of Greater London, probably at variable rates, in about 2010, preferably using the global positioning system (or the European Galileo). It was pushing ministers to consider a national 'electronic number plate' system, which would have wider uses, such as controlling licence and insurance evasion, and theft. Leeds was already experimenting with a shadow GPS scheme but London now had practical experience. The experiment conducted in London has taken urban road pricing out of its niche as a topic for transport economists and turned it into a practical tool of traffic management, to be considered as one option alongside others. Commentators in the financial press were even talking of a future in which business accepted that roads had a price that must be paid, either in the form of congestion or of charges.

Conclusion

Local government's role in transport in Britain is partly as an agent of the centre, but partly as an independent actor, and the story of the congestion charge in London illustrates that well. Yet London is a particular case because of its longer history as a very large metropolitan city strongly dependent on collective transport, its recent extraordinary concentration of power in one post-holder at the top of an all-purpose transport authority, and because of its political sensitivity as a capital city, of which one practical outcome was the Conservative government's decision to maintain public control over bus provision. What London can do may not be applicable to other local authorities. On the whole central government has since 1945 taken away responsibilities from local government. Detailed interventions in local authority finance and provision in recent years have further shifted control towards the centre, often in ways that seem hard to justify in rational terms: consider the dozen small grant schemes for implementing central government 'initiatives' that are all worthwhile but within the intellectual and technical capacity of local authorities to devise and fund for themselves had they the financial freedoms to do so; consider the refusal of the Home Office, the Education Department and, in part, the Transport Department, to allow the capital funding they have in any case decided to give each local authority to be put into a 'single pot' for the local authority to allocate according to local conditions.

On the other hand, Britain's international obligations under the Rio and Kyoto conventions and within the EU (see previous chapters and Chapter 4), are virtually imposing on its government a more devolved approach to transport policy. Not only must the changes be delivered at local, and especially, metropolitan level (it is in the metropolitan areas that problems of pollution and congestion are most sharply experienced: see Chapter 5), but also allowing local authorities to implement decisions that are unwelcome to key electoral audiences is both sensible (they can organize consensus better than national governments) and politically astute. The Labour government arrived in 1997 with a transport policy and a manifesto that promised a better relationship between local and central government (see Chapter 1), and some departments, including those under John Prescott and his junior ministers, seem genuinely to have promoted that agenda, especially at regional level, where spatial and transport strategies will now set the context for local authorities. But other ministers were more sceptical, the

Transport Minister and the Chancellor of the Exchequer notably and openly hostile to the London congestion charge until the day after the scheme was introduced. They left the Mayor to take the political blame if anything went wrong. Their lack of political support to the several major cities that had initially proposed adopting urban tolls even undermined the government's own *10 Year Plan* (Transport Committee, 2002a: para. 15). But the success of the charge has given central government a better sense of the utility of metropolitan governments. The White Paper of 2004, *The Future of Transport*, not only had the confidence to make road pricing (or at least a debate on road pricing) a big theme, but also offered the possibility of transferring PTA subsidies to PTA control so that the metropolitan authorities could choose how to distribute their funding between 'rail and other modes of transport'. They would have more power to specify additional rail services; and TfL would be given some responsibilities for commuter rail services. Such changes would move some transport decision-making power away from the centre and to the cities, and only the churlish would note that the requirement to show value for money would guide local choice for rail towards central government's preference for buses.

Chapter 4

The European Union and United Kingdom Transport Policy

When most people did not travel very far from home, and only the most expensive luxuries, such as silk and spices, had to be transported over great distances, there was little need for governments to coordinate their transport policies, but this changed as the Industrial Revolution gathered pace in the eighteenth and nineteenth centuries, leading to rapid growth in the transport of passengers and freight both nationally and internationally. In the twentieth century growth was held back briefly by two world wars, but has otherwise continued apace with the globalization of world trade. Europe's oldest surviving international transport organization is the Central Commission for the Navigation of the Rhine, established in 1815 under the Congress of Vienna. The Bern Convention on the international transport of goods by rail dates from 1890, though its antecedents date back to the Union of German Railway Administrations, established in 1850.

Britain was a founder member of the Rhine Commission, but this had little impact on British transport policy for obvious geographical reasons. It was 1952 before the inclusion of rail–sea transit provisions persuaded Britain to sign the Bern Convention. On the other hand, the international context has always been of critical importance to British policies for sea and air transport. Although the 'freedom of the seas' allows any vessel to sail through international waters, and to compete for the carriage of goods, the operation of regular timetabled services for mixed cargoes led from the nineteenth century onwards to the establishment of 'liner conferences' whose function was to fix tariffs at levels which would enable such services to be maintained on a profitable basis (in the longer-term interest, it is claimed, of both shipping companies and their customers). Airlines developed similar mechanisms to protect their markets, reinforced by bilateral agreements between governments. The need for internationally-agreed safety regulations both at sea and in the air gave rise to numerous agreements, now over-seen by the International Maritime Organization (IMO) and the International Civil Aviation Organization (ICAO). Britain played an important part in the negotiation of the Chicago Convention (1944) which laid the foundations of the international air transport regime, and the importance of Britain in international shipping was recognized by the location of IMO's headquarters in London. These and other international transport organizations remain relevant to British transport policy, but their significance has been progres-sively eclipsed by that of the European Union. This chapter sketches the development of the EU's common transport policy, the process by which EU policy is made, and its growing impact on British transport policies.

The common transport policy of the European Union

The omens at the birth of the common transport policy were not auspicious. The transport experts at the inter-governmental confer-ence which negotiated the Treaty of Rome (1957) were deeply divided between a majority favouring extensive state intervention in the provision of transport services and a determined minority, led by the Netherlands, who refused to give up an approach based on the liberal polices which best suited their more open trading economy. As a result the transport articles of the Treaty – cobbled together in a hurry when it was decided that transport was too important to leave out, but not important enough to wait for – are an awkward compromise. The germ of a liberal policy is buried deep in the apparently innocuous wording of Article 70, which requires the member states to pursue the objectives of the Treaty within the framework of a common transport policy (Article 70 was originally Article 74, but we use throughout this book the text of the Treaty as amended by the Treaty of Amsterdam, 1997, and the Treaty of Nice, 2001). The objectives of the Treaty, as set out in the preamble and principles, are essentially liberal. But Article 71(1) requires the Council to take account of the 'distinctive features of transport', which Nigel Despicht (Despicht, 1964: 35) described as 'a perma-nent pretext for treating the transport sector differently from the rest of the economy'. Indeed, most of the member states saw the transport articles as a defence against the general provisions of the Treaty governing such matters as competition, state aids and the freedom to provide services, which in their view could be applied to transport only within the framework of a common transport policy taking due account of its 'distinctive features'. In the absence of such a policy, more general Treaty provisions applying to the generality of economic activities could not yet be applied to transport.

Within the transport Title, most decisions affecting inland transport were supposed to be taken by qualified majority vote after the end of 1965, which should have made it easier to reach agreement, but ministers were reluctant to impose controversial policies on one another, as indeed they are to this day. Besides, Article 71(2) provides for the Council to take decisions by unanimity 'where the application of provisions concerning the principles of the regulatory system for transport would be liable to have a serious effect on the standard of living and on employment in certain areas and on the operation of transport facilities'.

If the development of a common policy for inland transport was frustrated by persistent disagreement over the policy to be followed, the application of the Treaty to sea and air transport was even more uncertain, since Article 80(2) merely provided that 'the Council may, acting unanimously, decide whether, to what extent and by what procedure appropriate provisions may be laid down for sea and air transport'. Until this Article was amended by the Single European Act (1986) to provide for decisions on sea and air transport to be taken by qualified majority, the Council treated it as granting explicit permission to exclude sea and air transport altogether from the ambit of the Treaty.

A single market in transport services

For over two decades progress towards agreement on a common transport policy was almost imperceptible. Indeed, in 1983, a senior member of the Commission's own transport directorate wrote that 'time and again the common transport policy has been the saddest chapter in the history of European integration' (Erdmenger, 1983: 89). However, the ice was about to crack. In 1983 the European Parliament (EP), frustrated with the continuing lack of progress, brought an action against the Council in the European Court of Justice (ECJ), seeking a declaration that the Council had infringed the Treaty by failing to introduce a common policy. The EP was only partially successful in its submission, because the obligation to establish a common transport policy was not expressed in the Treaty of Rome in sufficiently specific terms for an action for infringement of the Treaty to succeed. However, the underlying complaint could not seriously be contested, and the Court did find, in its judgment of 22 May 1985, that the Council was in breach of the Treaty on a narrower but still fundamental point, the obligation set out in Articles 71(1)(a) and (b) to ensure freedom to provide international transport services within the Community, and to lay down the conditions under which non-resident transport carriers may operate transport services in a member state (Case 13/83, *European Parliament* v. *Council of the European Communities*, ECR 1513–1603).

In 1986 a further landmark judgment of the Court, known as the *Nouvelles Frontières* case after the travel agency involved, confirmed that the fundamental principles of EU competition law, set out in Articles 81 and 82 of the Treaty, applied directly to transport even if the Council had laid down no regulations or directives to guide their application (Cases 209–213/84, *Ministère Public* v. *Asjes*, 30 April 1986). Since these Treaty articles ban anti-competitive agreements among companies and any abuse of a dominant position, the Nouvelles Frontières company was free to sell air tickets at bucket-shop prices not approved by the French government, which had endorsed the fares agreed within the International Air Transport Association (IATA). This judgment, with its implied threat that the terms of competition among the airlines would be determined by judgments of the Court if the Council failed to act, was wonderfully effective in compelling the member states to agree the first package of air transport liberalization measures in 1987, including a regulation which applied the competition rules of the treaty to air transport in an acceptable manner.

Important as the Court's judgments were, they were not the only factor which caused the Council of Ministers to take action. In June 1985, Lord Cockfield's White Paper on completing the internal market (Commission of the European Communities, or CEC, 1985) had identified hundreds of obstacles to the operation of the Community's internal market, many of which could be overcome only by the increased use of qualified majority voting to drive them through the Council. Political commitment to the implementation of this programme, at the level of the European Council, focused attention on areas including transport policy where the establishment of a single market had been frustrated. As a result a large number of Treaty articles were amended by means of the Single European Act (1986), to apply qualified majority voting to areas where unanimity had been an obstacle, among them sea and air transport.

Under these pressures, substantial progress was made between 1985 and 1992 towards the establishment of a single market in each of the main transport modes. What follows here and in the next section is a summary of developments before and after 1992; for more detail see Stevens (2004). Road transport led the way with a progressive relaxation, from 1984, of the bilateral quotas governing the transport of goods between member states. Quota restrictions were abolished altogether from the end of 1992, and a further agreement governing cabotage – the right to carry goods between two points within another member state – was phased in gradually between 1993 and 1998. Meanwhile, in 1985, a directive governing the maximum weights and dimensions for heavy lorries, which had been under discussion for two decades, was finally adopted, albeit with an exemption for the UK and Ireland to 1999 to allow time for the strengthening of roads and bridges. On the Community's inland waterways, the freedom to provide services – which signatories to the Rhine Convention already enjoyed – was extended to all EU member states in 1985, and cabotage rights were approved in 1991.

Only on the railways has progress towards a single market been slow. In 1991 a start was made on freeing up access to railway services. Directive 91/440/EEC, which provides for railways to be commercially managed, with separate accounting for infrastructure and transport operations, also provides for access and transit rights for certain international services. In 1995 Directives 95/18 and 95/19 provided for the licensing of railway companies, which has allowed Arriva, for example, to operate in Denmark, and Connex (a French company) in the UK. Further steps were taken towards the liberalization of rail freight services in 2001, with yet another package of liberalization measures proposed in 2004, but the Commission had to take a majority of the member states to the ECJ in 2003 for failure to implement the 2001 directives. In practice it remains extremely difficult to take trains across EU borders except with the mutual agreement of the dominant railway companies on either side, often with long delays (especially for freight trains while new crews take over, and new locomotives are attached). As a result of such restrictions, and the priority accorded to passenger services, the average speed of cross-border rail freight services in 2000 was just 18 kilometres per hour (CEC, 2001: 28).

In the air a minimal liberalization of inter-regional air services had been agreed in 1983. This was followed by three further packages of regulations in 1987, 1990 and 1992, which progressively liberalized the rights of airlines to carry passengers on any route within the EU, ended restrictions on capacity, frequency and fares, and even provided for the gradual phasing-in of cabotage rights between 1993 and 1997. At sea a package of regulations agreed in December 1986 freed up the provision of maritime services between member states, applied the Treaty competition rules to maritime transport, and made provision for levies to be imposed against the unfair pricing practices of subsidized foreign carriers. In 1989 the Commission sent the Council a second package of shipping measures. State aids were covered in a document, not requiring Council approval, setting out the conditions under which they would be allowed. The Commission's 1989 proposal to open up cabotage was finally adopted at the end of 1992, albeit with an exemption to 2004 for all Mediterranean cabotage and the Atlantic coasts of Portugal, Spain and France.

Since 1992 the Commission has continued to develop its transport policies on a pragmatic modal basis with a strong emphasis on measures required to buttress the single market. There was still much to be done in all modes, but especially on the railways, to complete the single market and to ensure that new barriers to competition were not continually erected as the old ones were taken down. Obstacles remain even today, particularly in respect of bus and rail services, but solid foundations have been laid for policies which can reasonably be regarded as consistent with the intention – always present in Articles 71(a) and 71(b) – to make provision for all Community transport operators to provide both international services within the Community and services within other member states. To that extent, it can reasonably be claimed that the foundations of a common transport policy were successfully laid in the period leading up to 1992.

Beyond the single market

Having observed the success of the Single European Act in supporting the single market programme, the Community embarked on a succession of further Inter-governmental Conferences generating Treaty amendments. The Treaty on European Union (or TEU, 1992) and the Treaties of Amsterdam (1997) and Nice (2001) each included further changes which have had profound consequences for the development of a common transport policy.

First, under the Treaty on European Union, the addition to Article 71 of a clause authorizing 'measures to improve transport safety' has provided a solid base in the Treaty for the development of safety-related policies in all the transport modes. Safety had already been a factor in decisions concerning European standards for equipment used in road transport (for example, safety belts), but until 1992 the member states had preferred to look after maritime and aviation safety on an inter-governmental basis, acting on their own authority within IMO, or ICAO and its European regional body, the European Civil Aviation Conference (ECAC). The provision of Treaty powers to regulate safety, together with the development of Community policies advocated in *A Common Policy on Safe Seas* (CEC, 1993), provided the foundations on which extensive Community policies for maritime safety were constructed during the 1990s, when political commitment was galvanized by a succession of maritime disasters in European waters. There have not been so many dramatic incidents in civil aviation – a consequence of the high standards required under ICAO – but the inconvenience of separate national arrangements for the safety certification of aircraft and equipment led first to inter-governmental cooperation under the umbrella of ECAC, and then in 2002 to the establishment of a European Aviation Safety Agency under the EU. A similar development occurred in relation to air traffic control where, in response to growing congestion in the skies, the logic of inter-governmental cooperation within Eurocontrol was gradually strengthened through the 1980s and 1990s, but finally gave way to the more powerful logic of EU regulation when proposals for 'a single European sky' were adopted, also in 2002. Finally, although the 11 September 2001 terrorist attack on the World Trade Center did not occur in European airspace, the shock which it caused throughout the aviation world was sufficient to compel the Council of Ministers to take new powers to control aviation security. The precedent set by the establishment of safety agencies for sea and air transport is also being followed on the railways, where a European Railway Agency is being set up between 2004 and 2006 to reinforce both safety and inter-operability.

Second, the addition of three new Articles (now 154–6), providing for the development and financing of Trans-European Networks, opened up a substantial new field of activity. Transport and Finance Ministers had been reluctant to grant the Community powers over infrastructure since cross-border routes were not a high priority for most of them, and they feared that an emphasis on such routes would distort national priorities. However, Trans-European Networks (TENs), not just for transport but for energy and telecommunications as well, figured prominently alongside the development of economic and monetary union in the Commission's 'White Paper on Growth, Competitiveness and Employment' (CEC, 1993a), the over-arching policy document which was intended to carry forward the European project after the 1992 completion of the single market. In December 1994 the European Council adopted a list of 14 major transport projects, including four of interest to the UK. The selection of these projects was the outcome of a negotiation at the highest levels of government (they had to be 'of common interest', but at the same time every member state had to claim a prize). New legislation was also put in place during 1995/96 to govern the selection and financing of a substantial programme of smaller projects. The largest projects have political appeal, even if the economic value of such investments is often questionable, and the programme is likely to continue to grow as efforts are made to integrate into the European economy the ten new member states which joined the EU in 2004. However, the terms of the Treaty Articles themselves, and especially of Regulation 2236/95 which governs the financing of TENs projects, give the member states a large measure of national control over the programme, so that it remains debatable how far the programme supports Community as opposed to national transport objectives. Much of the finance is provided by the European Investment Bank and the European Investment Fund, but projects in the EU's poorer regions also receive substantial support from the Community's regional and cohesion funds.

The third major change of scope affecting the common transport policy has been the development since the 1980s of a Community policy on the environment. Not mentioned at all in the Treaty of Rome, the environment made its first Treaty appearance in the Single European Act as a Community action. Meanwhile, international pressures were gradually moving environmental issues further and further up the agenda. *Our Common Future*, the report by the World Commission on Environment and Development (1987), stressed the need for development to be sustainable and environmentally sound, and this theme was picked up by the conference at Rio de Janeiro in 1992 which focused on the growing evidence of environmentally-related climate change, to which transport is a major contributor. In 1992 the TEU included a statement that 'environmental protection requirements must be integrated into the definition and implementation of other Community policies', and this was reflected in the White Paper, *The Future*

Development of the Common Transport Policy (CEC, 1992), which carried the sub-title: *A Global Approach to the Construction of a Community Framework for Sustainable Mobility.* In 1997 the obligation to integrate respect for the environment into the definition and implementation of other policies was further reinforced when Article 6 of the Treaty of Amsterdam placed it among the Principles on which the European Community is based, and made its application to transport (and other) policies explicit by reference to the policies and activities listed in Article 3.

When the UK held the Presidency of the EU in the first half of 1998, John Prescott, who was himself Secretary of State for Transport and the Environment, took the opportunity to summon a joint Council of Transport and Environment Ministers. This in turn prompted the Commission to draw up a paper, *On Transport and* CO_2 (CEC, 1998), which spelled out the responsibility of transport for the rising level of carbon dioxide in the atmosphere. In 1985 transport already accounted for 19 per cent of carbon dioxide emissions, but by 1995 this had risen to 26 per cent, and was set to rise to 40 per cent by 2010. This trend was incompatible with the commitment given by the Community, at the Kyoto Conference in 1997, to reduce emissions by 8 per cent by 2008–12. Moreover, since transport of passengers and freight by road and air generates much more carbon dioxide per passenger/kilometre or freight/ton than transport by rail or sea, the paper identified a range of transport policies which could be expected to make air and road transport cleaner and encourage a shift towards transport by rail and water. The environmental policy impetus remained an important factor in the Commission's 2001 White Paper on transport policy (CEC, 2001), which seeks not merely to influence the trends in modal use in favour of the more environmentally-sustainable modes – railways, inland waterways and short sea shipping – but, even more ambitiously, to break the linkage which has hitherto associated growth in transport with economic growth. Of course the aspirations of a White Paper are one thing; the policies adopted by the Community may not follow the Commission's lead. As John Whitelegg asserted in 1988, the EEC had up to that time failed in its transport policies to support those modes which could benefit the environment, whilst positively encouraging the further development of those (such as road and air transport) which were most likely to cause damage (Whitelegg, 1988). These policies have not been reversed, even if the Commission and indeed the member states would like to see a greater emphasis on rail and sea transport.

Transport and the institutions of the Community

Under the terms of the Treaty of Rome, as originally agreed, the procedure for the development of EU policies and the adoption of EU law was relatively straightforward. The Commission made proposals, which were sent to the Council of Ministers and the European Assembly (as the Parliament was then called). The latter gave its opinion, which the Council and the Commission were under no obligation to follow, and the Council then decided what to do, subject only to the constraint that the Commission had to approve any changes to its proposals. Under this arrangement the Council was the dominant force. Nothing could happen without its consent and, as we have seen, until about 1985 nothing much did happen, since the Council was divided about the nature of the transport policy to be adopted, and Ministers were deeply reluctant (as they still are) to impose policies on one another by qualified majority voting even where they had the power to do so, as was the case in respect of inland transport policies from 1966.

Since 1957, new EU institutions have emerged – notably the European Council – whilst the balance of power amongst the others has evolved very considerably, as may be seen from Figure 4.1. In particular, the Commission, the Council of Ministers and the EP are now more or less equal partners in the process of debate and negotiation which takes place under the co-decision procedure. Introduced by the TEU and applied immediately to the legislation required to implement Trans-European Networks, the co-decision procedure was extended to all transport legislation from 1997 under the Treaty of Amsterdam. The details of this procedure are complicated, but the essence is that legislation proposed by the Commission now has to be acceptable to an absolute majority in the EP and to a qualified majority in the Council of Ministers. The Commission, which remains the sole formal initiator of legislative proposals, plays an important part in reconciling its own preferred position with those of the Council and the EP.

The Council and Parliament, as the joint legislative authority of the EU, can adopt legislation in the form of regulations, directives, decisions or recommendations (Article 249). Whereas regulations are of general application, binding in their entirety and directly applicable in all the member states, directives, although binding as regards the objective to be achieved, have to be translated into

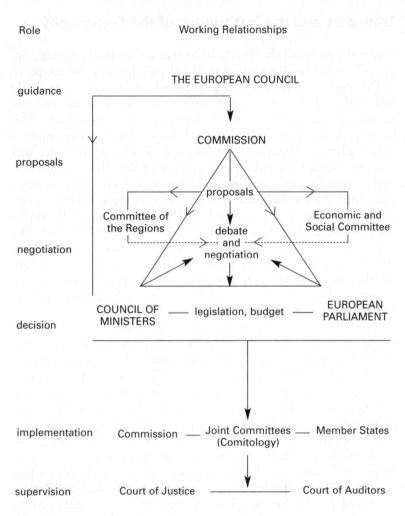

Role   Working Relationships

guidance   THE EUROPEAN COUNCIL

                                    COMMISSION

proposals

                                      proposals
              Committee of   Economic and
              the Regions   debate   Social Committee
negotiation   and
                              negotiation

              COUNCIL OF ── legislation, budget ── EUROPEAN
decision   MINISTERS   PARLIAMENT

implementation   Commission ── Joint Committees ── Member States
                               (Comitology)

supervision   Court of Justice ───────── Court of Auditors

FIGURE 4.1   *The role and working relationships of EU
institutions*

Source: Reproduced from Anne Stevens with Handley Stevens, *Brussels
Bureaucrats?* (Basingstoke: Palgrave Macmillan, 2004), p.5.

national law in each of the member states; this process leaves room
both for delay, and for considerable variations in practical effect. It
is significant that whereas regulations have been widely used in air,
sea and road transport, directives have generally been preferred in
the case of rail transport.

The European Council

The European Council dates from 1975, when the occasional summit meetings which had taken place before then became a regular event. The Council has no executive authority over the institutions of the European Community – that is to say, it cannot give them formal instructions – but Article 4 of the Treaty on European Union, drawing on a text which first appeared in the Single European Act, states that it 'shall provide the Union with the necessary impetus for its development and shall define the general political guidelines thereof'. The Presidency of the European Council goes with that of the Council of Ministers, and guidance takes the form of Presidency conclusions agreed at the meetings of the European Council, which take place at least once in each half year. Since 1985 these conclusions have frequently included some reference to transport policy, usually in the form of an appeal to the Transport Council to make further progress in their negotiations on one dossier or another. Such appeals remind ministers in the Transport Council that there is a wider political context to what they are doing, and rather more urgency about bringing matters to a satisfactory conclusion than they might otherwise perceive. Besides, each head of state does have substantial influence over the members of his or her government who constitute the Council of Ministers in its various forms, so it is reasonable to expect that they will feel under some obligation to implement the European Council's conclusions.

The Commission

Although Commission, Parliament and Council are now more equal partners in the negotiations which generate Community law, the Commission guards jealously its sole right to initiate any proposals for legislation or expenditure, which may be required in order to achieve the objectives of the Treaties. All such proposals have to be endorsed by the Commission, which in this formal sense means the Commissioners themselves, who meet every Wednesday to transact such business. The Commission's proposal takes the form of a communication addressed to the Council of Ministers and to the EP, to which is attached any draft legislation which may be required. This initiates the process of debate and negotiation, which may eventually lead to an agreed programme or legislative text. But such communications are themselves the result of what may be a long process of debate and negotiation both within the Commission itself and between the Commission's staff and external organizations representing those whose interests will be affected.

Once a case for action by the Community has been identified, someone within the services of the Commission will be charged with responsibility for drawing up proposals. According to the Commission's DECODE report (CEC, 1999: 7–12), there were in 1998 just 327 staff in the transport Directorate General (DG), of whom a little over half were A grade officials (staff in the A grade are those recruited at graduate level to work mainly on policy development). Since 1 January 2000, transport and energy have been combined in a single DG with about 650 staff, but the numbers working on transport have probably not changed very much. Even when it is remembered that the Commission has little or no responsibility for the implementation of transport policies, beyond trying to ensure that Community law is implemented by the member states, staff numbers are tiny by comparison with the resources committed to transport policy in any of the member states: for example, the British Department of Transport had just over 12,000 staff in 1996, including 936 in the senior grades broadly equivalent to the Commission's A grades (DoT, 1996a: 14).

There is an important distinction between the role of the Commissioner and the transport services of the Commission, headed by the Director General for transport. Despite the growing number of member states, and hence of Commissioners, there has always been an even larger number of DGs and other Commission services. The distribution of portfolios among Commissioners varies with each Commission, depending on the particular interests of the Commissioners themselves and the importance attached to different policies from time to time. Since the days of Lambert Schaus, the first Commissioner, transport has usually been seen as a significant, middle-ranking portfolio, but the Commissioner has often been responsible for more than one DG/service, and since 1999, the transport DG has itself been amalgamated with Energy.

The process followed by the services of the Commission in drawing up a proposal in any policy field is described by David Spence (Edwards and Spence, 1997: 111–18). Most transport issues will arise from (or be allocated to) the transport directorate, where the proposal will be developed primarily by a lead official working within his or her own hierarchy. This usually runs up through Head of Unit, Head of Division, and Director to the Director General. However, these arrangements are quite flexible in practice, so that it is common for a dossier to be 'owned' by one individual and over-seen by perhaps just one more senior official. In addition, the Commissioner's *cabinet* will also need to be kept informed, and may intervene at any stage in the directorate's consideration of both the substance of the proposal and its presentation.

At first the Commission may have only a very general idea of the issues which need to be addressed. In order to identify the problem more precisely and to explore how Community action might help, the lead official (or a more senior colleague), together with colleagues from other Commission directorates, may consult inter-ested parties individually, or convene a working group chaired by the Commission, or pay for detailed work to be carried out under contract. Those to be consulted may include industry representa-tives, users, and possibly other organizations, particularly where the intention may be to give the force of Community law to techni-cal agreements devised in some other more specialized forum. Few dossiers will concern transport alone, so there will be a requirement for any proposals, once settled within the lead directorate, to be coordinated with other Commission services (for example, those concerned with competition policy, or the environment).

Once the directorate is satisfied that the consultation process has gone as far as it can usefully be taken, both externally and internally, it embarks on the formal process which leads to the adoption of its proposal by the Commission. The Commissioner responsible for transport conveys the proposal to the Secretary General, for circula-tion to all Commissioners, under cover of a note which explains briefly what the document is about, and draws attention to any outstanding differences of view between the different directorates which may have an interest in it. Every effort will have been made to resolve such differences, or at least to agree the terms in which they are expressed in the covering note. Before the proposal can be put on the agenda of the Commission, it will be considered by *chefs de cabi-net*, who meet every Monday. If further work is needed, they may set up a small group of those most closely involved, known as 'special chefs'. Once the *chefs de cabinet* have done all they can to resolve the differences (or at least to clarify them for debate among the Commissioners), the proposal will be placed on the agenda for the Commission itself, either as an A point, if it can be taken on the nod because there is nothing to discuss, or as an item for discussion. Proposals do not have to be adopted unanimously, but there may have to be further iterations of this procedure if one or more Commissioners remain fundamentally opposed.

The Council of Ministers

When a proposal has been finally adopted by the Commission, it is sent to the Council and the European Parliament. The Council meets in a variety of specialized formations, of which transport has normally been one, though since 2001 it has been part of a wider Council bringing together ministers of transport, telecommunications and energy. Each member state takes it in turn for a period of six months (January to June, and July to December) to chair the Council of Ministers, and all the working groups which prepare the Council's meetings under the overall guidance of the Committee of Permanent Representatives (COREPER). Since the Transport Council meets only once, or at most twice under each Presidency, its work has to be carefully prepared in COREPER, which in turn relies on its Working Group on Transport Questions (TWG) to examine the Commission's proposals.

The regular members of the Working Group on Transport Questions are the middle-ranking officials attached to the offices in Brussels of the permanent representatives of the member states, but they are frequently joined at meetings by more specialized staff from national capitals. The offices of the permanent representatives are similar to an embassy, acting as the main channel for the dialogue which constantly takes place among the member states and between the member states and the institutions of the Union. Like embassies they report to Ministries of Foreign Affairs, which is important in respect of their formal instructions, but because of the impact of Community law on domestic law and policy they often include a number of officials from other departments (including transport) who maintain close links with their parent departments. Visiting specialists are likely to know much more about the policy under discussion than the TWG committee member from the permanent representation, but they must operate within any instructions agreed across government. Meetings are reported by the staff of the permanent representation, and when the dossier moves up from TWG to COREPER it is the Deputy Permanent Representative and his staff who must take responsibility for its further progress. The success of this double act depends heavily on the effectiveness of any machinery for the coordination of European policy in national capitals, such as in Britain the European Secretariat of the Cabinet Office, and in France the *Secrétariat Général du Comité Interminstériel pour les questions de coopération économique* (SGCI). Member states which do not have such a strong central executive authority, or which have less disciplined arrangements for inter-departmental policy coordination, find it more difficult than the British or the French to speak with authority and hence to exercise influence in the TWG.

As the debate progresses, the Presidency, with the help of the staff of the Council Secretariat, will prepare a note identifying the main points of difference among the delegations. Gradually, over a succession of meetings, the differences may be refined and whittled down to a few key issues. These in turn may be further refined and reduced in COREPER before the dossier goes to the Council itself, where ministers may succeed in bridging the last gaps, or alternatively may fail to do so, returning the dossier to COREPER and if necessary to the TWG for further consideration, perhaps with some indication of the parameters within which ministers think that agreement should be reached. In these negotiations, which can extend over many months or even years, ministers and their officials are very reluctant to use qualified majority voting to impose agreement on an unwilling partner, but they are equally reluctant to find themselves in a minority which could be over-ruled, and the political tension between these points of view tends to ensure that in the end member states do not hold out for concessions in isolation unless they really have to. Sometimes, for domestic political reasons, a minister may prefer to be overruled rather than be seen to make a concession; at other times a concession may be used to facilitate a linked set of agreements, which can be presented in each member state as a broadly acceptable outcome. Of course, some ministers play a better hand of poker than others, but their colleagues are for the most part seasoned campaigners too, with a well developed sense of how far a colleague can be pushed in a politically-sensitive negotiation.

The European Parliament

The third major partner in the legislative process is the EP. Corbett, Jacobs and Shackleton (2000) tell the story of the long struggle by which it gradually won increasing power, first over the budget and then over legislation. When the EP receives a proposal from the Commission, which it does at the same time as it is sent to the Council, the first step is to allocate it to one or more of the Parliament's 17 committees. Most transport proposals are allocated to the Committee on Regional Policy, Transport and Tourism. These committees work by appointing a *rapporteur* for each communication received, or other matter to be reported on. The *rapporteur*, who drafts the committee's report, receives representations from the interests likely to be directly affected by the legislation, as well as from national sources. In Britain the Cabinet Office, in France the SGCI, provides advice to ministries on how to influence this process, both directly through briefing the *rapporteur* and indirectly by briefing other MEPs. Within the committee, any member can propose an amendment. When the *rapporteur* presents the committee's report to a plenary session of the Parliament, amendments can be proposed by the responsible committee, by party groups, or by any group of not fewer than 32 MEPs, and in each case the *rapporteur* comments on what is proposed.

The European Court of Justice

The last of the five major institutions of the European Community with a significant influence on transport policy is the ECJ. Although the ECJ is not directly engaged in the negotiation of Community law, still less Community policy, the implications of its decisions can be very far-reaching indeed. The composition and powers of the Court are laid down in Articles 220–45 of the Treaty. The Court itself, which consists of one judge from each member state, is assisted by eight Advocates General, whose function is to lay out the issues of national and European law which arise in a particular case, and make proposals for the eventual ruling. The main function of the Court is to police the implementation of obligations under the Treaty. The classic action is therefore that brought by the Commission against a member state, under Article 226, for failure to fulfil an obligation under the Treaty. Under Article 232 such actions may also be brought by one institution of the Community against another. Under Articles 230–1, acts of the Community institutions may also be annulled, either on procedural grounds or because they are not securely based in the Treaty. All these powers have been used from time to time, usually but not always by the Commission seeking to assert the authority of the EU (and incidentally its own authority) over the member states. The Court cannot take the initiative, but the rulings it handed down during the 1970s and 1980s did much to establish the foundations on which the Council was eventually obliged to construct an internal market in transport services.

Such cases provide a direct opportunity for the Court to influence legislation adopted under the Treaty, but similar opportunities may also arise more indirectly when national courts apply for a preliminary ruling on the interpretation of the Treaty under Article 234. This was the procedure used in 1984 in the important *Nouvelles Frontières* case (see above). The Court is careful not to trespass on the right of the lawmaking institutions of the Community (the Commission, the Council and the EP) to define the content of policy. The Court is not political in any ordinary sense, but Article 234 requires it to give rulings concerning 'the interpretation of this Treaty', which must necessarily have a bearing on policy: for example, by narrowing the range of options open to the law-making institutions of the Community. In relation to transport policy, the Court's rulings have tended to favour the liberal market approach which is deeply embedded in the Treaties, setting limits to the anti-competitive adjustments which might otherwise be made in recognition of the 'distinctive features' of transport.

Actions before the Court can be very long drawn out. In the case of infringement proceedings, the Commission will normally begin by making informal enquiries of the member state concerned, and may tolerate considerable delay if the matter is obviously sensitive; but, if the matter cannot be satisfactorily resolved through such consultations, the next step is to prepare a reasoned opinion, allowing the member state time to comment on it. This too is a negotiating process in which the member state may make some concessions to the Commission in the hope of heading off formal proceedings, but when this process has run its course the Commission delivers its reasoned opinion to the member state, giving it a certain time to comply. Only if the member state fails to comply within the time laid down does the Commission finally bring the matter to the Court of Justice. Time then has to be allowed for the member state concerned to file its defence, and for other interested parties (for example, other member states) to comment, and for the Commission to comment on their submissions, but eventually the Commission makes formal application for judgment. There may then be a further extended period while the Advocate General assigned to the case takes evidence and makes his assessment, and then yet another wait before the Court itself determines its judgment and publishes it. In the cases brought by the Commission against the member states in connection with their US air services agreements (see below), enquiries began in 1994, the Commission's reasoned opinion was issued in March 1998, and judgment was sought at the end of that year, but the Advocate General did not deliver his opinion until January 2002, and the judgment itself was not received until November 2002, which was more than eight years after the process was set in motion. The delivery of preliminary rulings under Article 234 is generally rather quicker that that, but the Court has a heavy load of such casework, and commonly takes up to two years in controversial cases.

The legal competence of the Community in external affairs

The Court has also played an important part in establishing the role of the Commission in dealing with third countries and international organizations on behalf of the Community. This is an area which has been fiercely contested, since the member states are understandably reluctant to concede any part of their sovereign right to conduct their own international relations. The step-by-step extension of the Commission's external competence dates back to 1970, when it sought to annul an agreement, known as the AETR agreement, which the member states had struck within the wider forum of the United Nations Economic Commission for Europe concerning the work of crews of vehicles engaged in international road transport. The Commission lost its case on a technicality (as the Parliament 'lost' its case against the Council in 1983), but the Court went on to lay down a number of far-reaching general rules, including the following:

> In particular, each time the Community, with a view to implementing a common policy envisaged by the Treaty, adopts provisions laying down common rules, whatever form they may take, the Member States no longer have the right, acting individually or even collectively, to undertake obligations with third countries which affect those rules or alter their scope. With regard to the implementation of the provisions of the Treaty, the system of internal Community measures may not be separated from that of external relations . . . With regard to agreements in the sphere of transport policy, the Commission is entitled to make proposals and negotiate, whilst it is for the Council to conclude the agreement. (Extract from summary of judgment, Case 22/70)

The immediate impact of this judgment was quite small at a time when the extent of internal Community rule-making was itself very limited, but its impact has been progressively widened by subsequent rulings, particularly Opinion 1/76 concerning Rhine navigation and Opinion 1/94 concerning the competence of the Community to conclude international agreements relating to trade in services and intellectual property (Stevens, 2004: 225–31). And the Commission continues to push at the boundaries. In 1998, in Cases C-466/98 and seven parallel cases, the Commission challenged the 'open skies' air service agreements which eight member states had signed with the USA on the grounds that the rights available under these agreements were in each case restricted to the airlines wholly owned and effectively controlled in that one member state, thus discriminating unlawfully against the airlines of other member states. The Court took the view that the member states ought to have insisted on EU ownership and control clauses, even though such clauses, when proposed, have been rejected by the Americans. Ultimately, if the Court's judgment is to be respected, there will have to be an agreement between the EU as a whole and the USA, negotiated by the Commission under a mandate agreed by the member states within the Council. Moreover, since similar considerations would apply to all other bilateral air service agreements between EU member states and third countries, the implications for the whole network of international air services are profound.

Making policy in the European Union

Whilst each of the five major institutions has its own procedures, none of them is an autonomous agent in the business of policy-making, which takes place within the triangle of relationships at the heart of the institutional structure illustrated in Figure 4.1, where proposals for legislation as well as action programmes are debated and negotiated among the three principal partners: the Commission, the Council and the Parliament. A proposal enters this triangle when it has received the formal endorsement of the Commission. In the case of a legislative proposal subject to the co-decision procedure – the normal situation for transport proposals – the early stages of the long drawn out negotiating process will be concerned with staking out positions separately in the Council working group (TWG) under the guidance of the Presidency, and in the relevant committee of Parliament under the guidance of the *rapporteur*. Parliament has to act first, sending its opinion to the Council, so the *rapporteur*'s report is adopted or amended by a plenary session and sent to the Council. Unless all the EP's proposed amendments are acceptable, the Council responds with a 'common position' setting out its proposals with reasons. The Council's response, drafted in the Working Group, is refined in COREPER and finally at the Council itself before being sent back to the Parliament.

By now the positions of the three protagonists are becoming fairly clear. If they are not too far apart, the next stages can be launched, but these have firm deadlines: three months for the EP to propose amendments to the Council's common position, and three months after that for the Council to approve the proposal as amended by the EP. These periods can be extended by one month each if necessary. If there are still points of disagreement, a Conciliation Committee has to be set up within six weeks. This again has six weeks in which to arrive at a joint text, and the joint text then has to be agreed by the EP and Council separately within a further period of six weeks. Any of these six week periods can be extended to eight weeks; but if agreement has not then been reached by Parliament, acting by an absolute majority of the votes cast, and by the Council acting by a qualified majority, the proposal falls. These time periods add up to about ten months, which may seem like a long time, but in practice ten months is not very long if there are fundamental differences to be overcome. Ways have therefore been found to ensure that there is a good chance of reaching agreement before the time-controlled process is definitively engaged.

The device is called a trialogue. Since the setting up of a Conciliation Committee requires the agreement of the President of the Council and the President of the Parliament, they can agree to defer taking that step. There is no point in engaging a process which will result in the legislation being lost altogether, if both parties want it to succeed but need more time to arrive at an acceptable compromise. In these circumstances the Council calls for discussion without formally rejecting the amendments which the EP has proposed at its second reading. This stops the clock for so long as both parties are committed to a constructive negotiation, and since the Commission is also involved as honest broker, the process is called a trialogue. In a trialogue, the EP is represented by the Chair and *rapporteur* of the relevant committee, the Council is represented by the Deputy Permanent Representative of the current Presidency (who may be accompanied by the Deputy Permanent Representative of the successor Presidency as an observer), and the Commission is represented by the Director General or Director responsible for the legislation on the table. According to Michael

Shackleton (Corbett, Jacobs and Shackleton, 2000), all three nego-
tiators come with a supporting team of officials, but those present
will often number less than 25, of whom only four or five speak, the
bulk of the discussion taking place between Council and
Parliament. The meetings are based on a paper prepared jointly by
the Council and EP secretariats, after TWG and COREPER have
considered the EP's second reading amendments, stating which
amendments the Council could accept, which it could not accept,
and where there may be scope for compromise. Normally a trialogue will be concerned with a single measure or group of related
measures, but linkage to other dossiers is also possible.

Once agreement has been reached within the trialogue, the way
is clear for the formal Conciliation Committee to be convened. This
meeting, chaired by a Minister from the Presidency, brings together
representatives of all the member states at the level of COREPER
Deputies, facing a similar number of EP representatives, who
together endorse the outcome of the negotiation which has already
taken place. The texts so agreed can then go forward for approval
to a plenary meeting of the EP, and finally to the Council of
Ministers. The matter will appear on the agenda of the Council of
Transport Ministers if it is thought that the issue needs to be
debated, so that ministers can make statements explaining the
concessions they have made or the way they propose to interpret
the agreement which has been reached, for example. If there is no
need for the compromise to be publicly endorsed in this way, the
agreement can be taken as an 'A' point, without discussion, at any
Council meeting (Stevens, 2004: 81–5).

The role of the British Houses of Parliament

All legislation proposed for adoption by the Council is subject to
parliamentary scrutiny not only within the EP but also in each of
the member states. The focus of British parliamentary scrutiny is on
the implications of proposed European legislation for UK law and
policy. Each House brings its views to the attention of ministers by
means of reports and debates, so that they in turn can take the views
of Parliament into account in their negotiations within the Council.

As soon as the Commission sends to the Council any formal
document, and particularly any proposal for Community legislation, the Cabinet Office arranges for the document to be deposited
with both Houses of Parliament. This triggers the scrutiny process,

TITLE – of document and responsible department
SUBJECT MATTER
MINISTERIAL RESPONSIBILITY – normally in the case of transport
documents the Secretary of State for Transport, but other ministers will
be mentioned if they have an interest as well.
LEGAL AND PROCEDURAL ISSUES – including the legal basis in the
Treaties, the relevant procedure in the European Parliament, the voting
procedure within the Council (unanimity or qualified majority vote) and
the impact of the proposal on UK law.
APPLICATION TO THE EUROPEAN ECONOMIC AREA – much, though not
all, EU legislation applies to EEA countries such as Norway, Iceland and
Liechtenstein which are not EU members.
SUBSIDIARITY – comments on whether the proposal requires
Community action, or whether it could more appropriately be carried out
by member states.
POLICY IMPLICATIONS – some indication of how the proposal affects
British policy, including a compliance cost assessment, where
appropriate, evaluating the possible impact on business costs and
employment.
FINANCIAL IMPLICATIONS
TIMETABLE
OTHER OBSERVATIONS
ANNEXES – frequently used to summarize the history of past scrutiny of
related documents.

FIGURE 4.2   *Structure of an explanatory memorandum*

which may proceed in parallel in the two Houses. The first step is
the preparation of an explanatory memorandum (see Figure 4.2 for
its structure and content). The DoT prepared more than 30 memoranda in 1994. This short document, which must be sent to
Parliament within ten working days, describes what is proposed
and how it might affect British interests. All explanatory memoranda of any substance must be approved and signed by a minister,
though an unsigned memorandum (the DoT submitted seven in
1994) is considered sufficient where a document sets out amendments of little or no consequence, or where a factual report has no
legal or policy implications. EU documents, together with their
explanatory memoranda, are considered by both the Commons and
Lords scrutiny committees who decide what parliamentary action
to take on them. The Commons committee meets each Wednesday
when the House is sitting, to decide whether the documents before
it raise questions of legal and/or political importance, and whether
they should be debated. Another option is to ask for further information, which the department provides in the form of a

Supplementary Memorandum: six of the memoranda submitted in 1994 were prepared in response to requests of this kind.

If the scrutiny committee recommends a debate, the private secretary of the relevant transport minister must write within four weeks to the private secretary to the Chief Whip (whose task it is to manage the government's business in Parliament), with copies to other interested ministers. The document should set out the scrutiny committee's recommendation, giving a preferred date for the debate to take place having regard to tactical considerations including the progress of negotiations in Brussels, naming the minister who will take the lead in the debate, recommending whether the debate should be in committee or on the floor of the House, and setting out the exact wording of the motion. Debates usually take place on an extended 'take note' motion; that is to say, the committee is invited to take note of the Commission's proposal, but the motion will go on to give some general indication of the government's position, perhaps inviting the committee to support the government's view that the proposal will need amendment if it is to be acceptable, or that further measures will be needed. The department will consult the scrutiny committee clerk before writing to the Chief Whip's Office, and the terms of the draft motion will be agreed, where necessary, with other interested departments.

The arrangements for debates are negotiated by the Chief Whip's Office through the usual channels. Debates are usually held in one of the two European standing committees (Committee A for Transport), but may take place on the floor of the House if they are of major importance. If the debate is in committee, the chair will first allow the minister to make a brief introduction, followed by questions. Officials are present and can pass notes to the minister if necessary. After a maximum of one hour, the chair brings questions to a close and invites the minister to open the debate itself by moving the motion, usually with a short speech. Any amendments to the motion will normally have been tabled on the preceding day. At the end of the debate the chair puts the question on any amendments which have been debated, and then on the main question or the main question as amended. The minister has the right to intervene in the course of the debate, and to wind it up, but only members of the committee are entitled to vote. There were four debates arising from the explanatory memoranda which DoT sent to Parliament in 1994, all of them in committee.

The final stage of the Commons scrutiny procedure takes place a few days later on the floor of the House when a motion is tabled which is usually the same as the resolution reached by the standing committee. Such motions are taken, and if necessary voted on, without debate. If the government is not able to accept the terms of the committee's resolution, it may put its original motion to the floor of the House, or another motion which differs from that reached by the committee; but in those circumstances the minister, after consulting his colleagues (and particularly the Chief Whip), would need to write to the chair and members of the committee explaining in some detail how the government intends to proceed.

Whereas consideration by the Commons Scrutiny Committee is focused on the need for and terms of motions for debate, scrutiny in the House of Lords (under the aegis of the Select Committee on European Legislation) is more inclined to the investigation of issues in some depth through the work of five sub-committees which call expert witnesses and prepare reports with recommendations that may go well beyond the terms of the immediate proposal under consideration. Transport proposals are referred to the sub-committee on energy, industry and transport. The government has undertaken to respond to the reports of the Lords Scrutiny Committee normally within two months of publication, and no later than a week before a debate. Debates in the Lords are usually on a straightforward 'take note' motion.

Every effort is made to complete the scrutiny procedures before decisions have to be taken in the Council, and there are arrangements for speeding matters up when necessary, but there may occasionally be cases where national parliamentary procedures are not complete in time. If ministers are unable to delay a decision in the Council, it is possible to enter a parliamentary reserve pending completion of the scrutiny process, but such reserves are of a formal nature and it is not clear what would happen if Parliament were to pass a motion which precluded the lifting of such a reserve. Ministers can also decide to agree Community legislation without scrutiny clearance, but they must have good reason for doing so, and they need to explain themselves afterwards.

Most important transport legislation, and certainly anything controversial, is discussed and agreed at a meeting of the Transport Council, even if it may be adopted in final form as an 'A' point at another Council when any final drafting points have been resolved. The Secretary of State normally reports the outcome of each formal meeting of the Council to Parliament by means of an arranged Parliamentary Question or, if the business is sufficiently weighty, an oral statement. This action brings the parliamentary procedure to a conclusion.

The Europeanization of British transport policy

Héritier and others (2001) have shown that, despite the best endeavours of the Commission, with recourse to the Court where appropriate, the implementation of the Community's transport law differs widely across the member states, particularly where it takes the form of directives, depending on such factors as the prevailing ideology in each member state, the domestic political climate, and the capacity for implementing reform. Policy in some member states has been strongly influenced by Europe but not so far in Britain, where the EU's single market legislation required little change to British transport policies. The UK road haulage market was substantially liberated in the 1970s, long before such policies were accepted in Brussels, and although the privatization of British Rail took place in the mid-1990s, after the adoption of Directive 91/440, it was driven by a strong ideological commitment on the part of the Conservative government to the privatization of public utilities generally, and the introduction of competition into the regulatory arrangements governing their provision, which was more liberal than the European directive (Knill, 2001). There was no need to liberalize access to British maritime freight trade, including cabotage, when these policies were adopted by the EU because British trade was already open to ships of any nationality. Similarly, the liberalization of the European aviation market followed the model already adopted wherever possible in the UK's bilateral relations with other EU member states, having been strongly advocated by British Ministers within the EU even before the Commission came forward with its proposals. Liberalization looks more like a British export than a Community policy to which the UK has had to adjust.

It is the social and environmental aspects of European policy which have tended to cause more difficulty in Britain. The directive on the maximum weights and sizes of large lorries, which was almost ready to be adopted when Britain joined the Community in 1973, was blocked till 1985, and then allowed to go forward only on the basis of a long derogation to 1 January 1999 for the UK, to allow time for British roads and bridges to be strengthened. The British authorities had to be compelled by the ECJ to take effective steps to insist on the installation of tachographs (the spy in the cab) to monitor lorry drivers' working time, and Britain has fought hard since the 1980s to maintain as much flexibility as possible in the application to road transport of the 48-hour week. In maritime and aviation affairs, British ministers have often taken the lead in devising inter-governmental forms of cooperation – for example, the Paris Memorandum of Understanding (1982) governing the safety inspection of foreign vessels in EU ports – in preference to supranational arrangements under Community law. British reluctance to make concessions on access to Heathrow has been the main obstacle to an air services agreement between the EU and the USA.

Thirty years after Britain joined the EU, the list of contentious issues is remarkably short, but that is mainly because the principal thrust of the common transport policy has been towards the creation and development of a liberal, open market for transport services which is broadly consistent with British policy. However, many Europeans have always had quite different ambitions for a common transport policy as an instrument of economic, regional, environmental and social policies. We have seen this in the development of substantial infrastructure programmes, supported by the Cohesion Fund, first in southern Europe and now in the new member states of central Europe. We have also seen it in the application of environmental policies to transport: for example, in Directive 85/337/EEC, which requires an environmental impact assessment for all projects 'likely to have a significant effect on the environment', and now in Directive 2001/42/EC, which requires the strategic environmental assessment of all plans and programmes. Such measures can be accommodated well enough within British policy: indeed, Planning Minister Keith Hill claimed that application of the 2001 Directive to the planning system would help 'deliver the integrated treatment of economic, environmental and social issues which is a key principle of the Government's sustainable development strategy' (ODPM, News Release 2004/48, 2 March 2004), but there is a risk that the future development of the common transport policy will be less comfortable for Britain than has been the case hitherto. That remains to be seen. What can be said now is that EU law and EU policy-making have become deeply embedded in the process by which transport policy in Britain is made.

Chapter 5

Planning

At national level it is not just individual planning decisions which may be controversial but planning itself. The Labour manifesto for the 1997 general election (see Chapter 1) stated unequivocally that 'a sustainable environment requires above all an effective and integrated transport policy at national, regional and local level'. The Conservative governments of 1979 to 1997 would not have agreed with that judgement. Their objections were expressed most characteristically by Cecil Parkinson, Transport Minister 1989–90. He thought an integrated transport policy was 'socialist' and a 'way of keeping well-paid bureaucrats occupied' (Truelove, 1992: 8).

However, it would be a mistake to make a clear association of 'Labour' with transport planning, and 'Conservative' with leaving transport decisions to the market and to the private sector. First, even the Conservative governments of the 1980s, so distinctive in their insistence that markets should decide where transport investment would take place, included more interventionist ministers such as Michael Heseltine, who introduced the 'planning' devices of Urban Development Corporations. While seeking to attract the maximum private investment by the minimum of regulation, these government-sponsored bodies relied heavily on government intervention, especially in the London Docklands. The irrationality in technical terms of some of this investment, such as the Limehouse Link road, 'the most expensive road ever built in Britain', or the Jubilee Line Extension's 'high-level poker game' over the ratio of public to private contributions, was an indicator of their political significance (Brindley, Rydin and Stoker, 1996: 202; Newman and Thornley, 1996: 138).

Second, doubts have accumulated across the political spectrum about the value of trying to predict and prescribe patterns of land and transport use. The 1947 Town and Country Planning Act represented for many who demand an 'integrated transport policy' the ideal basis at local level, since it asked local authorities to set out their expectations for land use over the following decade. But rapid changes in population and road use in the 1950s made such plans

133

out of date almost before they were formally approved. The Buchanan Report on *Traffic in Towns* in 1963, and reactions to it, showed not only the unrealistic nature of the planning system, but also called into question the assumption that plans could or should meet transport demand. There was a serious loss of confidence in planning in the mid-1970s when urban motorways, inner-city redevelopment and the destruction of historic buildings came under challenge from a broad range of groups, from community activists to conservation societies.

Third, in the last years of the Thatcher government, vigorous campaigns against some large-scale road projects, an emerging scientific consensus on global warming, and a transfer of votes to the Green Party put pressure on all political parties to adopt an environment-friendly discourse: the Conservatives and the Liberal Democrats created or reconstituted 'Green' sections and the Labour Party spoke of an integrated transport policy. The *National Road Traffic Forecasts 1989* (DoT, 1989a), estimating that road traffic would double by 2025, and whose massive impact in concrete terms was set out in the road programme, *Roads for Prosperity* (DoT, 1989), helped fuel the debate about whether the provision of road space could continue to be demand-led.

In this climate of opinion John Major's government signed the global warming and biodiversity treaties negotiated at the Rio Earth Summit in 1992. These world-level accords obliged the British government to consider the consequences of traffic growth for the level of greenhouse gases and air pollutants. Its agreements within Europe to assess the environmental impact of major projects started to bite: the DoT dropped its East London River Crossing project in 1993 rather than continue to argue with the EU and the defenders of Oxleas Wood. The Houghton Report's conclusion that even the development of less-polluting vehicles would not keep the UK within its emissions targets, and that road traffic growth must be cut back (Houghton Report, 1994), together with the advice of the Standing Advisory Committee on Trunk Road Assessment (1994) that new road infrastructure generated more traffic, encouraged a return to a more 'planned' approach to transport.

By 1997 there was near-consensus that government had to constrain demand for road use, even if the Right looked more towards market-based solutions ('the polluter pays'), and the Left to collective solutions (public transport). When the new Labour government brought transport, environment, and land-use planning into one Whitehall department, the DETR, there was already a large measure of support for a more interventionist transport policy both in time and space: it was felt that government should try to adjust future patterns of transport demand towards other patterns, less harmful to the environment, and to use the land-use planning system to encourage individuals and developers to live, work and build where they would not generate additional traffic.

Forward planning

In the context of British transport planning *Transport 2010: The 10 Year Plan* (DETR, 2000) was a triumph, both for having obtained Treasury approval for annual budget headings for the coming ten years, and as a technical document. Ministers soon admitted it would not reduce congestion; they stopped mentioning its 50 per cent goal for rail traffic growth (*Financial Times*, 16 January 2003). The Plan had almost dropped out of view by the time it was subsumed into *The Future of Transport* (DfT, 2004), extending budget figures to 2015 (see Chapter 8), but it had served a useful purpose by publicly and formally overcoming the long-standing reluctance of the Treasury to entertain any commitment or even expectation of public expenditure extending beyond the customary three-year planning cycle.

Road traffic forecasts

The *National Road Traffic Forecasts 1997* (DETR, 1997a) predicted that road traffic growth would slow. An additional 28 per cent (in vehicle-kilometres) was expected between 1996 and 2011, still a substantial increase, but lower than the 35 per cent the 1989 forecasts had suggested for that period. Economic growth had not continued at the high levels of the 1980s; and its downward effect would outweigh the upward effect of a trend towards single-adult households. In addition, transport statisticians had introduced a new element into their equations: 'the nominal capacity of the network'. The 'moratorium' on road-building would lead to congestion, and some drivers would decide not to make their journey.

By 2000 the Blair government had already changed two assumptions of the forecasts: it added road capacity with its 'Targeted Programme of Improvements' (DETR, 1998a), and abandoned the real terms rise in fuel duty which it had said it would keep until

TABLE 5.1   *Forecast growth in road traffic and congestion (England)*

Baseline case for 10 Year Plan	All roads					Inter-urban trunk roads
	All areas	London	Other conurbations	Other urban areas	Other areas	
Congestion in 2000 (England = 100)	100	367	212	98	35	57
Increase in road traffic 2000–10	22%	14%	16%	21%	24%	29%
Increase in congestion 2000–10	15%	13%	15%	15%	36%	28%

Source: Compiled from DETR, *Transport 2010: The Background Analysis* (DETR, 2000a), Figures 6 and 7.

2002 (DETR, 1998). The European Commission's agreement with vehicle manufacturers to improve fuel efficiency, reducing emissions but also driving costs, would significantly promote road use. Traffic and congestion would grow, though more slowly on roads already near capacity – in and around London, Birmingham and Manchester – because of the existing congestion.

Table 5.1 illustrates this point with the figures used in the 'baseline case' for the 10 Year Plan (the situation if the Plan were not implemented), which used the 1997 forecasts as amended for the three policy changes described above. The predicted increase in traffic by 2010 would be 22 per cent in England as a whole but only 14–16 per cent in the metropolitan areas; traffic and congestion would grow faster on the less congested roads outside urban areas. (In the Tables, 'inter-urban trunk roads' include the M25.)

Rail traffic forecasts

Neither Railtrack nor the SRA had undertaken studies on future passenger traffic in time for the 10 Year Plan; but the SRA had ordered a forecast of rail freight demand from MDS Transmodal.

The DETR developed a model for non-commuter passenger traffic: GDP, car traffic and ticket prices seemed the important factors. It predicted that demand for non-commuter travel would increase by 39 per cent by 2010, if regulated fares dropped by 1 per cent a year below the Retail Price Index (RPI), unregulated fares remained stable, and road congestion led some drivers to switch to rail. The DETR was not able to model the volatile changes to commuter traffic. It assumed the historically high growth rates would probably drop to an overall increase of 15 per cent between 2000 and 2010, of which 3 per cent would result from a reduction in regulated fares. However, there would not be enough room on the tracks for the combined increase in passenger demand of about 34 per cent. In the absence of Plan measures for rail, an increase of 23 per cent was more likely.

MDS Transmodal found that demand for rail freight depended on GDP and the cost differential between rail and road; it could grow by 38 per cent during the 2000–10 period, if it were not held back by the crowded network and narrow gauge clearances on many routes. Growth in rail freight by 2010 would be limited to 10 per cent without additional investment in the network (DETR, 2000a: paras 10–23). These forecasts all fed into the 10 Year Plan as baseline figures.

The 10 Year Plan

Though *The 10 Year Plan* offered only a small if worthwhile addition to transport public expenditure in real terms (its rail expenditure depended heavily on private-sector contributions), it was a sophisticated exercise in forward planning. The planners calculated the impact of their baseline case of traffic growth on congestion and vehicle emissions by 2010. They estimated the impact on traffic (including cross-modal effects) of the infrastructure projects and other measures, such as congestion charging in London and eight other conurbations, that were sketched out in *The 10 Year Plan*, and tested the impact of more ambitious scenarios. Finally the outputs of Plan measures were assessed in terms of savings in drivers' time and greenhouse gas emissions.

The impact on road traffic and congestion of the Plan is shown in Tables 5.2 and 5.3. Traffic would increase more slowly (less than the increase in GDP), and there would be an absolute reduction in congestion. Both effects would be especially large in London, and considerable in the other conurbations. A scenario that assumed 80 additional towns introduced city-centre charging showed no more

TABLE 5.2 *Road traffic in England: Plan scenarios*

Increase in road traffic 2000–10	All roads (%)					Inter-urban trunk roads
	All areas	London	Other conurbations	Other urban areas	Other areas	
Without the Plan	22	14	16	21	24	29
With the Plan	17	5	10	17	21	26
Plan + 80 more cities charging	17	5	10	17	21	26
Plan + some inter-urban charging	17	5	8	17	21	23
Plan + constant motoring costs	13	–3	6	14	17	21

Source: Adapted from DETR, *Transport 2010: The Background Analysis* (DETR, 2000a), Figure 13.

TABLE 5.3 *Road congestion in England: Plan scenarios*

Increase in road traffic 2000–10	All roads (%)					Inter-urban trunk roads
	All areas	London	Other conurbations	Other urban areas	Other areas	
Without the Plan	15	13	15	15	36	28
With the Plan	–6	–15	–8	7	16	–5
Plan + 80 more cities charging	–7	–15	–8	7	16	–5
Plan + some inter-urban charging	–9	–15	–12	7	11	–20
Plan + constant motoring costs	–12	–26	–11	4	9	–11

Source: Adapted from DETR, *Transport 2010: The Background Analysis* (DETR, 2000a), Figure 13.

effect on road traffic or congestion than the Plan alone. A few motorway tolls at congested times would have a large effect on congestion, but less impact on traffic, as drivers would continue to travel, although at different times. Holding the costs of driving constant in real terms, in addition to the Plan measures, would produce a substantial drop in traffic growth and congestion, especially in London (though, for inter-urban roads, less substantial than tolls would have produced). The statistics are testimony to the deleterious effect of acceding to the demands of some drivers in 2000, and to the impact that inter-urban road pricing could have.

Rail passenger traffic was forecast to grow by 23 per cent in ten years without additional capacity. With Plan expenditure on the track, rolling stock provided under renegotiated franchises (see Chapter 7), and fares remaining in line with RPI, or decreasing (RPI – 1), rail traffic could grow by 51 per cent. But more public subsidy would have to be given to fares and driving costs kept stable before there was a really significant change in the growth of car traffic. *Rail freight* would benefit under the Plan from track improvements and specific programmes for capital projects and operating subsidies. The 80 per cent increase in demand predicted for rail freight could even rise to 120 per cent if 'lorry costs' remained constant, and additional subsidies were offered (see Table 5.4). However, as it turned out, Railtrack's reaction to the Hatfield accident, re-franchising delays, soaring costs on the West Coast Main Line upgrade, cheaper motoring and higher fares made a nonsense of these forecasts.

TABLE 5.4   *Rail traffic in England: Plan scenarios, 2000–10*

	Input on fare prices		Outcomes for traffic		
	Regulated fares	Unregulated inter-urban fares	Growth in passenger traffic (GB)	Growth in car traffic (England)	Growth in rail freight (GB)
Without the Plan	RPI – 1	RPI	23%	21%	10%
With the Plan	RPI – 1	RPI	51%	17%	80%
Plan + constant motoring costs	RPI – 1 to RPI – 4	RPI to RPI – 4	83%	12%	[120%]

Source: Data from DETR, *Transport 2010: The Background Analysis* (DETR, 2000a), Figures 10 and 11.

The London Transportation Studies Model used by the Government Office for London provided forecasts for the overall demand for travel, choice of mode and routes in response to ticket prices, journey times, road congestion, and over-crowding on public transport. Plan spending on bus services (priority lanes, real time information, more buses), was expected to improve their reliability, attracting travellers from the Tube and reducing peak hour journey times on public transport. The greatest reduction in travel time would be on the Tube itself (see Table 5.5). Building CrossRail would have the greatest impact on congestion on the Tube (DETR, 2000a: para. 62). Of the various scenarios proposed by DETR (leaving out either CrossRail or mainline rail improvements or bus improvements), not building CrossRail would make the most difference to the Underground, though bus improvements would turn more of the very crowded sections into the merely crowded. The congestion charge was expected to reduce traffic in central London by 10–15 per cent (in the event it was 15 per cent); congestion there would fall significantly (see Chapter 3). Since London's road conditions depend on encouraging the use of public transport, but reducing over-crowding on the Tube depends on bus quality and, especially, on CrossRail, it is unfortunate for all modes that CrossRail will not be built by 2010.

TABLE 5.5   *Travel in London: Plan scenarios, 2000–10*

Output indicator	Change 2000–10		Measures contributing most to the change
	Without the Plan	*With the Plan*	
Public transport:			
(peak journey time) Underground	+0.2%	–5%	Bus priority, more buses
(peak journey time)	+2%	–7%	Bus reliability and speed
Crowded Tube links	+10	–2	CrossRail
Very crowded Tube links	+13	–6	CrossRail
Road traffic:			
central London	+2.5% to + 5%	–10% to –15%	Congestion charge
outer London	up to 10%	– 2% to –3%	Better public transport
Congestion	+13%	–15%	Congestion charge

Source: Data from DETR, *Transport 2010: The Background Analysis* (DETR, 2000a), paras 28, 62.

TABLE 5.6   *Vehicle emissions: Plan scenarios, 2000–10 (England)*

	Carbon dioxide (million tonnes)		Nitrogen oxide (thousand tonnes)		Carbon particles (thousand tonnes)	
	Road	Rail	Road	Rail	Road	Rail
2000	30.3	0.7	487	14	19.7	0.6
2010 without the Plan	31.0	0.7	198	15	10.5	0.6
2010 with the Plan	29.1	1.0	188	20	10.1	0.9
Plan + constant motoring costs, urban charges, inter-urban charges	27.9	1.2	180	24	9.7	1.0

Source: Data from DETR, *Transport 2010: The Background Analysis* (DETR, 2000a), Figures 14 and 15.

Emissions forecasts for road traffic showed that little increase in the 'climate change' fuel emission of carbon dioxide is expected by 2010, despite the growth of traffic, because manufacturers are introducing more efficient vehicles (see Table 5.6). The Plan would, however, bring road carbon dioxide emissions below the 2000 level, offset marginally by increased rail emissions (including those from power stations). The introduction of higher technical standards for vehicle emissions such as nitrogen oxides and carbon particles, which harm humans and biodiversity, should have a dramatic effect despite traffic growth. Although the Plan and the additional measures would bring emissions down further, the stricter vehicle standards make the most difference. Yet within the good overall outlook there are geographical variations. It appears likely that, even with all the scenario options in operation, central London and very busy roads in the rest of London and other conurbations will still have levels of nitrogen dioxide in 2010 above the EU's maximum limit (DETR, 2000a: paras 74, 75).

Plan outputs from what DETR termed its 'key components' (trunk roads; passenger rail traffic; rail freight; London; other local

TABLE 5.7   *Comparison of outputs from Plan components*

Plan component	Reduction in congestion 2000–10		Central spend per vehicle hour saved in 2010 (£)	Carbon dioxide savings in 2010 (MtC)	Further rail/bus user benefits
	All roads	Trunk roads			
Trunk roads	3%	13%	5	adds 0.1	none
Passenger rail	1%	1%	11	11	high
Rail freight	0.4%	2%	10	25	medium
London	3%	0%	12	0.1	high
Local transport	3%	3%	8	0.1	high
Sustainable distribution	0.5%	1%	13	very low	(savings to business)

Note: Carbon dioxide savings are expressed as 'million tonnes of carbon', MtC.
Source: Data from DETR, *Transport 2010: The Background Analysis* (DETR, 2000a), Figure 16.

authorities; freight logistics) were compared. The evaluation of each component assumes the other components are in place. However, the comparison is limited to three, and really two, criteria: the reduction in greenhouse gas emissions; the reduction in road congestion; and the cost to central public budgets of removing that congestion, per vehicle-hour saved (see Table 5.7).

Spending on trunk roads is shown to be the most effective and cheapest strategy for reducing road congestion but it encourages traffic growth and increases Britain's contribution to global warming. At the other end of the scale, 'sustainable distribution' (a small budget for 'greener' lorries and efficient road haulage) is relatively expensive for the limited output: 'Expenditure on rail freight outperforms all other quantified components by some margin on expenditure per tonne of carbon saved'. Other potential benefits to users which were not quantified for the Plan, such as the savings in time and discomfort for rail passengers of spending on rail, were 'equivalent to tens of millions of road vehicle hours saved at standard transport appraisal values of time' (DETR, 2000a: para. 80).

Evaluation in terms of road congestion and emissions did not cover all the criteria announced in the Integrated Transport White Paper: environmental impact, safety, economy, accessibility and integration. The House of Commons Transport Committee found the Plan too focused on improving traffic flow at the expense of social objectives such as quality of life, safety and access to transport (Transport Committee, 2002a: paras 30–7). The Cabinet Office's Social Exclusion Unit complained that the Plan was 'heavily skewed towards modes used by higher earners'; the poorest fifth of the population would benefit from 11 per cent of Plan spending: the richest fifth from 38 per cent (Social Exclusion Unit, 2002: para. 4.11). While the Plan's background documents provided extensive information on methodologies and assumptions, they did not make clear how the cost-benefits of potential policy options were compared before choices were made. The result was dominated by high-cost infrastructure projects instead of smaller measures, such as walking and cycling schemes, which might be equally effective. The overall effect was to help those who travelled most, rather than reducing the need for travel.

The Transport Committee expressed the frustration of some of its members that political leaders did not help the Plan deliver its promises. The Plan assumed that eight large towns, preferably 20, would be implementing congestion charging schemes by 2010. Yet the government failed to give political support to local authorities (starting with London) willing to introduce these contentious policies (Transport Commitee, 2002a: para. 51). The goal to make public transport cheaper with respect to car travel had been made even harder to reach when the fuel duty escalator was stopped, an especially disappointing action given that holding the costs of driving constant in real terms seemed to be a very effective strategy for reducing road traffic and congestion.

All that said, the political, financial and technical criticisms do not detract from the value of the Plan as an attempt to engage in a long-term and cross-modal approach to forward planning. At the very least it was a useful exercise in a public and official comparison of the impact of different transport policies. Indeed, it was probably too much of a public analysis of options for ministers, for whom rational decision-making can cut off possibilities for political fudge and manoeuvre. The Plan could have been revised, as the Transport Committee suggested. A revision was announced for July 2002, postponed to September and December, when a Progress Report 'committed' the government to a 'review and roll forward' in 2004. *The Future of Transport* certainly rolled forward annual headline figures for transport spending to 2015 (DfT, 2004: Annex A); but there was no technical analysis of options, not even a breakdown of the proportions to be devoted to each 'key component'. Instead there were 'key themes', of which 'planning ahead' referred to a commitment to debate road pricing, an ambitious political challenge and important transport policy but not 'forward planning' in the sense of the 10 Year Plan.

Forecasts for air travel

Despite the almost wholly privatized nature of the air industry, the government takes a close interest in trends in air travel because of its responsibility for deciding applications for airport expansion and for air traffic control. *The Future of Air Transport*, setting out its preferences for airport development within a context of environmental constraints, depicted the problem thus: '[In 2030] demand will be between two and three times what it is today. This would imply an average of around two return trips a year for each UK resident, compared to an average of just under one return trip each today' (DfT, 2003: para. 2.8). However, the government had decided to make provision for BAA and other operators to expand far in advance of the forecasters' technical ability to demonstrate need ('between two and three times'). The 2000 edition of *Air Traffic Forecasts* had covered only the period to 2020. It had estimated that the number of travellers using British airports would increase by 4.3 per cent a year in the period up to 2020, though the rate of increase was slowing as the market became saturated. 'Trend growth has declined in every decade since the 1960s', from about 14 per cent in the 1960s to 7 per cent in the 1970s and 6 per cent in the 1980s (DETR, 2000b: para. 3.8). The rate of growth in air travel is related primarily to national economic growth, but also to international economic growth, trading volumes, exchange rates, and the price of tickets. The recent entry of 'no frills' airlines has introduced greater uncertainty into forecasts because of the lack of historic data. A significant difference from road traffic forecasts is the assumption that the capacity of airports and air space would always be sufficient, in order 'to identify where and when the need for additional capacity will arise and to inform decisions about the provision of such capacity. Forecasts constrained by capacity would not give any useful indication of demand that would exist for new facilities' (DETR, 2000b: para. 2.7).

The Future of Air Transport and *The Future of Transport* were explicit on airport capacity. 'Simply building more and more capacity to meet potential demand . . . would not be a sustainable approach' (DfT, 2003: para. 2.14). 'Simply providing ever more capacity on our roads and railways, ports and airports is not the answer in the long term' (DfT, 2004: para. 8). The government made provision for 470 million passengers per annum (mppa) by 2030; and its statistical support (DfT, 2003: Annex A) rather struggles to demonstrate that the capacity being provided so far ahead is needed but does not represent 'predict and provide'. The DfT extrapolated the trends in *Air Traffic Forecasts* from 2020 to 2030, assuming a slightly lower growth rate, and suggested passenger numbers would reach about 500 mppa in 2030, with a spread of between 400 and 600 mppa. It debated the likely impact of changes since the 2000 forecasts: on the one hand, September 2001 and its consequences had led to a fall-off in business demand but, on the other hand, the 'no-frills carriers' traffic is growing; on the one hand, a 100 per cent fuel tax would reduce the central demand to 450 mppa, but on the other hand, its imposition would force airlines to work harder to reduce fares and add traffic:

> Together with a predicted recovery for the long-haul market as confidence returns, this should be sufficient to offset any suppressing effect of any environmental charge that might otherwise reduce air travel demand by ten per cent. The forecast of 500mppa in 2030, assuming airport capacity is accommodating, is therefore regarded as robust. (DfT, 2003: A.25)

The Future of Air Transport promised 'to update traffic forecasts in the light of trends' (DfT, 2003: para. 12.19). New editions of *Air Traffic Forecasts* (normally produced every two or three years) will help determine whether the government is taking a sustainable approach.

Maritime traffic

There are no official or national forecasts of maritime traffic related to UK ports or shipping, even though the government has responsibilities for approving port developments similar to those for airports. Perhaps because John Prescott had been a seafarer, the DETR produced two maritime White Papers. *British Shipping* (DETR, 1998b) had to depend on 'global' figures proposed by the Chamber of Shipping and others (a rate of growth in world shipping of 5 per cent a year over the next decade). However, its authors commissioned research into the future supply of ships' officers (Glen, 2005 is a more developed version), and the training scheme that resulted is one outcome of an attempt to plan ahead in maritime transport. *Modern Ports* (DETR, 2000c) was 'the first comprehensive statement of policy for ports in the United Kingdom since 1964'. The position adopted by the Paper – 'it is not easy to measure port capacity, or whether it will meet expected growth in demand', and 'the Government does not make or endorse forecasts of port traffic as it does for roads and airports' (DETR, 2000c: 2.4.1. and 2.4.16) – sounded inadequate and even complacent, since the government ought to have some independent intellectual basis for assessing the supply and demand arguments put forward by port developers.

Until the implementation in 2000 of the EC's Maritime Statistics Directive 96/64/EC on the origins and destination of port traffic, information was limited to that required by Customs & Excise. The lack of data (on accidents, infrastructure, the movement of goods to and from ports by different modes of traffic, revenue and expenditure, trans-shipment) drew scorn from the Transport Committee: 'Unfortunately, there appears to be a remarkable lack of information about the ports industry. We were astonished that many of the statistics we asked for in the course of this inquiry were not available' (2003: para. 26). The Transport Department told the Committee in 2001 and 2003 that it was discussing with ports how the information could be collected and published. By 2005 its Maritime Statistics division was well on the way to collecting labour-related statistics, but the data that would allow the planning of a growing and less environment-damaging transport mode seem as far away as ever. More than any other form of transport, the development of maritime traffic is left to private interests.

Spatial planning

In spatial planning the Labour government introduced a more goal-directed system for England and Wales in 2004; the Scottish Executive introduced its own variant the same year, with the same objective of 'sustainable development'. Transport planning is only one aspect of the new system (for a wider picture of the role of local authorities see Chapter 3), but from the transport viewpoint there is much continuity – mainly because the most controversial reform was dropped – and, where there is change, it should lead towards a more purposeful planning system without a corresponding loss of democratic participation.

Since the Town and Country Planning Act 1971, local authorities have not been expected to be specific in prescribing land use. That approach was taken further under the 2004 Act. The details of planning legislation vary over time but, in broad terms, transport considerations are incorporated into land-use policies at three geographic levels. National government gives directions to local and regional planning bodies, and makes decisions on major projects. In England, regional institutions set frameworks for local councils within the national constraints. Councils draw up development plans and decide most planning applications, but if the project is large or contested the Secretary of State decides. The Scottish Executive and the Assembly in Wales have the planning powers once exercised by the Scottish or Welsh Secretary of State. Under their guidance, Scottish and Welsh local unitary authorities draw up structure plans and more detailed local plans and decide applications. All are linked by the strong powers given to ministers over the last 50 years to direct local authorities. Whether or not ministers choose to intervene, their approach to planning and transport is a strong determinant of the outcome.

Reforming spatial planning

By 1997, criticism of the land-use planning process was widespread. Business associations complained of councils' delays in drawing up plans or deciding planning applications. Local authorities, professional bodies, residents' associations and environmental groups objected to the way central government decided major projects; for example, when it over-ruled councils that had rejected applications to build shopping malls that would increase car traffic, or when ministers approved or rejected port developments without reference to a broader national strategy. People who lived near but not on the site of a transport project, or who rented their accommodation, were not adequately compensated for their contribution to the public good. The Labour government's reform of land-use planning was slow but the outcome seems to reflect fairly the conflicting aims of the interested parties.

The Planning and Compulsory Purchase Act 2004 implemented the DETR's *A Better Quality of Life: A Strategy for Sustainable Development for the UK* (1999), as well as providing more generous compensation payments to those disrupted by transport projects. There had been a lively debate between the Treasury and DETR over the goals of the reformed system; the former wanted it to have 'an economic basis', while the latter agreed to 'Business

Planning Zones' but not out-of-town supermarkets (*Financial Times*, 10 November 1999). In *Planning: Delivering a Fundamental Change* (DTLR, 2001), the government proposed introducing a parliamentary procedure for major projects, and a local planning system that increased the strategic role of regional assemblies while reducing that of county councils. The House of Commons opposed the new parliamentary procedure, and there was much opposition from local councils to the suggested reforms to planning (Transport Committee, 2002: para. 5). In 2003 the government gave up the parliamentary procedure, but pursued the local planning reforms, while making some concessions to county councils.

The 2004 Act required planning authorities in England and Wales, including the Secretary of State and the Welsh Assembly, to 'exercise the function with the objective of contributing to the achievement of sustainable development' (S.39). The Royal Commission on Environmental Pollution had said that planning would continue to oscillate 'between conflicting ideologies' unless it had a statutory objective; and the planning minister, Lord Falconer, agreed it would be 'to promote sustainable development' (Transport Committee, 2002: Q.886). It was the first time the planning system in Britain had been given a statutory aim. When English and Welsh local councils, English regional assemblies and the Welsh Assembly draw up local or regional plans (see Chapter 3), they must demonstrate with a sustainability appraisal that they have integrated transport into land-use planning. The National Assembly for Wales, on the basis of its consultative document, *Planning: Delivering for Wales* (January 2002), had already decided that there should be a Wales Spatial Plan, linking economic development, transport and protected areas. After consultation and a sustainability appraisal the Wales Spatial Plan for 2005–25 was agreed by the Welsh Assembly in November 2004. When Welsh local authorities draw up their development plans they must 'have regard to' the Wales Spatial Plan as well as to 'national [UK] policies' and the evolution of the 'transport system and traffic of the area'.

Scotland made a similar but non-statutory change at its national level. The Scottish Executive had conducted a Review of Strategic Planning, which showed widespread support for a *National Planning Framework*. This document, adopted in 2004, identifies the priorities and opportunities for Scotland and its regions up to 2025, and provides a spatial context for local plans and planning decisions. It will be taken into account when the Executive decides transport priorities, and reviews transport project and appraisal procedures. 'Sustainable development' is the first principle guiding Scottish councils' structure plans; and planning applications to councils must show arrangements for access and the effect on the environment.

There is no over-arching spatial strategy for England or the UK. The Commons Committee asked the Westminster government to consider establishing a National Spatial Strategy (for the UK) that would provide the context for major infrastructure proposals such as airport and port development, the North–South high-speed rail route and a strategy on rail freight (Transport Committee, 2002: paras 15–16). Ministers refused, arguing that it would be 'unnecessarily complicated' to combine into one spatial strategy the government's policy statements (for example, the White Paper on Air Transport), planning policy statements (government's instructions to planning authorities, see below) and the regions' spatial strategies (ODPM, 2002: para. 10).

Regional spatial planning in England

The strategic role of the regional tier in England was reinforced by the 2004 Planning Act. Local councils have long collaborated at regional level on land-use planning and transport. Standing regional conferences of councils offered advice to Environment and Transport Secretaries on the Regional Planning Guidance which the government had issued as a framework for local authority plans. Some councils worked voluntarily on transport strategy with other neighbouring authorities: East Anglian counties coordinated roads planning from the early 1980s. These initiatives responded to local desires for a longer-term and larger-scale approach to transport planning during periods when formal structures or ministerial interest were inadequate. Local government officers were among those who wanted Labour's planning reform to create stronger regional strategies with statutory authority (Transport Committee, 2002: Q.271, Q.274).

The drive to strengthen the regional planning structures and strategies became more pronounced in the 1990s, first of all because of environmental concerns: for example, the Houghton Report recommended that the standing regional conferences should decide major road proposals which crossed council boundaries. Second, the Major government started to replace the two-tier system of county and district with 'unitary authorities' which were too small for transport planning functions. It created Government Offices of the Regions to coordinate policies such as planning and transport and urban regeneration. Third, the Labour manifesto of 1997 promised to create 'regional chambers to coordinate transport, planning, economic development, bids for European funding and land use planning'; in time, these would be directly elected. Regional chambers were indeed set up, as explained in Chapter 3, though the first region to vote rejected the idea of directly-elected councils. Nevertheless, at the time the planning reform was prepared, there were many reasons to base it on planning and transport strategies produced by regional authorities which would set the framework for local plans by the unitary or district council.

The eight regional assemblies (and the Greater London Authority) were designated as regional planning bodies (RPBs), and their main task under the 2004 Act is to prepare a Regional Spatial Strategy (RSS), which is to include a Regional Transport Strategy (RTS). The scope for regional autonomy over the content of these strategies is in the end determined by central government, because the Regional Spatial Strategy must be submitted to the Secretary of State, who can require changes before approving it. 'The Regional Spatial Strategy must set out the Secretary of State's policies (however expressed) in relation to the development and use of land within the region' (2004 Act: 1 (2)). The Planning Policy Statement PPS11, *Regional Spatial Strategies* (ODPM, 2004a), specifies nine government documents the assemblies must take into account in drawing up the Regional Transport Strategy, such as the Integrated Transport White Paper (DETR, 1998), the 10 Year Plan, *The Future of Transport* (DfT, 2004), *The Future of Air Transport* (DfT, 2003) and *The Future of Rail* (DfT, 2004e), as well as more detailed Planning Policy Statements or Guidance, such as *PPG13: Transport* (DETR, 2001). The ODPM warned planning bodies to keep up with revisions! PPS11 sets out the government's expectations on how the Regional Spatial Strategy should be prepared, implemented, monitored and reviewed, including arrangements for community involvement. It must provide 'a broad development strategy for the region for a fifteen to twenty year period'. The Regional Transport Strategy is required to set out how national transport policies will be delivered in the region; to outline the transport and related land-use policies and measures required to support the spatial strategy; and to provide a long-term framework for transport in the region. It must provide the regional and sub-regional context for the Local

Transport mode	Content of the Regional Transport Strategy
Transport investment and management across the modes	Sets out regional objectives and priorities to support the spatial strategy and delivery of sustainable national transport policies depending on the region's transport system, project value-for-money, and likely resources
Airports and ports	Gives a strategic steer to port and airport development that is consistent with national policy
Trunk roads, regional and sub-regional roads	Provides guidance on the priorities for managing and improving the network, to include those enhancements already agreed in principle by the Department of Transport
Sustainable freight distribution	Gives advice on its promotion, such as by identifying general location of multi-modal freight interchanges, and seeking to maximize the use of existing infrastructure
Public transport	Guides location of new development accessible by public transport, and identifies public transport priorities to improve access to jobs and services for those without a car
Parking policies	Gives advice on setting parking standards appropriate to different parts of the region
Traffic demand management	Identifies locations where demand management could reduce congestion and suggests criteria for approving schemes

FIGURE 5.1 *Main aims of a Regional Transport Strategy*

Source: Compiled from information in ODPM (2004a), *Planning Policy Statement 11* (TSO, 2004), pp. 58–67.

Transport Plans that are prepared by county councils and unitary councils (see Chapter 3); and must enable local authorities in their own planning documents to encourage housing or business expansion where public transport is or will be provided. The main items that the government asks the assembly to address in its Regional Transport Strategy are summarized in Figure 5.1.

Few regional planning bodies are starting with a blank sheet, as the case of the South West Regional Assembly illustrates (see www.southwest-ra.gov.uk). In 2005 its Regional Spatial Strategy was the existing Regional Planning Guidance of 2001, which the Assembly revised before starting to develop its Regional Spatial Strategy for 2006–26. The Regional Transport Strategy of 2001 was also revised to take account of subsequent multi-modal studies in the region and *The Future of Air Transport*, and to revise the priorities for transport investment. This RTS of 2004 was used by the county councils and unitary authorities, such as Bristol, as the framework for their own five-year Local Transport Plans submitted to the DfT in the summer of 2005. Consultation then started on the Regional Transport Strategy that would form part of the new Regional Spatial Strategy. The Assembly decided to promote integration by creating a joint Regional Spatial Planning and Transport Group to oversee the development of the Spatial Strategy. The South West Regional Development Agency and the Government Office for the South West attend Group meetings, and the Group works with the regional office of the Highways Agency and (until 2005) the SRA. Collaborative working did not prevent disputes, such as over the relative priority to be given to the Highways Agency's Targeted Programme of Improvement road schemes in the South West and a list of public transport schemes for Bristol and other urban areas (*Local Transport Today*, 24 November 2005).

The most controversial aspect of the spatial planning reform was the refocusing of tasks at the level of regions and unitary or district councils, which seemed to ignore the county council's responsibility for Local Transport Plans (see Chapter 3), and left a large gulf between local experience and regional strategic planning. The 2004 Act therefore required the regional body to use counties as technical advisers, and to enable counties to take the lead role in developing any sub-regional strategy envisaged by the assembly. In any case, county councils are represented on the regional body (for example, they have four members on the South West's Planning and Transport Group, alongside four unitary councils and ten district councils), and counties and unitary authorities remain responsible for drawing up Local Transport Plans within the framework set by the Regional Transport Strategy. There is much continuity with the old in the new development plan process, even if the organizational structures have changed.

Major infrastructure projects

Though local plans must accommodate major road schemes, new railway lines or airport terminals, the far-reaching effect on land use and the environment means they are properly decided at national level. However, no process has yet been found for authorizing or rejecting these projects that is acceptable to all concerned, despite a continuous attempt at reform since at least the 1970s. At the heart of the problem is the tension between the 'owners' of the project (whether the Transport Department or a private developer) and those objecting to it (local or environmental groups): the former want a swift process and the others want a fair chance for their arguments to be taken into account. (For an excellent first-hand account of an important case through the cycle of consultation, public inquiry and political campaign, see Barbara Bryant's *Twyford Down*, 1996.) The inevitable conflict of opinion is intensified by the adversarial traditions of the British party, parliamentary and judicial systems. Yet the only sites for a national debate on the issues relating to a national project seem to be Parliament or a public inquiry, or a mixture of both.

A *public inquiry* is the usual forum for examining large road, airport or port developments. An independent inspector appointed by the government hears witnesses and reports to Transport and Planning Ministers on the objections, other proposals, and technical assessments offered by transport officials and other witnesses (see Chapter 8 for the technical assessments). The report recommends whether the infrastructure project or development application should be accepted, perhaps with modifications, and sometimes suggests a different solution. The inspector decides which non-statutory objectors, such as representatives of environmental groups, will be heard. The planning inspector examining the case for Heathrow Terminal Five, for instance, selected as witnesses 1,000 individuals and 70 representatives of airlines, airport operators, local businesses, trade unions and local groups opposing the proposals, such as HACAN (Heathrow Association for the Control of Aircraft Noise) and FHANG (Federation of Heathrow Anti-Noise Groups).

Witnesses may raise issues only about the project which is the subject of the inquiry, not its place in a national air or road policy. Public debate about transport policy becomes fragmented into a series of arguments around a number of large infrastructure investments. Approval for a controversial scheme, such as the stretch of the M3 that cuts through Twyford Down, may be given because it is the last link in a route whose general need is not in dispute, whereas a consideration of the whole route could have produced a less destructive scheme. The court-like atmosphere of the inquiry is another constraint. To present an effective case against the technical and legal expertise of departments or developers, environmental groups and other objectors have had to take on professional advisers and barristers. The 'inquiry' has become an expensive argument between experts, for and against the department's road scheme, the new airport runway or terminal. Local community groups can feel sidelined.

After the inquiry the minister is entirely free to reject the inspector's recommendations. Because of possible electoral consequences, ministers can take decades to make controversial decisions, as with the A34 bypass (of the bypass) around Newbury, deferring time after time to 'relook at the evidence'. The political overtones add to the list of criticisms, because they make it harder for objectors to accept that an unfavourable outcome is the best decision for the nation.

Parliamentary legislation has long been the way in which British Rail, London Underground and other corporate bodies obtained planning consent for new infrastructure, such as the Jubilee Line extension; they used the private or hybrid bill procedure. (The procedure for a hybrid bill is similar to that for a private bill, but has the benefit of formal support from the government.) In either case, the public inquiry is replaced by a parliamentary committee holding hearings in public, although only those whose property is directly affected have a right to appear. Other objectors can only submit petitions. By choosing the hybrid bill procedure for the Channel Tunnel Rail Link, the government was able to remove the protection of conservation law from the historic buildings and gas holders at St Pancras and King's Cross, and English Heritage could not give evidence (Lord Kennet, *HL Debates*, 21 May 1996: 810). The examination must be confined to the route presented by the developer or minor modifications. Planning through legislative procedures also has the disadvantage that small concessions made to petitioners (for example, on noise reduction measures) run the risk of setting a legal precedent. The Treasury scrutinizes bills carefully for these problems; the negotiating flexibility inherent in a ministerial decision is thereby reduced.

Two new parliamentary procedures for approving transport projects were introduced in the 1990s. The New Roads and Streetworks Act 1991 permitted the granting of concessions to private firms to design, build, and run new motorways in return for toll (or shadow toll) income, and was intended to meet the government's desire for speedier approval and completion of road schemes than through public inquiries and government expenditure. The first road project to be authorized under this Act was the private-sector M6 toll road near Birmingham, submitted to public consultation before the concession agreement in March 1992, but not given the definite go-ahead until July 1997. It opened in 2004, and although most heavy traffic continued to prefer the congested but toll-free M6, it was soon treated as the model for a further stretch of toll road parallel to the M6 to the north of Birmingham.

The Transport and Works Act 1992 (applying in England and Wales) replaced the private bill procedure for railways and tramways. It responded to complaints by backbenchers about the amount of their time taken up by private bills, especially because of the surge of interest in urban rail schemes. The Act gave the Secretary of State for Transport power to agree small-scale rail projects by laying a 'negative procedure' Order before Parliament: one of the houses would have to pass a resolution against the Order to annul it, a rare occurrence but one which provides some safeguard. Larger-scale projects must have Parliament's positive consent; the proposals must be approved by both Houses. In this case, Parliament is expected to discuss just the 'general features' of a major project and endorse (or reject) it. If approval is given, the constructor is expected to seek detailed planning consent from the local authority, though the Secretary of State can waive that requirement. Whether the project is minor or major, if there are objections from the public the Secretary of State can decide to hold a public inquiry; but if a local authority objects there must be an inquiry. The final decision is made by the Secretary of State (see DoT, 1992).

The Transport and Works Act (TWA) saved much parliamentary time. By summer 2001, when the procedure was reviewed as part of the planning reform, 83 applications had been made, almost all of them small schemes treated by the 'negative procedure', such as extensions to the Manchester Metrolink and Heathrow Express, or the reconstruction of the Welsh Highland Railway between Porthmadog and Caernarfon by the Ffestiniog Railway. Applications for 29 projects were unopposed; the department was able to settle objections on 15 projects by letter, and seven applications were withdrawn. Thirty schemes went to a Public Inquiry. However the process was still lengthy, as far as developers and residents suffering 'planning blight' were concerned. The average time from application to decision for those that went to an inquiry was 26 months; it was 16 months where objections were dealt with by letter, and even 11 months for those that no one opposed (MVA, 2002: 12).

There had been only two major applications by 2001 that required the 'positive procedure': Central Railway's draft Order was rejected by the House of Commons; and the Channel Tunnel Rail Link (Stratford Station) Order, promoted by Eurostar, was accepted by both Houses of Parliament. Even so, the whole process took three-and-a-half years. The application by Central Railway plc on 22 May 1996 to construct and operate a 'lorry on rail' freight line between the Midlands and the Channel Tunnel attracted 13,000 letters of objection. The Secretary of State announced within two days that he had decided to submit it for parliamentary debate; it was rejected by the Commons on 24 July by 172 votes to 7 on a free vote. The project was not the finest test of the Act: Clare Short, Labour's shadow transport minister, summed it up justly as 'well-intentioned but not properly considered' (*HC Debates*, 24 July 1996: 419). The minister warned that 'Parliament's endorsement of the principle of the project would be bound to carry weight with the inquiry inspector in making a recommendation' (*HC Debates*, 24 July 1996: 408). Thus the fate of the project rested on a 90-minute debate in which MPs from constituencies along the route expressed the anxieties of their constituents; in that forum it would have been hard for other MPs to defend a much better project. Parliamentarians were annoyed to have been asked to debate it:

> This application shows the need to review the Transport and Works Act 1992 . . . The Government cannot justify a system in which a minor company makes proposals without adequate thought and planning, and then expects to get it through on the ground that it can spell out the detail later once Parliament has approved it. I appeal to the Minister to learn from this lesson. The Act must be amended. (Clive Soley, *HC Debates*, 24 July 1996: 429)

It was therefore surprising that the government in December 2001 suggested that major infrastructure projects should be examined by Parliament.

Major Infrastructure Projects: Delivering Fundamental Change (DTLR, 2001a) outlined the government's reform proposals. Parliament would consider the broad principles; if it approved the 'need' and the 'location' there would be a public inquiry on the details. The inquiry inspector would not be able to recommend against a principle that Parliament had agreed, but the minister could halt proceedings if the inquiry identified insuperable problems. The government would publish up-to-date policy statements setting out the national framework to avoid objectors trying to debate government policy at the inquiry. It would strengthen the inquiry inspector's powers, and restrict both the time for cross-examination of witnesses and the inquiry's terms of reference.

The Commons Transport, Local Government and the Regions Committee said it preferred inquiries. First, inquiries 'provide rights of hearing to the principal parties and to other persons at the inspector's discretion . . . In general, the inquiry system commands wide public confidence and respect' (2002: para. 134). Affected parties would have the right only to lobby their MP. 'A debate in parliament constitutes a debate in public but not a public debate', and risked challenges under the Human Rights Act 1998 (Huggett, 2002: 30). Second, the EC directive on Environmental Impact Assessment (EIA) requires expertise and an 'open-minded consideration' that was incompatible with party political whipping (M. Grant, 2002). When Lord Falconer told the Committee that 'it would be inappropriate for there to be whipping', he was assured by a former DoE minister that there was whipping, such as on the Channel Tunnel Rail Link bill. According to the Committee chair: 'The crucial thing [on planning through private bills was] who got the chair', and 'that was done as a deal between the Whips, and everything that was said was often a waste of time because you knew the outcome' (2002: Q.958–64). Third, the parliamentary process was likely to take a whole session (November to July) to examine a major project, which is longer than many inquiries. Many major road inquiries were over in 50 days: only a few development projects, notably terminals or runways at Heathrow, Manchester and Stansted, took more than three months (2002: para. 151). Ministers themselves held up the planning process. 'The announcement of the decisions has on occasions been delayed for political convenience' (2002: para. 170). The most that the Transport, Local Government and the Regions Committee would offer the government was an extension to the 1992 Act. For its part, the Procedure Committee said that even considering such a reform was likely to take Parliament some time, and reminded ministers that it had taken five years to negotiate the 1992 Act (2002, para. 9): 'As Parliament decided when it enacted the Transport and Works Act 1992, there is only the most limited capacity within Parliament for dispute resolution regarding the location of major works' (M. Grant, 2002).

In the face of these objections, the government abandoned the parliamentary procedure, and turned back to improving the traditional public inquiry. It reiterated its intention to produce up-to-date national policy statements, and published *The Future of Air Transport* in 2003, and *The Future of Rail* and *The Future of Transport* (mainly roads) in 2004. A policy statement on ports was expected in late 2005, but only after ministers had dealt with a number of planning applications for new ports (*Financial Times*, 28 March 2005), and these decisions were still being made on a case by case basis in spring 2006. The Planning and Compulsory Purchase Act 2004 shortened inquiry procedures by appointing additional inspectors to consider aspects of the application concurrently rather than sequentially; new inquiry rules should enable inspectors to timetable the hearings more efficiently. The right to object was extended to a wider group of people, and compensation for compulsory purchase was made more generous to occupiers as well as owners in order to reduce objections. Finally, the government tried to enforce speedier decision-making on itself with the 2004 Act by requiring the Secretary of State to set out a timetable for making decisions, with an annual report to Parliament on his or her performance. Ministers have set themselves goals for reaching decisions on 80 per cent of applications. It remains to be seen whether the politically-sensitive decisions will remain part of the 20 per cent of decisions that are not taken within these limits.

Conclusion

Parliament seemed to many reformers the ideal democratic location for debating and deciding national transport issues yet, despite the serious interest taken by a few MPs, the procedures and habits of Westminster do not encourage sustained attention from a large core of parliamentarians. The normal party-dominated legislative procedures of Parliament cannot be guaranteed to settle a debate to general satisfaction. On the one hand, government legislation on national policies that raise issues of principle is decided on party lines. The Act implementing rail privatization was passed by Parliament only because some Conservative MPs who had spoken against rail privatization in public put aside their reasoned arguments to vote for it in the cause of maintaining their party in government. On the other, the constituency basis of representation makes it difficult for MPs to consider the general and strategic interest when asked to decide practical details of implementation. Infrastructure bills seem to combine the worst of both worlds. Party whipping removes the interest for committee members of considering and then deciding (in secret) a case on its technical merits; personal, party and constituency allegiances encourage 'nimbyism' (not in my back yard) in open debate in the chamber, inhibiting the expression of considered opinion.

The Cabinet is the only body within the British political system with the authority and power to decide and impose a national transport strategy. Transport programmes, because of their highly technical content, are easily assumed to be objective and ideology-free. Yet there is no ideal transport policy, or even an ideal roads programme on which all will agree, but a variety of possibilities each of which would help bring about a different array of economic and social goals. The collective judgment and responsibility of the Cabinet must be engaged in reconciling the political, economic and social goals of transport policy. Although a final decision would be promoted by the Secretary of State with the primary responsibility for transport, the support of the Cabinet as a whole is crucial. The 10 Year Transport Plan and the Planning and Compulsory Purchase Act 2004 illustrate, each in its own way, the collective nature of transport policy-making at national level: the former an integrated strategy, for all its faults, combining in its preparation the efforts and commitment of finance, environment, road and rail-oriented ministers and officials; the latter giving regional and local government, environment, transport and finance ministers and officials what they wanted in separate sections of the package (regional assemblies; a more 'planned' and participatory local land-use policy process; sustainable development at local level; deregulated business zones; and quicker, less-disputatious decision-making on large port and airport developments).

For any minister's policy to succeed, Treasury ministers have to be as committed as others to allowing spending to be directed in line with policy. But there are particular problems facing a Transport Secretary who decides to implement a transport plan because of the long time-scale needed to build infrastructure and to change travel patterns. The political system is geared to a four- (or at most a five-) year maximum period between elections. That is why the 10 Year Transport Plan was so significant, and such a disappointment when it failed to receive consistent support across government and from the top (harder to accept than the well-understood real-world problems of implementation). However independent and expert a forum is, and however widespread the public support for its recommendations, if the government does not like the political effect of the recommendations it will not implement them. Reports from

Royal Commissions and expert committees will be ignored, at least in the short term, if the recommendations are not politically convenient. The reality is shown by ministers' decisions after a planning inquiry that do not reflect the inspector's report. Forensic examinations of 'major infrastructure transport projects' (the third London airport, or Twyford Down) reveal a transport planning system which all too often fails to act in accordance with the technical, economic and procedurally rational arguments that appear in policy documents.

Chapter 6

Influencing Transport Policy

Central and local governments, Parliament and European Union institutions are formal actors in transport policy-making, given express authority to make decisions. Trying to influence these structures are the informal actors called interest groups, pressure groups or lobbies. As in other policy domains, the 'transport lobby' is made up of very diverse groups: some expressing the 'self-interest' of their own section of society, such as the FTA, the Transport and General Workers' Union (TGWU) or the Pedestrians' Association; others promoting changes that are in the 'general interest', such as Transport 2000 (Transport Scotland north of the border), which campaigns for increased public transport provision, the Royal Society for the Prevention of Accidents (RoSPA), or Friends of the Earth (FoE). All want transport services to be improved, but they have different – and conflicting – priorities, and therefore differ on what they want done and where, and how they want it to be funded.

The use of the convenient word 'groups' should not distract attention from the influence of professional bodies, companies and some individuals, and of others who are portrayed as neutral or 'holding the ring' (public bodies, the media or ministry officials). Andrew Marr noted a decade or more ago that the national debate over road-building was not taking place in Parliament (where parties were split on this issue), but between two opposing line-ups: on one side, the DoE, Transport 2000, the Council for the Protection of Rural England (CPRE), FoE, and the National Trust: on the other, the DfT, the big road construction companies, the retail motor trade, oil companies, gravel firms, the Automobile Association (AA) and the Royal Automobile Club (*Independent*, 27 September 1994). Any analysis of how transport policy is made would need to consider all these participants, and many more, including those at local level for and against particular projects.

The principles of interest-group action

Interest groups fit uneasily with British views of representative parliamentary democracy, yet the fundamental idea of a liberal democracy is that groups are free to organize and express their opinions; they also provide a channel of professional expertise to decision-makers alongside party representation in Parliament.

According to the pluralist theory of democracy, policy is, and should be, made through individuals and groups competing freely for influence at many levels and places in society (Dahl, 1956). However weak the theory turns out to be in practice, it sets a standard for government behaviour. Ministers are keen to show they have consulted relevant interests, and the DfT has increasingly opened up its consultation procedures (see www.dft.govt.uk, topic 'consultations'). The Department's mobility unit in 2004 asked 60 organizations or firms to advise on legislation that would give disabled people the same rights of access to transport as they have to shops and offices. Half were organizations representing users, such as the Rail Passengers Council, the Disabled Persons Transport Advisory Committee (DPTAC), and Mencap; and the other half providers of transport services, such as Arriva, the Green Flag break-down firm and the TGWU. None the less, participation in British policy-making is not guaranteed: in contrast, say, with the 'remiss' system of Sweden, which automatically incorporates the opinion of any interested group into parliamentary discussion. Neither do British interest groups have the access to government documents that Swedish citizens take for granted. British officials may provide and explain the data on which groups rely to develop policy, but the internal advice on which ministers make their decisions remains protected. The eventual implementation in 2005 of the Freedom of Information Act 2000 did not bring rapid change: the government refused, on cost grounds, to release papers relating to Stephen Byers's decision to declare Railtrack insolvent (*Independent*, 11 February 2005).

'Elite theorists' question whether decision-making can be pluralist, arguing that power is dominated by elite groups, such as business leaders, top professionals or senior civil servants. Public policy decisions may constitute only one face of power. There may also be a 'restrictive face of power' or 'veto power' (Bachrach and Baratz, 1962; Lukes, 1974), exercised by elite groups when they diffuse values or procedures that keep other issues off the policy agenda. The 'cost–benefit' formulae for infrastructure projects operated in this way by emphasizing criteria linked to the economy, and by regarding landscapes, habitats, communities and history as inadmissible. Transport economists have since the 1960s developed ways of evaluating in monetary terms some social benefits such as reductions in accidents and journey times. The DfT's cost–benefit analysis of road schemes (see Chapter 8), and the Scottish Executive's procedures for rail freight grants incorporate quantified environmental advantages such as noise reduction and removing lorries from urban areas, yet some considerations remain out of reach of quantitative techniques. While new ports could reduce road traffic, 'how do you compare the impact of roads killing an estimated 5000 barn owls each year with the loss of intertidal habitat?' (Huggett, 2002: 29). Second, this 'econocratic' approach (Self, 1975) is criticized for being not only less value-free than it seems, but also reducing the transparency of decisions. Despite the existence of participatory techniques that allow groups affected by a transport project to weigh up options according to their own priorities (Chevroulet, 2002), decisions are still guided by procedures operated by a small group of bureaucrats and ministers in ways they themselves have largely determined.

Lindblom's variant of elite theory emphasized the crucial power of one elite group, business (1977: 172). This group had special power, Lindblom argued, because its main interest (economic growth) was regarded as the public interest, and governments automatically took its views into account: this policy is often summed up as 'what is good for General Motors is good for the country'. Lindblom's theory seemed somewhat questionable in Britain in the 1970s when organized labour was able to obtain large pay increases, led notably by Ford workers at Dagenham, and rail unions could disrupt commuter services over long periods. But in the 1980s workers were called to order with legislation restricting unions' freedom to strike, and privatization of the transport manufacturing and service industries. Political leaders listened less to manufacturing business, instead seeking views on public policy from a newer financial elite, such as members of the Institute of Directors (IoD) and accountancy firms, who represented economic growth and efficient management. On rail privatization, ministers took advice from management consultants and marketing firms rather than the Railway Industry Association and the heads of the old transport industries, with the added irony that the consultants were paid substantial fees to express their opinions.

Governments automatically seek out the views of leading firms and commercial associations on policies relating to their business, especially where their technical information is vital. Thus, when the

European Commission in 2003 proposed a common size of Intermodal Loading Unit (container or 'swap body' or palletized load) to make it simpler to transfer freight from road to other modes, the DfT invited comments from seven firms and nine associations of firms operating freight transport services. Yet, though commercial firms dominated the DfT's consultation process (DfT, 2003a), it was not so much because of a desire to pay attention to the views of 'business' (or capitalism) as a wish to hear those of the narrow sector concerned; and private interests figured strongly because provision was in the hands of private operators. In contrast, the European Commission, because of its aim to take freight off roads, consulted the *users* of inter-modal services too: the chemical industry, shippers of manufactured goods, freight forwarders and car logistics firms.

In Britain the consultation of interest groups is left mainly to the discretion of officials. This contrasts sharply with the situation in many other European countries, and in the European Union, where such consultation is frequently built into the legislative process. For example, the European Union's Economic and Social Committee (see Chapter 4) gave its formal opinion on the Commission's proposal for Intermodal Units before it was considered by the European Parliament. In France the same proposal was debated extensively in the *Conseil National des Transports* (CNT), an official consultative body of 8 parliamentarians and representatives from 9 local passenger transport authorities, 18 ministries, 13 user associations, 29 public and private transport operators and 25 trade unions of various political persuasions. While CNT members made the same criticisms of the Intermodal Units as had the British port and shipping interests (British rail and road interests were more favourable), the CNT heard a more rounded picture than was presented to the DfT (quick, safe transfers between modes; savings to logistics operators and to distributors and thus to consumers: CNT, 2004).

Writers on corporatism put this point more generally when they criticize the pluralist 'free-for-all' and argue that interest group activity should be more systematically organized. They envisage policy being made by permanent negotiation between the government bodies and the interest groups relevant to a sector; groups would promote the interests of their members in the discussions and help implement decisions through their members (Cawson, 1986: 38). Policy-making in Britain is far less corporatist than in some other European countries (Austria, Germany, Scandinavia), though in sectors where the number of professional groups is small, policy-making can often be corporatist in nature, the close relationship between the road construction lobby and highways officials having been the classic example (Wistrich, 1983: 102). The formal organization of transport interests is more in evidence in Britain at times when coordinated policy-making is being stressed, such as under the Heath and Wilson governments of the 1970s. In the 1976 Transport Policy consultation document, produced by the Environment and Transport 'Super-Department', a National Transport Council was proposed, in which employers, trade unions, local authorities and users would examine major projects and pricing structures; it was rejected by the re-created Department of Transport a year later.

A revived Department of Environment and Transport, headed by John Prescott, set up the Commission for Integrated Transport in 1999 (CfIT). The careful selection of Commission members from the transport industry, local government, user groups and voluntary bodies made it a microcosm of the sector, at least in the road and rail domains (little attention was given to air and none to maritime transport). An official review of CfIT concluded that it engaged effectively in key debates (paying for road use, congestion charging); had published useful research reports with 'dispassionate perspectives' (comparison of motoring taxes in European countries); and that its excellent study of the bus subsidy regime had 'made an important contribution to policy making'. Overall, CfIT had shown the 'unique contribution' to policy-making that could be made by a body representing a broad range of interests and authoritative expertise. However, the task it was subsequently given of monitoring the 10 Year Transport Plan (see Chapter 5) 'adversely affected' CfIT's relationship with the DfT. Furthermore, the government took one component of CfIT's advice on raising maximum lorry weight to 44 tonnes without implementing the counterbalancing measures CfIT proposed for rail (DfT, 2003b: 2–4, 19).

Interest representation is complex: while none of the major theories about how interests might contribute to decision-making apply very well to British transport policy, all have some relevance. The pluralist ideal is not universally accepted, but there is a very lively presence of transport groups notwithstanding, and consultation and access to information are improving. Ministers and their civil servants form an elite set of decision-makers with their own prejudices, but there is little sign of the technocratic power seen in France. Finally, although corporatism as such is rejected, there was a stronger inclination by the early Blair government to set up 'task forces' to bring together the varied interests within one sector (see Table 6.1). Some were launched mainly for political reasons, such

TABLE 6.1 *Department of Transport advisory bodies*

Organization and year set up		Membership	Role
Rail Passengers Council	2005 (1947)	16 members appointed by ministers and devolved assemblies	Take up passengers' complaints with operators, press for better performance.
Disabled Persons Transport Advisory Committee	1985	21 members, most of whom are disabled; DfT secretary	Advise on matters affecting transport needs of disabled people.
Shipping Working Group	1997	DETR official, Chamber of Shipping, NUMAST, RMT, TGWU, 4 other ministries	Prepare and oversee implementation of *Shipping* White Paper (DETR, 1998b).
Cleaner Vehicles Task Force	1997	DETR, Trade ministers, official; SMMT, RAC, FTA, oil firms, local government, green groups	Develop a package of practical solutions for cleaner road vehicles.
Road Haulage Forum	1999	Transport and Treasury ministers; RHA, FTA, NFU, CBI	Discuss costs and problems 'with particular respect to competitiveness and modernisation'.
Advisory Group on Motorcycling	1999	Minister, 11 officials, police, 5 motorcyclists' groups, manufacturer, AA, RAC	Advise on role of motorcycling in integrated transport.

Commission for Integrated Transport	1999	Academic; local government, CPT, Network Rail, DPTAC, Highways Agency, RPC, CAA, FTA, Post Office, RAC, Transport 2000, TGWU, CBI	Advise on implementing an integrated transport policy; identify and disseminate best practice; refresh the transport policy debate.
Motorists' Forum	2000	RAC, AA, local government, disabled drivers group, police, WI, DfT roads, SMMT, CBI, Ford, oil, environment group	Represent motoring interests and car users' views in the development of national and local policies.
Road Safety Advisory Panel	2000	Minister, government agencies, police, safety groups, AA, RAC, SMMT, road safety officers	Advise on and monitor road safety targets to be delivered by 2010.
Aviation Health Working Group	2001	DfT, Health Department; aviation industry	Tackle problems of passenger welfare (thrombosis; cabin air quality).
Bus Partnership Forum	2002	DfT, bus industry, local authority officials	Identify problems hindering growth in bus use and propose solutions.
Sea and Water	2003	Academic; members from 100 'sea/water' groups	To develop short sea and water shipping; represent UK interests to EU.

Notes: NUMAST, National Union of Marine, Aviation and Shipping Transport Officers; RMT, Rail and Maritime Transport Union; RHA, Road Haulage Association; NFU, National Farmers' Union; CPT, Confederation of Passenger Transport; RPC, Rail Passengers' Council; WI, Women's Institutes.

as the Road Haulage Forum to halt the hauliers' demonstrations in March 1999, or the Motorists' Forum to counter the 'anti-car' image of Labour identified by Blair's advisers (*Financial Times*, 15 November 2000). However, others have more thoughtful origins: for instance 'Sea and Water', created to develop this mode of transport, a variant of the Water Freight Forum recommended by the Freight Study Group (2002), itself set up by DETR in 2000.

Explaining group influence

It is hard to evaluate the impact of particular groups on particular decisions. The decision-makers themselves may be unaware how much their 'own' ideas were stimulated by organized pressure. Current methods of examining how interests wield their influence fall into two broad categories, though neither enables definite conclusions to be drawn (see Dowding, 1995). The first examines individual participants for characteristics which seem to aid influence: key information or technical expertise, valid claims to represent their section of society, financial resources, economic weight, and access to decision-makers, itself a product of the others. The Society of Motor Manufacturers and Traders provided the standard example: the government sought its opinion in the 1960s on the question of making car seat-belts compulsory because its members had the technical information about providing safe anchor points, and also because it represented all car manufacturers in the UK, a source of valuable exports and employment which no government would damage lightly. (This approach to understanding group influence will be explored in a later section.)

The second method examines the networks of groups acting in each policy area (see Marsh and Rhodes, 1992; and also Vigar, 2002, for a development of this approach, applied to mobility). The term 'policy community', at one end of the policy network spectrum, refers to the close working relationship which forms between a division of a government department and the organizations it subsidizes, regulates or expects to implement government goals. It is based on some shared professional understanding or economic interest; the close relationship between the road-building lobby and the Transport Department's road engineers has long been the typical example. It applies more widely, as seen when UK Major Ports (a pressure group) said it was 'more comfortable' with the DfT deciding marine planning applications than the DoE, because the

DoE was more likely to take the views of environmental groups into account than 'the needs of transport infrastructure'. Similarly, 'the conservation agencies will feel more comfortable with' DoE (Environment Committee, 2004: para. 11 and Q.94). The concern most frequently expressed is that a ministry will become so familiar with the circumstances faced by certain groups that it identifies with them. The DfT seemed to be in that position in the 1990s, when it was reluctant to require members of the Confederation of Passenger Transport (or CPT: bus and coach operators) to fit seat belts, and emphasized their difficulties: the cost-benefit case was weak, even allowing for such elements as pain and suffering; there were technical problems regarding attachment points; British coach manufacturers and operators would be put at a disadvantage since the government could not legally impose similar rules on operators from other EU countries; and EU legislation would be needed.

In contrast, at the other end of the policy network spectrum is the 'issue network', a more volatile arrangement connecting a larger number of participants of varying resources and limited mutual agreement. The issue is commonly one for which no government department serves as an obvious focal point, either because the problem cuts across departments (which may hold different views on the solutions), or because it is new to the political agenda. The Civic Trust and the CPRE were put on the 'consultation list' for lorry regulations in 1969, but only because an MP pressured by constituents affected by heavy lorry traffic persuaded the transport minister. This action brought environmental concerns into transport policy discussions (Richardson and Jordan, 1985: 6, 127).

The emergence of a more pluralistic issue network on coach seatbelts changed the common position held by the DfT and CPT (see Figure 6.1). An unusually large number of accidents in 1993 affecting this normally safe means of travel brought the topic onto the agenda. The Consumers' Association, the RAC and the British Safety Council (an organization for improving workplace safety) called for seat-belts to be installed. The National Consumer Council (an official body that advises the Department of Trade) and its Northern Ireland counter-part put pressure on ministers. A parents' group, BUSK (Belt Up School Kids), which was already campaigning in Gwent, soon had 43 branches. It presented a petition with 156,000 signatures to Parliament to which the Transport Minister responded sympathetically, revealing the pressure he was under from MPs (*HC Debates*, 29 April 1994: 377; 23 May 1994: 54). Strathclyde Council gained authorization from the Department for

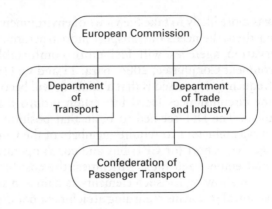

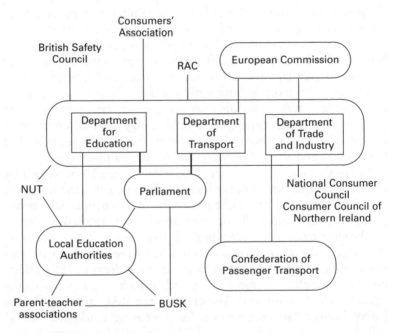

FIGURE 6.1   *Seat-belt networks*

Education to spend money on seat-belts. Several ministries were coming under pressure from a variety of organizations. *The Independent* campaigned for seat-belts on its 'education' pages. The National Union of Teachers (NUT) asked government for grants for minibus seat-belts. Under pressure from BUSK and parent–teacher associations, some local education authorities made belts compulsory for school bus contractors and lobbied MPs for a change in legislation. The traditional actors, the DfT and the CPT, moved in stages to meet the demands of the new players. In March 1995, the day before the minister had to appear before a Commons committee examining transport safety, draft rules for consultation on seat-belts were sent out; regulations were issued in February 1996.

A series of tragedies had brought together a disparate set of interests to put effective pressure on government. No really new technical or financial information had become available, but the political priorities changed. In addition to illustrating the varied types of relationships there can be between interest groups and central government departments on transport issues, the development of coach seat-belt regulations demonstrates how groups from outside the institutions designated to deal with a transport question can bring about policy change. Usually several groups or events come together to shift the balance of opinion on an issue. A small organization such as BUSK in Gwent could not by itself bring about regulatory change, but its activity gave real-life substance to journalists' reports and statements from public bodies, which in turn lent authority to the campaign.

Characteristics of transport interest groups

The success or failure of a campaign is strongly influenced by external factors, such as the attitude of the government of the day to group pressure or popular opinion on the particular cause, but internal factors relating to the characteristics of the groups themselves are critical too. In general, the characteristics of an interest group that matter most are its type and size, how well it can claim to represent its membership, its resources and the sanctions it can impose on government (W. Grant, 2000: 197–204). The transport domain is no exception.

Types of group

Sectoral groups predominate in transport policy-making, either promoting the interests of businesses or workers in the sector at national level, or defending residents from unwelcome infrastructure projects at local level.

The two main business organizations, the CBI and the IoD, are long-standing contributors to transport policy-making (see Table 6.2).

TABLE 6.2 *Business interest groups*

Organization	Membership	Staff	Aims in 2005 from their web-sites
Society of Motor Manufacturers and Traders	5,000 vehicle manufacturers, importers	Policy unit; press office	Represents members to government at home and abroad on key industry issues.
Institute of Directors	55,000 directors	Policy unit of 11 staff; press office	To support and set standards for directors. For road-pricing, road-building.
Confederation of British Industry	200,000 businesses	80 policy staff in Brussels, US	To create and sustain conditions in which business prospers. Wants transport investment to be focused on strategic inter-modal network.
Freight Transport Association	About 11,000 firms and hauliers	40 policy staff; press office	Campaigns for the legal, cost and structural infrastructure most conducive to efficient freight movement.
Road Haulage Association	Over 10,000 road hauliers	Press officer; 16 staff for member services	Campaign on fuel prices, M6 toll, EU working time directive, lorry road user charge. Works with local councils.

Organisation	Members	Staff	Aims
Confederation of Passenger Transport	1100 bus, coach, and light rail operators	20 staff in Wales, Scotland, EU; 3 press officers	Sustain commercial environment in which members can provide an efficient, cost-effective service to customers; campaigns on coach parking; welcomed fuel duty freeze.
Chamber of Shipping	125 ship owners, plus associate members	22 policy staff and administrators	Align tax regimes with overseas competitors; reduce burden of customs procedures; coordinate recruitment and training and input to maritime law issues.
British Air Transport Association	BA, Virgin Atlantic and 8 other airlines	3 officers	Encourage safe, healthy and economic development of UK civil aviation. Active on airports strategy and regulation, air traffic control, environmental impact, safety.
British Ports Association	98 small and medium port operators	3 officers; Scottish Committee	Wants equitable, transparent ports industry; promotes shipping as environmentally sustainable transport.
Association of Train Operating Companies	26 passenger train operators	Office and press office	Helps members meet their obligations, cooperate to promote use of passenger services.
Rail Freight Group	150 suppliers, customers, operators	3 officers (15 board directors)	Increase the volume and market share of freight carried profitably by rail.

For road transport, the traders' associations include the SMMT, CPT, FTA and the Road Haulage Association (RHA). The RHA's members are road hauliers, often with only a few lorries, whereas the FTA includes large companies sending their own or other firms' goods by rail or air as well as road; the two groups therefore have different interests. The Chamber of Shipping brings all commercial shipping interests together into one association. British airlines have combined themselves into one British Air Transport Association (BATA); however, British Airways and Virgin Atlantic, not to mention BAA (the former British Airports Authority) are influential in their own right. The ports and rail sectors are both internally divided. There are two associations of port operators: the UK Major Ports Group of the eight largest companies (including Associated British Ports, the Port of London Authority and Mersey Docks); and the British Ports Association, which has a large membership of smaller ports, some as much concerned with fishing as with transport. The Rail Freight Group of about 150 companies includes users and providers, whether train or terminal operators, equipment suppliers or developers of new freight schemes. However, the smaller Association of Train Operating Companies (ATOC) is a more important player, reflecting the volume and political significance of passenger traffic.

Transport trade unions (see Table 6.3) are still in part divided by mode, as seen in the Associated Society of Locomotive Engineers and Firemen (ASLEF, for train drivers), the British Airline Pilots' Association (BALPA), and the National Union of Marine, Aviation and Shipping Transport Officers (NUMAST, for professional mariners at sea and in ports). However, the Rail and Maritime Transport Union (RMT) works on behalf of engineers and 'blue-collar' staff in those two modes, and the Transport Salaried Staffs' Association (TSSA) for 'white-collar' staff across the transport and travel industries. The largest union, the TGWU, defends manual workers throughout the British economy but has a large transport section. These unions have long histories but have had to adapt to changes in society and in transport organization. Fewer people join unions, a factor in the creation of the RMT from the National Union of Railwaymen and the National Union of Seamen in 1990. Rail privatization brought new recruits into the industry, some of whom rejected the traditional unions: several train drivers formed their own group, Associated Train Crew Union (ATCU) in January 2005.

Travellers are a disparate group, difficult to organize, and they

TABLE 6.3   *Transport trade unions*

Organization and year set up	Membership	Aims in 2005 from their web-sites
ASLEF (1880)	17,000 train drivers on rail, light rail, Underground	'For a return to public ownership' but 'keen to win the best for its members whatever the system'.
TGWU (1922)	900,000 members: 200,000 in transport 88,000 in passenger services 11,000 on docks 47,000 in air transport 90% of bus drivers	Campaigns on air rage, drivers' working time, pay rates for women, wages, working conditions on buses, health and safety, pensions. Aims to have 'good working relations' with main passenger transport firms.
BALPA (1937)	8,000 members: over 75% of airline pilots	To improve status of pilots, working conditions, pensions; to promote UK safety standards in the enlarged EU. Intervened in sky marshal debate, drugs and alcohol, airport expansion, flagging-out.
TSSA (1951)	33,000 in rail, Underground, TfL, travel trade, maritime, road haulage, buses	Works to protect members' interests, e.g., campaign on Virgin's call centre in Dingwall. Supports TUC campaign against UK 'long hours culture'.
NUMAST (1985)	19,000 ships' masters, officers, cadets, professional staff at sea, on oil rigs, in ports	To encourage national flag shipping; and maritime skills base; and fairer seafarer income tax rules. Approves EU directive on conditions of service and wages. Works to control sub-standard foreign ships in UK waters; to improve conditions on UK ships.
RMT (1990)	70,000 rail workers, including drivers (former NUR), and seafarers (former NUS), some bus and road freight drivers.	Protect and promote members' interests. Promote better public transport through political and industrial influence. Against Caledonian MacBrayne privatization. For rail re-nationalization.

Note: See chapter text for full names of unions.

cannot match the strength of transport producers. The Rail Passengers' Council (see Table 6.1) is a statutory body whose members are appointed by the Secretary of State for Transport (or, for London, by the London Assembly), and whose official role is to take up passengers' complaints with train companies and press for improved performance. The special transport problems of people with disabilities are represented by several groups: DPTAC, whose members are chosen by the DfT, has statutory rights to consultation: for example, to be consulted by the Rail Regulator on a code of practice for protecting the interests of disabled people after privatization. Although there was no legal obligation on operators to adopt the code, DPTAC and the Rail Passengers' Council, working with the Rail Regulator, established Disabled People's Protection Policies for each train operator.

Other groups do not have an official status. The Pedestrians' Association (better known by its campaigning slogan, Living Streets) is a voluntary body close in spirit and activity to 'public interest' groups (see Table 6.4). While the AA and RAC often 'represent' motoring interests in government-sponsored bodies, they are difficult to classify as user groups, since their members join for the breakdown services. Both organizations to some extent also promote the public interest (see the web-site of the RAC on reducing accidents to pedestrians (www.rac.co.uk), or that of the AA on car pollution (www.theaa.com). The two national bodies that represent consumers – the National Consumer Council and the Consumers' Association (an independent charity) – sometimes discuss transport issues, such as coach seat-belts, rail privatization, the 'price-fixing' of new cars, and the quality of garage servicing, but they do not concern themselves permanently with transport policy. Indeed, the National Consumer Council in 1977 wanted a National Transport Council to be created as a specialized forum (Wistrich, 1983: 48).

Cause groups that promote transport issues, such as Sustrans (which encourages cycling and other low-energy modes), the Inland Waterway Association and RoSPA, are few in number. The Inland Waterway Association is a long-established interest group now more focused on leisure and heritage than reviving waterborne traffic. *Freight on Water* (Freight Study Group, 2002), recommended setting up a more broadly-based organization that would treat the logistics chain as a whole (from barge-owners and freight forwarders to seaport operators). Sea and Water had over 100 members by 2005, including NUMAST, the FTA and ports and shipping groups. The best-known transport 'cause group', Transport 2000, which promotes public transport, was initiated in 1972 by a rail workers' union, part-funded from 1977 by British Rail, and then by public service providers such as Arriva and EWS (English, Welsh and Scottish Railways, the largest freight train operator).

TABLE 6.4 *Established transport interest groups*

Organization and year set up	Membership	Income (2003)	Aims from their web-sites and annual reports
RSPB (1889)	1 million	£55m.	To conserve wild birds and their environment: 'Changes in how we plan transport and use vehicles are urgently needed to protect our environment'.
RAC (1897)	6 million	[£67m.]	RAC Foundation promotes 'environmental, economic, mobility, safety issues relating to motor vehicles'.
AA (1905)	15 million	Trust: £2m.	AA Motoring Trust 'champions the interests and safety of Britain's road users'; carries out road safety research.
CPRE (1926)	59,000	£3m.	Campaigns for protection and enhancement of countryside: beauty, tranquillity, diversity.
RoSPA (1928)	'growing'	£8m.	Promotes safety, especially on roads; against hand-held mobile phones; for 'meeting without moving'.
Living Streets (1929)	68 branches	£0.5m.	To make local streets worth strolling, relaxing in; to persuade local authorities not to give priority to traffic.
Inland Waterways (1946)	36 branches	£0.9m.	Campaigning for the conservation, use, maintenance, restoration and development of inland waterways.
Civic Trust (1957)	850 groups	£2m.	To promote thriving towns and villages through communities, government and businesses partnerships.
FoE UK (1971)	100,000	£6m.	Reduction of traffic and promotion of alternatives to cars; fears airport expansion will harm environment.
Transport 2000 (1973)	39 bodies	Trust £0.3m.	Works for policy framework that relies less on cars and roads and more on sustainable transport.
Sustrans (1984)	40,000 supporters	£12m.	To promote and organize safe routes for cycling, walking, and low energy transport.

RSPB = Royal Society for the Protection of Birds

The most high-profile cause groups in transport policy-making are the conservation and environmental groups, especially FoE, CPRE and the Civic Trust, which are all members of Transport 2000, and the Royal Society for the Protection of Birds (RSPB). They are often in agreement on transport issues, even if from different perspectives. All three opposed the introduction of 44-tonne lorries. The FoE said heavy lorries were responsible for much of the pollution in cities, used more fuel and were less safe than rail freight; the CPRE and Civic Trust that heavy lorries are noisy and damage buildings, and physically divide the communities through which they pass. Even the proponents of heavier lorries (FTA, RHA) felt obliged to argue their case on environmental grounds, maintaining that larger vehicles with more axles would mean fewer journeys, and thus less damage and less pollution. Both FoE and the RSPB were significant objectors to the proposed airport at Cliffe on the Thames estuary: the RSPB because it would destroy wetlands of international importance; FoE because of the impact of airport expansion on the level of pollutants. However, while FoE consistently criticizes cuts in fuel tax, the CPRE, conscious of the disadvantages of rural life, stressed that the main issue in the fuel tax protests of 2000 was the lack of public transport (*Independent*, 12 September 2000).

Local environmental groups, campaigning against transport projects, are frequently supported by one or more of these national groups. The Twyford Down Association was given practical help by FoE during the later stages of its campaign. The M3 cutting at Twyford Down destroyed parts of a Site of Special Scientific Interest, two Scheduled Ancient Monuments and an Area of Outstanding Natural Beauty. The Countryside Agency had decided not to object, after it was given an exaggerated impression by DfT of the damage that an alternative route would cause to one Ancient Monument (Bryant, 1996: 45). The group of middle-class local residents who became the Twyford Down Association fought a sophisticated campaign of reasoned argument through a re-opened Inquiry, a judicial review and an appeal to the European Commission. Nevertheless the government decided in favour of the cutting, mainly because the intervention of the official environmental agencies came too late, allowing the DfT to think it had found an acceptable solution: Barbara Bryant's well-documented and thoughtful study of this important case shows that 'the time to alter decisions is before they are made' (Bryant, 1996: viii, 34). Once the government decision was announced, opposition moved to non-violent direct action, first organized by the FoE and then by the 'ecowarriors'. The 'new-style, anti-roads protest was born' at Twyford Down (Porritt, 1996: 301).

These single-issue campaigning groups, sometimes called 'fire-fighting' groups, are the most visible face of opposition in transport policy-making (for examples, see Table 6.5). They are usually

TABLE 6.5 *'Fire-fighting' or single-issue campaign groups*

Organization	Membership	Aims from web-sites and press
Rail Future	'Hundreds of volunteers' and 17 branches	Campaigns for re-opening of stations and lines for benefit of community, economy and environment.
HACAN Clear Skies	3 officers, including 1 policy researcher	Led opposition to Heathrow Terminal 5; responds to consultations using well-researched arguments.
Association of British Drivers	'Britain's beleaguered drivers and motorcyclists'	Demands 'an end to the abuse of speed cameras for extorting money from drivers'.
BUSK	Parents and 43 parent–teacher associations	Campaigned for seat-belts in school transport; now promotes safety of children in all vehicles.
Road Alert		Gives advice on roads inquiries and anti-road campaigning – 'non-violent action tool box'.
Reclaim the Streets	Eco-activists in protests at Newbury and Manchester	From reclaiming streets for inhabitants, pedestrians and cyclists to more radical anti-capitalist campaign.
TransAction	2000 radical hauliers later backed by RHA	Against high fuel prices, rise in duty, and cabotage by foreign firms; blocked Park Lane; action at Dover.
People's Fuel Lobby	Farmers, hauliers, taxi-drivers, rural car owners	Demanded cuts in fuel duty by organized protest; threatened to disrupt 2001 and 2005 elections.
Freedom to Fly	BAA, BA, Virgin, CBI, IoD, TGWU and Amicus unions	Wants increased airport capacity, 'to avoid chaos of rail network', and reduce delays or higher prices.
Stop Stansted Expansion	Essex and Herts Preservation Society, FoE, local MPs, many local councils	To contain the development of Stansted Airport within sustainable limits; to protect quality of life of residents, and the natural environment.
Alliance against Urban 4×4s	FoE, Transport 2000, Mayor of London, Green Party; Liberal Democrat MPs	To remove 'sports utility vehicles' from urban streets to reduce fuel consumption, high emissions and damage to other road-users in accidents.
Portswatch	FoE, CPRE, RSPB, Transport 2000, Wildlife Trusts and marine groups	Draws attention to proposals for port development; campaigns for a national ports strategy, not a 'purely market-driven provision of ports capacity'.

transient, disbanding once the issue is resolved one way or the other. Some, such as BUSK and the Twyford Down Association, have strong credentials as cause groups. Others are sectional in nature: examples include Trans-Action, the road hauliers' group that blocked roads in autumn 1999, arguing that Continental hauliers had access to cheaper fuel (though they also paid higher social welfare charges and road tolls); the Association of British Drivers, demanding on behalf of 'Britain's beleaguered drivers and motorcyclists . . . an end to the abuse of speed cameras for extorting money from drivers' (www.abd.org.uk, April 2005), or 'nimby' groups, such as householders protesting against a bypass, airport extension or re-opened freight line that would reduce their own quality of life.

Size

Size is an important criterion for exercising influence: other things being equal, groups with a larger membership are more likely to command attention from ministers and officials. The RSPB, with over a million members, could not easily be ignored when it protested against the choice of Dibden Bay for a new port or Cliffe for a new airport. The general secretary of NUMAST noted that 'the sorry sight of oiled seabirds' after the sinking of the *Prestige* drew more public and political attention to maritime safety than had the annual loss of 350 mariners' lives (letter to *Financial Times*, 22 November 2002). Groups themselves believe that size matters, as their 'home' web pages show: 'BALPA is among the world's largest flight crew associations – second in size only to the US Air Line Pilots' Association'; NUMAST is 'one of the world's largest organizations representing Merchant Navy officers'; the CBI is 'the largest UK lobbying organization'; 'Welcome to RMT – Britain's largest specialist transport union'.

To acquire the impact of scale, groups may establish an 'umbrella' association. Thus eight environmental groups, including FoE and Transport 2000, constituted Portswatch when operators made multiple applications for 'super-port' development. Its 'manifesto', *Troubled Waters,* published on its members' websites (for example, www.foe.co.uk), called in February 2004 for a national spatial strategy for ports if south-east England were to avoid the destruction of coastal sites, increased traffic congestion and planning blight. Although the government had just told the Commons Transport Committee that 'it would be neither justifiable nor practicable to formulate now an integrated national ports plan' (DfT, 2004f: 11), it announced in July 2004 that it would draw up a national ports strategy, although only after existing development applications had been decided (*Financial Times*, 28 March 2005). Despite this partial success, size is not the only criterion: trade unions representing more than a million workers seem far from achieving their demand for re-nationalization of passenger services.

Representativeness

The proportion of people in the relevant section of society that a group can claim to represent is as important to its credibility as its absolute size. The Chamber of Shipping's 125 members are responsible for '90 per cent of British shipping', and it 'represents all sectors of the shipping industry' through the associate membership it offers to such institutions as the Baltic Exchange. The UK Major Ports Group represents the largest ports but not the majority of ports. 'The UK ports industry is seen as being weak and fractious . . . it cannot do what most other industries . . . seem to be capable of doing – namely, speaking with one voice'; 'the benefits of speaking with one voice can be considerable, not least when trying to influence politicians and change the unyielding minds of civil servants' (The Port of Dover and NUMAST in DTLR, 2002: 42, 43).

Trade unions have less influence than cause groups because civil servants do not see them as representative of their client group (W. Grant, 2000: 197). Employees join trade unions for many reasons, and may even feel pressed to do so. Though BALPA already includes 'well over 75% of all airline pilots', that did not seem to be enough: 'A challenging agenda . . . will mean constantly improving our membership levels' (BALPA, 2004). With two unions, ASLEF and RMT, already claiming to represent train drivers, ASLEF's disquiet at the loss of 'a breakaway group of a dozen or so disaffected rail workers' (www.aslef.org.uk, 12 January 2005) was understandable.

The larger and broader a group becomes, the more difficult it is to please all members. The RHA followed rather than led its membership in the escalating action on fuel duties: in spring 1999 it distanced itself from TransAction's blockades, and joined the government's Road Haulage Forum, but its members were joining the protest groups, and it organized its own demonstration in July. The same feature can be seen in campaigns against road-building, when the 'non-hierarchical, spontaneous' groups such as the 'Dongas' at Twyford Down reject the strategy of the large environmental groups, who try to influence road proposals much earlier in the decision-making process (Porritt, 1996: 303).

Resources

Financial resources are important because groups benefit from employing policy analysts and press officers who can monitor forthcoming legislation, including EU directives, and then try to influence its content by making a good case to the appropriate officials and the wider world (W. Grant, 2000: 202). RoSPA (2004) had the capacity to make submissions to 15 consultation exercises on diverse transport issues in a single year: five to the DfT (for example, on whether delivery van drivers should be exempted from wearing seat-belts), another five to DfT agencies (including on driving tests and MOT inspections), three to the devolved governments in Northern Ireland and Scotland, and two responses to the Commons Transport Committee (on traffic law enforcement, and 'cars of the future').

No group can be effective without the resources to do its job, but if additionally it represents a sector that makes a large contribution to the national economy, it is likely to have even more influence. The IoD has directors in 95 per cent of FTSE 100 companies (companies with the largest capital value on the Stock Exchange); and 'FTA members operate over 200,000 goods vehicles – almost half the UK fleet. In addition, they consign over 90 per cent of the freight moved by rail and over 70 per cent of sea and air freight' (www.fta.com). The ports operated by members of the UK Major Ports Group 'account for 70 per cent of all cargo handled in the UK . . . it is clearly in the interests of both importers and exporters that their business should be supported by an efficient and cost effective port industry' (UK Major Ports Group, 2001). The commercial interest of transport operators is often promoted by the government simply because it tallies with the national economic interest. The Sheen Inquiry into the sinking of the *Herald of Free Enterprise* (whose owner was a key member of the Chamber of Shipping) said that although DfT had wanted higher standards for roll-on roll-off ships, it did not want them as high as the US, USSR, Poland and Norway had proposed, because they 'would gravely impair commercial viability of the ferries' (DoT, 1987: para. 53).

Information

Information or expertise is a helpful resource for groups in a domain as technical as transport. Officials have to seek advice in the newer areas, such as ecological impact or noise envelopes, in the way that they once listened to manufacturers on suitable fixing points for vehicle seat-belts. Groups such as FoE, with a highly-educated membership, are self-confident and comfortable in meetings with civil servants; they are good at drafting papers and knowledgeable about the political system (W. Grant, 2000: 197). The RSPB was not only the expert on the impact on wading birds of a new port at Dibden Bay, but it was also able to produce forecasts of the shortfall in container port space by 2010 (RSPB, 1997). Many witnesses quoted the RSPB's figures to the Transport Committee's inquiry on *Ports* (2003), challenging the government's claim that it was not only unnecessary to plan for port capacity, but also too difficult (DTLR, 2002: para. 2.4.1). Even a very small group, such as the Heathrow Association for the Control of Aircraft Noise, which has one paid research post, could respond to DfT's consultation documents on *The Future Development of Air Transport* (DfT, 2002) with an analysis of the impact of airport expansion on noise and nitrogen dioxide; the effect of airline tax exemptions on passenger demand, runway capacity and the UK economy; the requirement for hub airports in south-east England; and alternative policies to runway expansion (HACAN, 2003).

Once the motoring associations adopted research-based campaigning with the creation of the AA Motoring Trust and the RAC Foundation, they were able to devote considerable sums both to expert studies and to their dissemination: £1.8 million by the AA Motoring Trust in 2003, including £0.4 million on road safety research (for example, on the 'high-risk roads' on which drivers were most likely to have accidents: AA Motoring Trust Annual Report, 2004).

However, ministers can ignore specialized expertise when other factors take priority. Following the accident to the *Herald of Free Enterprise*, the Royal Institution of Naval Architects (RINA), the professional body, insisted that only bulkheads could provide adequate safety on roll-on roll-off (Ro-Ro) ships even though they slow down the unloading of vehicles. The Sheen Inquiry report recommended that serious attention should be given to changes to Ro-Ro design, 'restricting the spread of water on the bulkhead deck' (the final words of the report: DoT, 1987: 72). The government introduced different regulations, which were less costly for ferry operators.

Sanctions

The sanctions that a group can impose on decision-makers can be important, especially economic sanctions. The blockade of fuel deliveries and 'go slow' convoys of road hauliers, farmers, taxi-drivers and car drivers in September 2000 'nearly brought the UK to a halt' (*Financial Times*, 1 October 2003). Car manufacturers might invest abroad if the home market comes under threat. BATA uses the argument that 'others will expand if London does not'. British road hauliers campaigning against high fuel duties and vehicle licence costs in 1999 threatened to set up in 'cheaper' European countries (those who tried found it complicated and expensive).

Legal sanctions became a practical option after the Environmental Impact Assessment Directive and then the Habitats Directive gave campaigners the possibility of appeal to the European Commission or the European Court of Justice (see Chapter 4). The RSPB's ports researcher warned that if the government chose to speed up planning applications by new parliamentary procedures that did not allow public participation, 'it should be prepared for challenges on human rights grounds' (Huggett, 2002: 30). The Stop Stansted Expansion group (see Table 6.5) and a consortium of local authorities sought judicial review of the Aviation White Paper of 2004, which had announced that another runway would be built at Stansted. While the judge did not require the government to rethink the consultation process as a whole (even commending the intellectual quality of the White Paper), the government was criticized for announcing the site of the Stansted runway before a Planning Inquiry had been held, and for giving a false impression that Luton's inhabitants had been consulted on development there; and the court proceedings exposed Treasury doubts about the viability of the runway that the DfT had been reluctant to reveal (*Guardian*, 19 February 2005).

Economically weak groups without legal recourse are left with using the threat of demonstrations or other forms of direct action. Reclaim the Streets blocked streets with parties or mass cycle rides, and tree-climbers and tunnel-makers delayed work on the Newbury bypass and Manchester's new runway. Yet, once construction starts, the only effect of the activity of protest groups is to add to the cost of the current project and perhaps influence the climate of opinion met by the next project.

The context of action

The influence of an interest group depends not only on its own characteristics but on those of the environment in which it operates. Chief among these contextual conditions are the attitudes taken by the government, other groups, and public opinion.

The government's own views affect the reception they give interest groups. Indeed the style of individual ministers can have an impact on the direction of policy (see Dudley and Richardson, 2001). The Thatcher governments rejected the neo-corporatism of the Wilson–Callaghan era, a stance reinforced by the part trade unions played in the downfall of the Heath and Callaghan governments. Mrs Thatcher and many of her ministers (Nicholas Ridley, Lord Young, Kenneth Clarke, Cecil Parkinson) regarded the 'vested interests' (including rail workers, dock workers and ships' crews) as being 'part of the problem not the solution'. Conservative ministers sought advice, notwithstanding, but from groups and individuals with 'New Right' credentials (Lord Sterling, chairman of P&O, a leading player in the Chamber of Shipping, was a special adviser to Lord Young and other Trade and Industry ministers from 1982 to 1990). The IoD, with City financiers and entrepreneurs as members, was preferred to the more conservative and industry-focused CBI. The IoD promoted market ideas, such as privately-built tolled motorways in the 1980s and more general road pricing from 1990 (Hillman, 1992: 228); the use of private finance to build roads fitted the government's ideology.

In contrast, New Labour took office in 1997 proclaiming its willingness to include many interests inside its 'big tent', and to listen to people's opinions (a promise reiterated to a sceptical electorate in 2005). Its intention to develop 'integrated transport', and to take account of the 'basic accessibility needs of all sectors of society' (DETR, 1997) implied collaboration with diverse interests. The DETR's forums listed in Table 6.1 illustrate the approach. Other Whitehall departments did likewise. However, while their 'task forces' worked to complete the integrated transport agenda in specific areas of policy (*Environmental Impacts* – DETR, 1999a; *Actions for Sustainable Transport* – DTI, 1999), Labour ministers implemented the goals of groups out of tune with the

Labour manifesto (reducing taxes on fuel and vehicles, and increasing maximum lorry weights), while not adopting the re-nationalization of rail services demanded by Labour supporters in the unions.

As an exception to the 'Third Way' approach to group participation, John Prescott, a Transport minister who had once worked on ships, established the Shipping Working Group, 'a partnership with both sides of industry' in classic corporatist style (DETR, 1998b: para. 3). Members were appointed from the trade unions (NUMAST, RMT, TGWU), the Chamber of Shipping and several ministries. The proposals they made for more jobs for British crew and improved training and safety were largely implemented, and linked to a new tax regime welcomed by ship owners that encouraged them to register their boats in the UK, where safety can more easily be monitored.

Opposition from other groups, especially those that claim to represent similar interests, is a great disadvantage. The defenders of Twyford Down competed with counter-claims from 'commercial interests to the south of Winchester and the road lobby', other conservation groups and local authorities. Winchester City Council, the Winchester branch of CPRE and the Winchester Preservation Trust at first supported the 'cutting route' (Bryant, 1996: 74). Hampshire County Council, Winchester College (though not all its 'old boys') and residents of one area of Winchester continued to do so (Bryant, 1996: 101, 108, 207). In contrast, the Oxleas Wood protest movement (East London River Crossing, which the DfT abandoned), had solid support from those who owned neighbouring properties (Twyford Down was owned by Winchester College), most national environmental organizations, the local council and local MPs (Porritt, 1996: 300). In the case of Heathrow expansion, residents and environmentalist groups face not only powerful commercial interests but also the trade unions whose members will find jobs in an expanding enterprise: 'Freedom to Fly' includes the TGWU and Amicus as well as BA, Virgin Atlantic, BAA, the CBI, IoD, the British Tourist Authority and air transport users.

Favourable public opinion can encourage a sympathetic hearing from ministers and, in turn, a group's campaign may stimulate public opinion to evolve. If popular environmental awareness came too late to change the decision on Twyford Down, the national publicity generated by the protests ensured ministers would tread carefully in deciding future projects. From 1987 opinion polls identified the 'environment' as an important issue, a finding that seemed to be confirmed by the 15 per cent vote for the Greens in the 1989 European Parliament elections. It became 'respectable . . . for loyal Tories to care about the environment' (Bryant, 1996: 122). The DoE reacted quickly to this favourable climate, with *This Common Inheritance* (1990). The DfT was either more reluctant to adapt its programmes (its documents continued to find justifications for road-building, such as congested roads producing more pollution) or more realistic, recognizing that people do not always connect environmental concern and travel behaviour, and that opinions change (MORI's polls show that, while over 30 per cent of people in 1989 and 1990 saw the environment as an important issue, less than 10 per cent have done so since 1991: see www.mori.com).

Public support is easier to organize on some issues than others. Though local opponents of new infrastructure schemes usually have the government machine and large businesses against them, at least they have the advantage of a support base that is more easily located and enthused to back the campaign. In contrast, the motorists and holiday-makers who will benefit from the new road or airport are not so easily harnessed in its defence. In preparing its case for Terminal 5, BAA deliberately stimulated a Heathrow Airport Support Group, bringing together the CBI and over 120 firms, trade associations and trade unions; it advised members to write to policy-makers and the media, and to issue company press releases; to introduce the case for Terminal 5 into normal business presentations; and to give evidence to the Inquiry. Trade unions should benefit from the organizational advantage of workplace structures but this advantage seems to be discounted by officials, who question the validity of the recruitment. Furthermore, the post-privatization fragmentation of the rail and bus industries, and a higher staff turnover, have made union organization more difficult. On the other hand, liberalized telecommunications (mobile phones, in-cab fax machines, the Internet) have made it easier to round up and help people with similar aims but who are geographically dispersed or concerned about legal restrictions on organizing demonstrations (drivers against speed cameras, fuel tax protesters, Reclaim the Streets, Road Alert). A small number of road hauliers used such methods to organize demonstrations on fuel prices in 1999 which attracted such public and media interest and support within the sector that the RHA had to follow its 'grass-roots' members; ministers then set up the Road Haulage Forum. After the thousand or so lorry drivers were joined in September 2000 by 'many thousands' of farmers, 500 taxi-drivers and 100 rural car owners who blocked fuel depots, inconveniencing many more thousands of car drivers who nevertheless largely supported and shared the lorry drivers' concerns, the Chancellor of the Exchequer announced forthcoming freezes on fuel and vehicle taxes.

Access: insiders and outsiders

The characteristics of the group and its fit with the aims of government determine the quality of an organization's access to decision-makers. For most organizations, the ideal is to become '*insiders*', working so consistently with government that they are seen by officials less as representing interests than as providing expertise and delivering implementation. Whilst BUSK was able (with the help of public opinion and some tragic incidents) to turn a technical issue into a political decision, it is the CPT which continues to put its technical and economic case to government departments: the most effective strategies are those that do not come to public attention.

Groups who gain insider access are those who understand the political process and copy officials' modes of operation and language (W. Grant, 2000: 202). They are on friendly terms with the head of the relevant ministry division: the Port of London Authority with the Ports policy division (DTLR, 2002: 11); the FTA with the Road Haulage Division (*FTA News Digest*, 20 November 2000). Groups may even recruit civil servants (P&O's Director of Communications was formerly Principal Private Secretary to the Secretary of State for Trade and Industry; Jarvis's Director of Communications was once the Prime Minister's press secretary). They invite ministers to their Annual Dinners and conferences: at one FTA Annual Dinner John Prescott suggested raising the maximum lorry weight to 44 tonnes (*Financial Times*, 26 April 1999); at another, Alistair Darling emphasized the road-building programme but also the need for more efficient road use by freight operators and charges for lorry road use (see speech of 26 October 2004 on www.dft.gov.uk).

Some insider groups adopt a higher public profile. They use the media and external events in a 'responsible' way to remind both government and their own clientele of their expertise and their political support. In one year the AA used their 'Awards' event, attended by Darling, to give its views on 'how motorists pay for the roads they use'; and organized a cross-party seminar in Parliament to which Darling contributed, and another that reviewed progress on the 10 Year Plan, especially its roads component (AA Motoring Trust Annual Report, 2004). Yet, if the need is to talk to government early, and certainly before a department 'goes public' within Whitehall (Bryant 1996: 124), less well-funded groups, such as the Joint Committee on Mobility of Disabled People or the Joint Committee on Mobility of Blind and Partially-Sighted People, whose meetings are attended by DfT staff (*HC Debates*, 29 Sept. 1999, col. 467), may be just as effective in modifying policy.

In contrast, '*outsider groups*' impinge on governmental decisions intermittently. Some, such as Reclaim the Streets, are ideological outsiders, rejecting collaboration rather than tone down their demands or their methods of operation. When some Scottish branches of the RMT voted in 2003 to donate funds to the Scottish Socialist Party, and some Welsh branches to support Forward Wales (not Labour), they must have thought there was little to be gained by 'insider' discussion. Most groups are anxious not to lose the chance of insider status by appearing 'irresponsible'. BALPA assured its members that its campaign on pilots' working conditions did 'not mean war with Government, regulator or operator, we aim to focus on an aspirational rather than adversarial approach' (BALPA, 2004). At Twyford Down the local association did not want to go beyond conventional campaigning; and FoE felt it could not go beyond civil disobedience to the 'confrontationalism' of the 'Dongas tribe' (Porritt, 1996: 300–2).

Political channels of influence: parliamentary committees

Parliament has an official role in transport policy-making and, as such, was examined in the previous chapter, where it was shown to be a poor forum for deciding transport projects. However, its Departmental Select Committees exercise a modest influence, almost in the style of a pressure group, through a symbiotic relationship with the relevant interests: the committees use group expertise, while themselves giving groups access to information and the stamp of their authority. A number of Committees investigate one aspect or another of transport issues from time to time (the Environment Committee recently discussed coastal planning; the Trade Committee fuel duty; and the Public Accounts Committee scrutinized the DfT's spending on Light Rail and the London

Underground), but naturally it is the Transport Committee which considers the domain as a whole.

Transport Select Committees have recently been chaired by politicians respected for their knowledge, investigative skills and independent minds: Robert Adley, appointed in 1992, and Gwyneth Dunwoody from 1997. The latter was so effective that Labour parliamentary managers refused to re-appoint her in 2001 but MPs prevailed then, and again in 2005. Yet even these redoubtable politicians could not alter the main thrust of government policies they opposed: rail privatization and the PPP scheme for the Tube went ahead.

The Adley Committee's examination of the White Paper on rail privatization (DoT, 1992a) was an opportunity for informed views to be heard in public. Its inquiry heard an extensive range of witnesses, including public officials, the private companies expected to run the new system, rail user groups, trade unions and Transport 2000 (Transport Committee, 1993). Some Committee recommendations were adopted by the government. The White Paper had proposed 'open access' to the track: the Committee found that open access would help freight train operators but impair passenger timetables and off-peak services (it suggested franchises or contracts). Another example was the insistence of ministers that regulations to make operators accept through-tickets issued by other operators were not needed, because companies would find it commercially sensible to work together: the Committee, persuaded by bus operators' experience, recommended a compulsory scheme and the government eventually agreed that 'operators will be required to participate in common ticketing and revenue allocation arrangements' (*HL Debates*, 15 June 1993: 1428). On the other hand, the Committee's advice on some fundamental principles of rail privatization was ignored by the government. The potential operators, rail unions, British Rail and the Committee wanted vertical integration, with the franchise-holder controlling both trains and track (Transport Committee, 1993: paras 95–107). The government rejected their arguments; franchisees were not given control over the track, and the case of rail privatization shows the limited impact of Parliament and interest groups when British government ministers are determined to impose their own solution.

With Gwyneth Dunwoody in the chair, the Transport Committee took a more comprehensive, 'integrated', approach than the government to policy questions. The Transport Committee's inquiry into *The Road Haulage Industry* (2000) was, like the government's Road Haulage Forum, stimulated by the hauliers' demonstrations against high fuel prices. Yet it also considered the working conditions and accident record of the industry, the environmental and economic impact of road haulage, and the effect on rail freight of an increase in maximum lorry weight. It took evidence from the actors in the government's Road Haulage Forum but also from the Rail Freight Group, 'Freight on Rail' campaigners and the TGWU, who provided a cross-modal perspective on the issue. The Committee's report said 'it had not accepted . . . that fuel prices and VED [vehicle excise duty] are too high, and should fall'. It argued that an increase in haulage rates (adding at most 2 per cent to the total price of goods) could produce 'a safe and clean road haulage industry' that reflected the true costs to society of road freight (Transport Committee, 2000: para. 109). The government gave more concessions to road freight companies than the Committee had advised, while not implementing the counter-balancing measures for rail freight demanded by the Committee.

Nevertheless, despite the weakness of its direct influence, the Select Committees improve the quality of transport policy-making indirectly. They examine witnesses who provide information for groups and their experts, as well as MPs, that otherwise would not be made available to them, although the Committee was unable to persuade a Treasury minister to attend their 2002 inquiry into the PPP for the Tube, despite having received evidence that 'the Treasury' was 'one of the principal instigators of the PPP scheme' (Transport Committee, 2002b: para. 86), or to interview Lord Birt, the prime minister's adviser on 'blue skies thinking' on transport (Transport Committee, 2002c).

Conclusion

The British political system gives interest groups wide freedom to express their points of view, even if that freedom with respect to organizing demonstrations has been legally curtailed since 1994, largely as a result of 'direct action' against road projects. Lobbying groups deploy a multitude of techniques to influence transport issues. They participate in consultation exercises, conferences, forums and commissions; and petition Parliament or government (a technique used by professional organizations such as the FTA and RMT as well as by parents worried about school transport).

Official advisory bodies, voluntary organizations and associations of private companies submit reports to government, and invite ministers to their Annual Dinners and conferences. They send letters and press releases to the media, hoping they will investigate further ('news' is very much driven by material supplied to journalists). They join forces with other groups at European level, or with those in policy areas that overlap, who may approach a different ministry (education or environment or trade rather than transport), just as those campaigning on seat belts or fuel duty did. They make formal objections at Public Inquiries (though the lengthy nature of Inquiries has led to government searching for shorter routes to planning permission), or they organize support in the project's favour (such as BAA and the Heathrow Airport Support Group). They appeal to higher legal authorities against administrative procedures or political decisions; warn of the potential loss of economic production or international competitiveness; or eventually take strike action, block roads or obstruct the work of road builders.

Although the crowded British transport policy-making arena gives the appearance of pluralism, these techniques are not all available equally to all groups and do not have an equal impact; the political environment values some interests more than others. First, a fair balance cannot be struck between the competing interests if conservation agencies decide not to defend the interests they are responsible for guarding (Bryant, 1996: 33); or departments do not include all pertinent parties in consultation exercises; or ministers refuse to answer Select Committee questions. Second, some groups are more likely to be heard. The producer groups (CBI, FHA, RHA and trade unions) have a greater presence than transport users, though the government-sponsored Motorists' Forum filled one gap, and DPTAC has helped people with disabilities gain improved access to transport. The larger the group in terms of membership (AA, RAC, CBI, FTA, RHA, TGWU, RSPB, FoE), or role in the economy (CBI, IoD, FTA, RHA, BATA, Chamber of Shipping, UK Major Ports, SMMT), the more likely the government is to take note of its views. Wealthier organizations (AA, RAC, IoD, RSPB, FTA, UK Major Ports) can more easily monitor and respond to opportunities for participation, although groups with a highly-motivated membership can supply effective arguments out of proportion to their income (Twyford Down Association, FoE, HACAN). Finally, for some transport groups (BATA, FTA, UK Major Ports, Chamber of Shipping) economic sanctions are sufficiently powerful to remain unspoken. Though environmental groups can threaten legal sanctions, strikes and demonstrations may be the last resort of trade unions and 'outsiders' unable to negotiate a solution around a table.

The 'insider groups' are those with the most favourable characteristics, bound to be consulted, representative of their section of society, with 'reasonable' aims expressed in a 'responsible' fashion, and whose knowledge and cooperation is needed by the government because of their economic leverage and veto power (CBI, IoD, FTA, BATA, Chamber of Shipping, UK Major Ports Group), or exceptional public support (wildlife groups). Policy-makers categorize groups into respectable 'insiders' and illegitimate 'outsiders' (W. Grant, 2000). Yet, as Geoffrey Alderman pointed out, an effective campaign can make use of two types of action, the public and the discreet (1984: 12–22). Consistent insider action by the CBI and FTA, coupled with the direct action of the more militant members of RHA, culminating in the demonstrations of the People's Fuel Lobby, which 'succeeded in forcing Gordon Brown, the chancellor, to offer concessions on fuel and excise duty beyond the expectations of many' (*Financial Times*, 15 November 2000), was an unbeatable combination.

Chapter 7

Engaging the Private Sector

The policy of the Conservative governments between 1979 and 1997 was to use market forces to improve the delivery of transport services by releasing them from the constraints of the public sector. Competition was increased in the provision of air, bus, rail and road freight services. The regulatory arrangements were adjusted accordingly to secure the public interest within the new structures. The Labour governments from 1997 onwards acquiesced in some of these policies and, in the case of the London Underground, positively promoted them. But Labour's 'headline' philosophy was to replace 'competition' by 'integration'. When events demanded positive action, as with the railways, they tended to re-establish government control.

In this chapter we discuss three case studies which illustrate the struggle to reconcile the wish to use competition and private sector provision with the special responsibilities of government and a changing political environment.

Competition and deregulation of bus services

The White Paper, *Buses* (DoT, 1984), took a simple line on competition. Regulation itself was seen as the important barrier which prevented competition. It was thought that significant barriers to entry to the industry could not be sustained by incumbent operators if the regulation were abolished: economies of scale, network effects and problems of imperfect information were not considered sufficiently important to cause concern. It was acknowledged that predatory practices had been observed in the past, but it was argued that it would not be commercially sensible, or even possible, for an incumbent to ward off competition on many fronts simultaneously without the sustenance provided by a protected, regulated sector.

The lack of concern about past anti-competitive practices was founded on several observations. There was pro-competitive legislation; corruption and criminal enforcement of cartels was not

194

likely to be as much of a problem in Britain as it is in some other parts of the world; and any combines, associations and territorial monopolies would be so constrained in their behaviour by the threat of competitive entry that they would have to behave almost as if the industry were perfectly competitive (the market would be 'contestable', to use the modern terminology). These propositions were strongly questioned at the time by opponents of bus deregulation (see, for example, Gwilliam, Nash and Mackie, 1985 and 1985a).

A major reason for adopting the policy of bus deregulation was that it was the method most likely to succeed in meeting the timetable for subsidy reduction set by the public expenditure requirements. The aim was to introduce genuine competition into bus labour markets by creating a competitive industrial structure: that is, to both deregulate and privatize. The tendering alternative was adopted in London.

Competition in labour markets

Competition in the market for labour was an explicit part of the 1984 policy. Earnings for drivers in the regulated bus industry were higher than drivers in comparable, competitive industries. The *Buses* White Paper (DoT, 1984) insisted that to achieve the labour market competition it was necessary to break up and privatize the state monopoly bus company as well as to deregulate the industry. Figure 7.1 shows full-time average hourly manual earnings for male bus drivers and for all male manual workers. Before the policy was enacted in 1985, average hourly earnings of bus drivers were slightly higher than those for manual workers as a whole. Afterwards there was an immediate fall and the gap has widened over the period. The change in pay rates undoubtedly contributed to the reduction in real unit bus costs of over 40 per cent which was achieved after bus deregulation.

Outside London, deregulation proper occurred in January 1987, although a transitional arrangement started in October 1986. In terms of the objective of bringing revenue support back to the public expenditure plan levels, the policy worked well, and was made possible by the predicted fall in bus operating costs per vehicle-kilometre. The real fall from 1983 to 1993 was 87 per cent in the former metropolitan counties, 58 per cent in the shire counties and 54 per cent in London. As Figure 7.1 illustrates, one source for these savings was a deterioration in terms and conditions of employment,

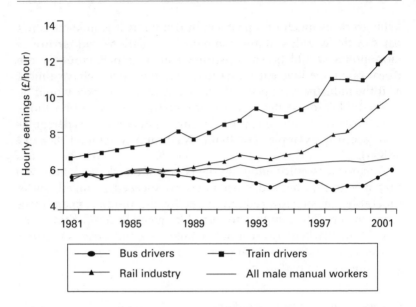

FIGURE 7.1   *Hourly earnings of bus and train drivers*

Note: Hourly earnings of full-time male railway workers, train drivers, bus drivers and all full-time male manual workers (1997 prices).
Source: Data from Office for National Statistics, *New Earnings Survey*, various years.

with real weekly and hourly earnings in the industry falling, against an increase in other industries. Another source of savings was the fall in numbers employed which, together with increases in output, suggests considerable increases in output per employee. These are superficial comparisons, but several authors have made careful analyses to understand what has happened in detail; they confirm the general impression given by the aggregate statistics (see Gomez-Ibanez and Meyer, 1989; Gwilliam, 1989; Tyson, 1989; P. White, 1990; P. White and Turner, 1990). The cost reduction must be counted as the success of the 1985 Act.

In the English metropolitan areas, fares rose by an average of 33 per cent more than retail prices over the period 1983 to 1993. They rose by only 10 per cent in the English shire counties. There was a remarkable increase in output where a decrease might have been expected: a 20 per cent increase in total vehicle-kilometres, 1983 to 1993 (but the average vehicle size has fallen: see below). As many vehicle-kilometres are now operated as a commercial service as the total service in 1985–86; outside the big metropolitan areas there are more. The proportion of the routes extant before deregulation that carried on afterwards as commercial propositions – well over 80 per cent – was more than anybody had predicted (see Gomez-Ibanez and Meyer, 1989).

The official statistics indicate that bus patronage outside London has not increased: between 1993–94 and 2003–04 patronage fell steadily, by a total of 17 per cent (DfT, 2004g). Gomez-Ibanez and Meyer (1989) and White and Turner (1990) argued that, after standardizing for the changes in fares, the decline in patronage is much as it would have been on the basis of secular trends, so the increase in vehicle-kilometres does not appear to have generated more patronage. Vehicle-kilometres have increased whilst passenger-kilometres have remained stagnant, so load factors have fallen and costs per passenger-kilometre have fallen little. The explanation given by Peter White (1990) is that the potential benefit of the extra distance run was not converted into better service quality, because of irregular running, or vehicle bunching, lack of service coordination, or confusion amongst passengers because of frequent changes, or some other factor.

There can be no doubt that some of these factors played a part; however, it is not at all clear that it is a complete explanation. In most detailed case studies bus output increase was accompanied by an improvement in observed or estimated service quality. Evans (1987) notes: 'This gap between estimated and expected patronage is a puzzle, both at the national level and at the level of the case-study towns.' Evans finds the most convincing explanation of the unexpected patronage figures, and the one accepted by other commentators, is that a known infrequent service has been replaced by an unknown frequent one, so that effective waiting times were not reduced.

Tendering for bus services: the London alternative

In London, buses were not deregulated. London Transport controlled fares strictly and determined which services would be provided. A programme of competitive tendering, route-by-route, was progressively introduced from 1985 in which the state-owned operator, London Buses Limited, was placed in direct competition with privately-owned providers. This was followed by privatization of the state-owned bus company in 1993. By 1995 the real unit cost of bus operations in London had fully halved compared to 1983 (see Kennedy, Glaister and Travers, 1995), and competitive route tendering was undoubtedly the most important factor in achieving the reduction in labour costs which made this possible. Crucial ingredients of this policy were that the contracts were not too large and were of reasonably short duration: three years in the first instance and more recently five years. At contract termination there was an open and reasonably actively-contested competition for the contracts. The state-owned monopolies – the National Bus Company and London Buses Limited – were heavily unionized but the unions seemed unable to protect the terms and conditions, and the level of union membership has now fallen considerably.

The cost saving from putting a given route out to tender net of administration costs was estimated to be 14 per cent, to which should be added any passenger benefits associated with new vehicles, and these are calculated to be 20 per cent on average (Kennedy, Glaister and Travers, 1995). These savings are of the same order as previously estimated in the contexts of contracting-out refuse collection and ancillary hospital services. Deregulation in London in 1985 would have reduced bus costs more rapidly, but after several years of tendering this advantage has been attenuated. The policy of route tendering and privatization in London has been highly successful. Whilst efficiency improved, the reliability of service to passengers also improved, partly because of enforceable quality clauses in the contracts with the service providers (Kennedy, Glaister and Travers, 1995, give estimates of the revenue benefits attributable to this increase in quality). It was easy for the regulatory authority to implement policies for protecting integrated ticketing and coordinated service planning.

In London bus patronage has continued to increase. Between 1993–94 and 2003–04 patronage grew by over 50 per cent; it grew by over 10 per cent in 2003–04 alone. Indeed, the growth in London has enabled the government to claim a success in increasing the national total bus patronage, in spite of the decline in the rest of Great Britain. The increase has been in part a consequence of active policy by the Mayor of London, elected in 2000. Fares were kept unchanged, and therefore fell relative to retail prices and earnings. Service levels were also substantially increased so that, with a little assistance from the clearer roads in central London attributable to the congestion charge, both frequency of service and reliability improved significantly (see TfL, 2004a: section 3.3). But these achievements came at the cost of increased levels of subsidy, from £44 million in 1999–2000 to over £450 million in 2005–06.

Proposals for reform

In the bus industry, exploitation of monopoly power may involve raising fares, reducing the quantum of service, or reducing other dimensions of service quality, either to make excess profits or to feather-bed inefficiency. If barriers to entry are negligible then this exploitation is unlikely to happen because sooner or later a competitor will enter, taking advantage of the opportunity created. By the mid-1990s the Monopolies and Mergers Commission had ruled on several cases. Some attempts to erect barriers were detected and prevented: for instance, the attempt to restrict the use of bus terminals by the bus companies which control them. Other barriers are alleged to have appeared since deregulation. Predatory behaviour has also been alleged in the bus industry. The tactics may involve one operator reducing fares or increasing capacity in the hope of driving another operator out of business. Although what looks like predatory behaviour is not uncommon, it is notoriously difficult to demonstrate objectively that it has occurred.

There are technical arguments that carry some weight which suggest that in these kinds of markets price competition will not work as it should, leading to excessive provision of services. But a theoretical demonstration of a tendency to over-supply the market, compared with a theoretical optimum, does not of itself demonstrate a case for restriction of output by regulation. That would imply that, in practice, an omniscient regulator could determine what the optimum actually was, and could enforce it without sacrificing other important benefits of competition or falling foul of the classic dangers associated with regulation (especially regulation which restricts the quantity offered).

The emergence of local monopoly in the bus industry is not, in itself, a bad thing, and it could offer some advantages in terms of making service coordination and integration easier. Local monopoly may facilitate making the physical layout of interchange points convenient, ensuring that different services run to timetables which minimize waiting times for interchanging passengers, ensuring that information is readily available in one place and that there is a central and comprehensive enquiry point, or a common ticket. These benefits to passengers may be delivered spontaneously by a local monopoly operator, but these possible advantages must be set against the usual public-interest concerns which surround monopoly.

There have been many calls for radical change in the regulatory regime for buses outside London, many of them urging that the

London system should be introduced universally. The Labour government itself appeared to be moving in this direction at one time. In its consultation document of August 1997, *Developing an Integrated Transport Policy* (DETR, 1997, para. 21), it said: 'Regulation will help achieve efficient, high quality bus services at the local level, providing an adequate framework and real choice.' However, both the 'Integrated Transport' White Paper (DETR, 1998) and the *10 Year Transport Plan* (DETR, 2000) gave remarkably little attention to buses and no major reforms were made. The position set out in *The Future of Transport* (DfT, 2004) is limited to a redeployment of some of the subsidy presently delivered in the form of a rebate on fuel duty, a promise of some extra funds drawn from a 'Transport Innovation Fund' and reliance on 'Quality Partnerships' and 'Quality Contracts' which were introduced in the Transport Act 2000 to 'allow local transport authorities to determine the routes, fares, quality standards and frequency of bus services in specified areas, where it is the only practicable way for them to implement their bus strategies'.

This policy stance is a far cry from the return to full regulation that some commentators advocate. It is less unfavourable towards the continuation of competitive provision of bus services than had been indicated by the new Labour government in 1997.

Competition and privatization of rail services

The British railway industry still retains much the same structure as that created under privatization legislation in 1993. A fundamental principle was, and to some degree remains, that both privately-owned infrastructure providers and train operators should be given incentives to be efficient – and thus to reduce the call on the taxpayer – by being made to suffer the financial consequences of their inefficiencies. Conventional disciplines were supposed to apply whereby failure to do well for the shareholders would normally be punished through the competitive market for corporate control, the threat of takeover and replacement of the management (see Glaister, 2005, from which parts of this section are taken).

The problem the government of the early 1990s was trying to solve was a familiar one with national railways: how to reduce the demands on the national taxpayer without unacceptable reductions in the scale of railway services. Competition was at the heart of the reforms.

In the original concept the following were some of the dimensions of competition:

(a) competition for passengers by privately-owned train operators;
(b) twenty-five contracts for specific passenger service groups referred to as 'franchises' to be let by competitive tender;
(c) three competing rolling-stock leasing companies;
(d) the rail freight businesses to be sold as a number of competing private businesses;
(e) the infrastructure owner and operator to be kept as a privately-owned but regulated monopoly, called Railtrack (its sole source of income was to come from access charges to users, the train operators).

Railtrack was created with relatively few direct employees (about 12,000) and it was to procure on the open market most of the services it needed, including engineering services for maintenance, renewal and enhancement. The existing rail engineering operations were broken into thirteen companies and sold to the private sector.

Explicit policy and political risk

The railways policy worked reasonably well for a period but it ultimately failed because the privatization legislation was pushed though in 1993 by a Conservative government (despite considerable opposition within the Party), whilst a Labour government elected in 1997 had to administer it.

The signal that there were severe political risks was transmitted in the *Prospectus* for the Railtrack Share Offer (SBC Warburg, 1996) which contains the text of a speech, dated 29 March 1996, by Clare Short MP, Labour Opposition Transport Secretary, which included the following phrases:

Should the flotation of Railtrack PLC proceed a Labour Government will make good its commitment to a publicly owned and publicly accountable railway by taking the following steps: . . .
[to] reconstitute British Rail as a fully publicly owned, publicly accountable company holding the public's interest in the rail network and charged with encouraging and fostering partnership

between public and private finance in the rail network on a long term basis to secure future investment; and
. . . dependent on the availability of resources, and as priorities allow, [to] seek, by appropriate means, to extend public ownership and control over Railtrack.

The train operating companies: policy risk

Immediately after the Railways Act 1993 had been passed, the government changed its policy to 'moderating competition' (DoT, 1993). The Treasury had realized one of the implications of open competition. Under the old regime some of the rail routes had been highly profitable and their profits had been used to cross-subsidize the loss-making parts of the railway. Open competition would have annihilated those monopoly profits. Since the government had committed itself to not allowing privatization to lead to any service reductions or withdrawals, the implication was that direct subsidies from the Exchequer would have to increase substantially. It was doubtful whether the degree of on-rail competition envisaged in the 1992 Railways White Paper was technically feasible.

The Rail Regulator responded (ORR, 1994) with a complicated set of rules designed to allow Train Operating Companies (TOCs) to protect what they declared as the core of their businesses whilst exposing them to competition on non-core activities. Competition amongst the TOCs fell far short of the scale that the original policy had envisaged. The 25 TOC contracts had two components: a minimum guaranteed level of services to be provided by the operator, and a degree of flexibility above this level which allowed the operator room to develop and improve services. But the competition was primarily over who would sign a normal commercial contract to meet the specifications for the smallest payments by government. The attractiveness of service improvements on offer was a secondary consideration. Competition for the contracts was strong and seemed to become more aggressive over time as bidders gained confidence. In many cases the bidders – especially the bus companies that won 15 of the franchises – were confident they could run the services with fewer staff. In others it was anticipated that large increases in passenger revenues could be generated by increasing both running speeds and service frequencies. Some were planning to both cut staff and increase services.

Figure 7.2 shows the total subsidies contracted for and the total subsides actually paid between 1997–98 and 2003–04. Had the contracts been honoured the subsidy would have fallen from £1.8

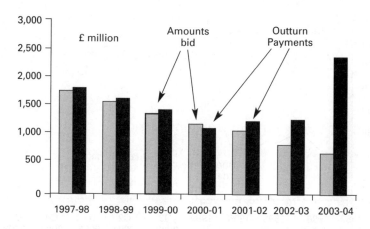

FIGURE 7.2   *Train Operating Company bids and payments*

Notes: Train Operating Company total agreed bids and outturn payments (current prices).
Sources: Data from OPRAF and SRA Annual Reports, various years.

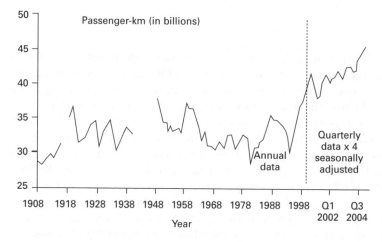

FIGURE 7.3   *Rail passenger-kilometres, 1908–2004*

Sources: Data from DfT, *Transport Statistics Great Britain* (various years), and Office of Rail Regulation, *National Rail Trends: July–September 2005* (2005).

billion a year to £0.7 billion a year. Things did go reasonably well for the first few years. Total subsidies fell only slightly less rapidly than anticipated. Moreover, as Figure 7.3 shows, passenger-kilometres grew from 1993 at a sustained rate which is without precedent in the last hundred years: again, a major triumph.

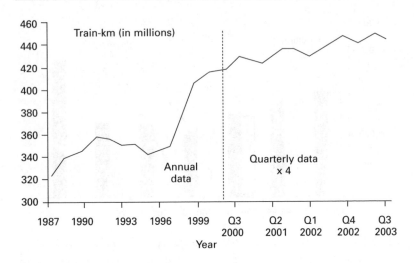

FIGURE 7.4   *Train-kilometres, 1987–2003*

Sources: Data from DfT, *Transport Statistics Great Britain*, and SRA Annual Reports, various years.

Behind these figures there were the beginnings of problems, however. Quite early on some of the TOCs discovered that they had been over-ambitious in reducing employee numbers and that they could not run the service with the numbers they had planned. Service deteriorated significantly on some commuter routes into London: the public quickly blamed it on 'Tory privatization'. Second, trains began to impede one another. When privatization had been designed it had been thought that, because of the long-term decline in the railways, there was spare capacity on the tracks and the big problem was to reduce subsidy whilst preventing further decline. But, as Figure 7.4 shows, the TOCs began to put on many more trains, to the point where congestion began to interfere with train reliability. The public felt the declining reliability – inevitably 'the fault of Tory privatization' – more than offset the benefits of more frequent and more varied services.

Some of the TOCs began to allege that they had run into difficulty in their negotiations with Railtrack to provide the new, high quality infrastructure they needed if they were to achieve the revenue growth to which they had implicitly committed themselves in their contracts. It increasingly became apparent that few, if any, major upgrades were commercially viable, and these required subsidy if they were to proceed. Railtrack was accused of being unresponsive and unwilling to take commercial investment risks. But Railtrack did enter into one monumentally risky agreement with Virgin, and that was to upgrade the West Coast Main Line infrastructure in order to provide for running at 140 mph rather than 125 mph and for the extra capacity Virgin had assumed it could achieve when it made its bid for its franchise. Because of inadequate costing this turned out to be much more expensive to deliver than the extra charges Railtrack had agreed.

Finally, there was the change of government in May 1997 which brought to power the party that had made its distaste for rail privatization very clear. In the first instance it decided to change nothing, perhaps because national budgets were unusually tight, the financial position of the railway was improving rapidly and the government had more urgent problems. However, there was a propensity on the part of the members of the new Labour government to draw attention to failings and to promise 'action', rather than to take the line that the industry was now the responsibility of the private-sector providers and the independent, public-interest Regulator, and that government should leave the industry to sort itself out like any other. The perceived failings eventually led the government to take action by replacing OPRAF with a new Strategic Rail Authority. While lack of strategic planning was generally accepted as a shortcoming of the privatized rail system, creating the SRA was not a high priority for the government and it took all of two-and-a-half years for legislation firmly promised in the 1998 White Paper to reach the statute book.

In late 2001 it began to transpire that several TOCs were in serious financial difficulty. Figure 7.1 shows that the pattern of reduced hourly labour costs in the deregulated bus industry was not repeated in the case of the railways. In the 1980s the average hourly earnings in the rail industry were close to the average for all manual workers and those for train drivers and assistants were about 10 per cent higher. After the structural change of 1993 rail industry earnings rates moved ahead of general earnings, and by 2002 they were nearly 50 per cent higher. Real earnings of train drivers increased even more, so that by 2002 they stood 80 per cent above general manual earnings. The labour unions had more success in protecting the position of their memberships in railways than they had in buses. So, if the TOCs had been counting on the competitive reduction in pay rates that they had enjoyed with bus deregulation, then they were disappointed. By July 2003 nine franchises had failed financially and had been allowed by the government to continue on some kind of cost plus basis (see Figure 7.2 and Transport Committee, 2004: para. 123). A crucial policy decision had been taken that the normal mechanism for enforcing commercial risk transfer – namely bankruptcy – was not going to be enforced.

Rail freight

Before privatization it had been policy for a number of years that rail freight services should at least cover their allocated costs, although that had not always been achieved in practice. Freight services on the privatized railway were always intended to be entirely by open access, competitive companies: that is, there was no attempt to create any analogous arrangement to the subsidized passenger rail franchises.

The government had intended to set up several rail freight carriers, but the market showed so little interest that one company, EWS, became the main operator. Subsequently there has been significant competitive entry by new rail companies but the main competitor is, of course, road haulage. It seems that competition for rail freight services has worked reasonably well. There has been significant innovation in both the nature of the services offered and in the methods used to deliver them. The official statistics are not comprehensive but it seems that growth has largely been in traditional sectors (e.g., moving coal to power stations over longer distances). There has been some, limited, success in winning new markets, and arguably more than in the days of the nationalized railway.

It must be acknowledged that, as in the past, rail freight is given an advantage relative to passenger traffic in that it is only required to pay the variable costs it imposes on the system, so it is making less of a contribution to the full costs. If it were required to 'pay its way', rail freight would reduce substantially.

Infrastructure maintenance

In the original design for rail privatization, engineering work for repairs, maintenance and enhancements – the major expense for the infrastructure company – was to be procured competitively. Elementary and damaging errors were made in this area at privatization. The first was that the companies were sold with the benefit of negotiated procurement contracts already put in place by government. There was no open competition to determine the terms on which Railtrack would procure.

A second error was that Railtrack failed to put in place adequate contract management arrangements: 'Railtrack didn't have a clear idea of what work was being done for the price paid' (National Audit Office, or NAO, 2004). When the contracts came to be renewed there seemed to be a lack of certainty about how the procurements should be managed and what should be the nature of the contractual arrangement. Accidents at Hatfield in 2000 (see below), Potters Bar in 2002 and Kings Cross in 2003 cumulatively cast doubt on the ability of Railtrack or Network Rail to manage private companies to perform infrastructure maintenance contracts safely. Eventually, in 2003, Network Rail made the decision to terminate its outstanding maintenance contracts and to bring the function back in-house, whilst continuing to procure enhancement work from the private sector. Some of the private sector providers (notably Jarvis) decided to leave the railway maintenance sector. Thus one of the major potential sources of efficiency gain from rail privatization – competition in the labour market for civil engineering work – was never achieved.

Railtrack and Network Rail

The failure of Railtrack is the best known of the difficulties experienced by the UK rail privatization. At first things seemed to go well. The shares were over-subscribed at flotation at a price of £3.90. That valued the company at £1.9 billion, less than half the historic cost book value of the assets. The share price reached a peak of £17.68 in 1998, *after* the change of government.

The first Chairman of Railtrack and, from 1997 a powerful Chief Executive, were both recruited from other industries. It is alleged that many of the best senior engineers were lost to the company during the restructuring of the industry in the mid-1990s, other managerial skills being preferred over theirs (see, for example, NAO, 2004: para. 2). This change in personnel may have contributed towards a tendency to under-estimate the extreme complexity of a large railway, having heavy, long-lived, safety-critical assets of many types all working together in a profoundly interdependent system. The accusation was made that Railtrack was spending too little on maintenance and renewals and too much on dividends to shareholders (one of the reasons for the rise in share price). Even though Railtrack did achieve higher rates of investment in its infrastructure than had been achieved before, the National Audit Office (NAO, 2004: Figure 2) confirmed the view that there had been a decline in some aspects of the health of the network, and in particular an increase in the number of broken rails which are an important railway health indicator. The Regulator had become concerned that the network was not being adequately maintained and, specifically, had warned that the increase in the number of broken rails was not acceptable. Further, the Regulator was concerned about the inadequacy of Railtrack's knowledge of the volume and condition of its assets.

Finally there were two major accidents, both in West London; one in 1997 at Southall in which seven people were killed and one in 1999 at Ladbroke Grove in which 31 people were killed. Both accidents involved trains failing to stop at red signals. The extent to which the infrastructure or privatization may have been a factor remains controversial. Rightly or wrongly, Railtrack was very heavily criticized by the press and by senior members of the government after the Ladbroke Grove accident. This was a crucial turning point. The public intervention by ministers greatly heightened the general public's perception that privatization had made the railways less safe in spite of the clear evidence that safety was improving before privatization and it continued to improve at much the same rate afterwards (see Evans, 2004).

All these factors came into play after another accident at Hatfield in October 2000. A train travelling at speed was derailed because of the failure of a decaying rail. Four people were killed. On investigation it was quickly established that the rail in question had exhibited symptomatic cracks before failure. The accident may have been a consequence of avoidable negligence, but it was not as serious as some railway accidents and it did not take the accident rate outside what was to be expected on the basis of historical trends. However, the way Railtrack managers responded did immense damage to the industry (see Foster and Castles, 2004). Railtrack all but closed the system by imposing very wide and restrictive train speed limits that caused many train cancellations. The disruption was compounded by one of the wettest autumns of recent years, leading to embankment slips and flooding which added materially to the service disruption. Railtrack lost income through failing to provide contracted train paths to the TOCs, and it suffered financial penalties under the performance regime.

Coincidentally the Regulator's Periodic Review of Railtrack's charges was published just after the Hatfield accident, having been in preparation for many months. During the proceedings for the Periodic Review it had become clear that Railtrack was facing a second, major financial problem because of the commercial agreement concerning the West Coast Main Line. In October 2001, without warning, the Secretary of State for Transport (Stephen Byers) took the opportunity presented to him. He invoked certain provisions of the Railways Act to put Railtrack into Railway Administration. Railway Administration is a special case of the 'administration' of a company that is unable to pay its debts, in which an administrator appointed by the courts runs the business while negotiating the division of assets between the company's suppliers and contractors and potential buyers of the company. The Railways Act 1993 ensured that the railways would continue to function even if Railtrack was about to become insolvent: first, by forbidding the company to sell parts of the network to pay its debts; second, by enabling the Secretary of State to ask the courts to wind up a failing railway company and appoint a special railway administrator; and third, by requiring the franchised train operating companies and other rail contractors to continue to fulfil their contracted agreements, including paying track access charges to the railway administrator; for its part, the government said it would provide funds to ensure the railway was run safely. The government might have acquiesced in a conventional takeover of Railtrack and there were companies that showed an interest in it. The normal competitive market for corporate control would have acted to change the management and rebuild the company. That would have kept the structure intact and avoided the damaging hiatus that ensued. But Stephen Byers was apparently determined to take the opportunity to destroy the privatized, shareholder ownership structure that the Labour Government had inherited in 1997, thereby fulfilling one of the promises made by Clare Short in the privatization *Prospectus*.

If the Left of the Labour Party had seen Railtrack's bankruptcy as the opportunity to completely re-nationalize the railway, they were quickly to be disappointed. The Treasury was unwilling to find the funds necessary to buy out the TOCs' contracts and other surviving private interests. In addition, and more importantly, Railtrack had considerable and rapidly increasing debt which the Office of National Statistics had classified as private debt on the grounds that the company was not under public control. The Chancellor was unwilling to countenance any move that would bring that debt on to the public balance sheet. This is a consideration that remains central to railways policy to this day.

At the point of putting Railtrack into administration the government announced that it wished to replace the existing company Railtrack, with a company limited by guarantee, Network Rail. Network Rail is run by an executive board accountable to 115 'Members', many chosen to represent one of a large number of public and private interests including train operators, railway employees and passengers. It was described as 'not for profit', thus appearing to deal with the objection to the earning of profit in a public utility. The company would be entirely financed by debt. In fact, it is more accurately described as 'not for dividend' since, in the original concept, profits earned would service the debts and build up a 'buffer fund' to absorb unexpected financial demands, and the residual would be ploughed back into the industry. Major new investments would continue to be undertaken by 'Special Purpose Vehicles' (SPVs): contractual arrangements with private sector providers.

The accountabilities and incentives under the new structure for Network Rail are unclear. As Parliament's Transport Select Committee said (2004: para. 13), it is hard to avoid the conclusion that the government: 'added another fudge by creating Network Rail, a private company without any private sector disciplines, seemingly set up simply to keep the enormous costs of the railway infrastructure away from the Government's balance sheet'.

In spite of the weaknesses in Railtrack's initial management, recent and careful statistical analysis by Kennedy and Smith (2004) confirms that:

> Railtrack delivered substantial real unit cost reductions in the early years after privatization (between 5.9 and 7.9 per cent for maintenance activity; and 6.4 to 6.8 per cent for overall maintenance and renewal activity) . . . However, these improvements were largely offset by the post-Hatfield cost increases, which resulted in unit cost increases of 26 and 38 per cent for maintenance and overall (maintenance and renewal) activity respectively.

There is little doubt that Network Rail now has better senior management. They are successfully re-introducing sound engineering practice into the way the business is managed. They are committed to bringing the runaway costs back under control. It is an open question whether the incentive structure they are working with will enable them to succeed in the long term.

The next railways policy: The Future of Rail

In July 2004 the government published the outcome of a review of its railways policy as a White Paper, *The Future of Rail* (DfT, 2004e). The legislation giving effect to the proposals was completed in early 2005. This review had been precipitated by a number of factors: the most immediate problem was caused by the outcome of the Rail Regulator's special review of Network Rail's access charges, undertaken in the aftermath of Railtrack's failure, and published in December 2003. The review contained bad news for the government because the Regulator judged that the basic costs of Network Rail were going to be higher than had been thought before Hatfield (see NAO, 2004). In 2004 public funding for the railway has risen to £3.8 billion, up from £1.8 billion in 1997–98 (DfT, 2004e: para. 2.2.1). In addition the year in which Railtrack waited in administration contributed towards a very rapid increase in Network Rail's debt, from £585 million at privatization to £9,404 million by March 2003 (see NAO, 2004: para. 3.10).

The increased annual bill for running the railway flew directly in the face of everything the Treasury had been trying to achieve for the railway for decades and, for a period, thought they had success-fully achieved with rail privatization. The DfT was additionally concerned because the increases in rail costs disrupted the 10 Year Plan for transport (DETR, 2000) which had previously been agreed with the Treasury. At base the problem was one which has bedev-illed government involvement in railway policy for decades. On the one hand, the Treasury was unwilling to find the relentlessly-increasing money that railways demand of the Exchequer and, on the other, the government was unwilling to face the political diffi-culties of reducing railway services.

The government's indecision is reflected in *The Future of Rail,* a rather vague document that proposed remarkably little fundamen-tal reform. The basic structure of the industry is to remain unchanged. Network Rail will remain as the regulated monopoly infrastructure provider, and privately-owned passenger and freight train companies will continue to operate on either a contracted or open access basis. The accountability of Network Rail presents an unresolved problem. The one major change proposed was to abol-ish the SRA and transfer its functions to the DfT. Since the SRA had always been a 'non-departmental public body', subject to Direction from the Secretary of State, this may not seem to be a very radical change. The major reason that the SRA came to be perceived as having failed was that it was never given enough money to deliver the task that government expected of it. However, there is little cause to suppose that the function will be better funded within the DfT.

There is one fundamental reason to doubt whether the structure now proposed for the railway can operate successfully for very long. Railtrack's year in administration, the subsequent increases in costs, the realization that more needs to be invested, the borrowing at the request of government in order to reduce current taxpayer-funded grants, government's aspirations to carry more rail traffic and its refusal to countenance large-scale closures all lead to one place: rapidly increasing debt for Network Rail. It is hard to see how Network Rail will ever repay – or even bring under control – debt on this scale. Government's refusal to write off unrepayable debt prevented the industry functioning properly throughout the 1950s, 1960s and 1970s. Distorting future managerial and commercial decisions in a vain attempt to repair the damage caused by past policy errors is not sensible. The government's determination to keep Network Rail in the private sector and to keep its debt off the public balance sheet, together with its reluctance to countenance a sufficient increase in access charges to enable it to deal with its debt problem, do not augur well for the long-term financial sustainability of Network Rail.

Unfortunately, the British experience on railways may illustrate the possibility of ending up with the worst of all worlds: to incur the costs of privatization in order to harness the forces of competition but then to intervene because it is found to be politically unacceptable to allow normal private-sector disciplines to operate, with the consequence that competition is prevented from delivering its benefits; and to end up paying private risk-bearing rates of interest on large debts without achieving any real risk transfer from the public sector.

The London Underground Public–Private Partnership (PPP)

In view of Labour's opposition to rail privatization and the way its leaders sought to modify it once in power, the simultaneous creation of the PPP for London Underground, announced in March 1998 and completed in spring 2003, is full of ironies and contradictions.

The government anticipated that the use of private-sector providers would achieve the same kind of efficiency gains as had previously been achieved in the privatized utilities. But, in order to meet the 1997 General Election *Manifesto* commitment not wholly to privatize the Underground, the privatization relates only to the fixed infrastructure, signalling and trains. It was a strange decision since the government had argued that it was in the maintenance and renewal of the infrastructure that the private sector performed so unsatisfactorily on the main railway. Operational staff – train drivers and station staff – remain as public-sector employees of the newly-created Greater London Authority. Thus, approximately 64 per cent of the staff have remained in the public sector. The others transferred to the private sector but, crucially, their terms and conditions were protected in accordance with the commitment made by the Deputy Prime Minister at the time the scheme was announced as well as by EU employment legislation (Transfer of Undertakings – Protection of Employment Regulations, 1981). In addition to this split between operations in the public sector and maintenance and renewal in the private sector, the private sector involvement is itself sub-divided into three separate contracts. Thus, whilst criticizing the fragmentation and vertical separation of British Rail brought about by the Conservative government, the Labour government simultaneously created a slightly different, four-fold fragmentation and vertical separation for London Underground.

This PPP (see Chapter 8) was proposed as a solution to the widely-accepted problem of historical under-investment in the upkeep and current maintenance of the London Underground. The hope was that a PPP procurement under a set of long-term contracts could achieve the provision of early capital investment without increasing explicit government borrowing. It would have the additional and considerable advantage of providing stable and predictable funding for the first time. The government's advisers anticipated continued growth in fares revenues from the Underground, and the government was persuaded that over a long period the revenues would prove sufficient to service the private sector's capital investment in full. This assumption led the government to design 30-year contracts in the belief that they would enable an infrastructure service charge to be negotiated that could be fully funded out of revenues, thus making the investments self-funding over such a contract period (HM Treasury, 1998: para. 8.4). Thus, the Underground would be brought up to a proper standard of repair, there would be some capacity increase (though the PPP only relates to the existing Underground and makes no provision for major new works such as new Underground lines), and yet the call on the Exchequer would be zero from the beginning. This hope proved to be wildly over-optimistic: in the event, the call on the Exchequer turned out to be over £1 billion a year.

The government divided the infrastructure into three 'Infracos' based on sets of lines: Jubilee/Northern/Piccadilly; Bakerloo/ Central/Victoria and District/Circle/Metropolitan/Hammersmith. However, during the competition for the contracts the government decided that the last two would be owned by a single consortium. The successful bidders were consortia of established companies: Amey/Jarvis/Bechtel and Atkins/Balfour Beatty/Bombardier/ Electricité de France. Some of these firms were new to the railway business and some were well known from their involvement in the privatized railway.

The contracts follow the PPP principle of being output-based. The contracts say little about how results are to be achieved, but they give financial incentives for achievement. The incentive payment regime has main components relating to 'ambience', 'capability' and 'availability'. The availability measure is probably the most important:

> Infracos are rewarded or abated depending on the performance of each line relative to its benchmark. Performance better than benchmark results in a bonus of £3 per Lost Customer Hour while performance below benchmark incurs an abatement of £6 per Lost Customer Hour. Performance below a level defined as 'Unacceptable' incurs an abatement of £9 per Lost Customer Hour. There are various additional contractual remedies available to LUL should performance fall below the benchmark or unacceptable levels.

The government's original intention was that the contracts would be completed and then transferred to the newly-elected Greater London Authority in spring 2000. However, this did not prove feasible, and final agreement on the main commercial terms was delayed until late 2002.

The first executive Mayor of London, Ken Livingstone, was elected in 2000. He was deeply opposed to the PPP, just as Labour had been opposed to rail privatization when in opposition. He recruited Bob Kiley from New York as Transport Commissioner for

London (the chief executive of TfL). There was never dissent that engineering services should, where appropriate, be competitively procured from private-sector providers; but Kiley recognized the difficulties that would be created by the monopoly power granted under very long contracts to non-competitive providers. It would be hard to secure good value for money, hard to ensure service delivery to the required quality, hard to manage safety and hard to secure changes to the terms of the agreements as the development of policy required it. He argued that he needed 'unified management control'. As an alternative he proposed a system of many more, much shorter contracts (TfL, 2001).

Further, Livingstone and Kiley pointed out that the PPP structure was not necessary to secure the required capital because bonds could have been issued, providing the government was willing to allow the debt on to the public balance sheet. But the government would not change policy, the suspicion being that the Treasury wanted to impose the contracts in order to fetter the power of the Mayor over spending on Underground infrastructure. The PPP certainly has that effect.

The Government has emphasized that this is not a 'conventional, Tory' utility privatization, even though the situation will be rather similar to the privatized utilities: private, for-profit consortia are in monopoly control of essential network facilities, receiving fees for access. But there is no regulator. Protection of the public interest for the next 30 years will depend crucially on a regime of contracts presided over by a Statutory Arbiter. In contrast to the duties of the Rail Regulator, those of the PPP Arbiter are to help enforce the agreements at the *time the contracts were signed*. The powers and duties are set out only in the barest terms in the legislation because the detail is explicitly delineated in the complex and inaccessible PPP Agreements.

Although there was initially an open competition for the PPP contracts, once the preferred bidders had been selected there was a long period of negotiation during which the risks accepted by the bidders were significantly reduced (see NAO, 2004a). The original draft contracts had already placed important caps on the liabilities faced by the contractors. Consequently, the final contracts greatly limit the magnitude of the risks that the investors are facing, and there is very little equity investment in any case (see Walder and Amenta, 2004). The end result seems to be that high service charges are being paid to monopoly service providers to guarantee them high rates of return on capital (see NAO, 2004a), whilst they bear little risk. This is again ironic given the objections of Labour to the earning of profit by infrastructure companies in the privatized railway.

Full responsibility for London Underground operations and for the PPP contracts passed to the Mayor and TfL in June 2003. It is too soon to have definitive objective evaluation of the outcome. However, there have been three preliminary official studies (NAO, 2004b and TfL, 2004b and TfL, 2005a). The second Tfl review notes that:

> There has been some progress in the first two years, but there are also some worrying trends and overall there is a shortfall compared with the expectations created by the private sector Infrastructure companies' bids. In short, performance is not good enough and is less than what was promised.
>
> In some areas the Infrastructure companies (Infracos) have delivered improvements in asset reliability, but this is neither consistent across all asset types, nor is it the level of improvement that was promised for all asset types. There has been some progress in the delivery of renewals but again this is inconsistent and significant parts of the capital programme are late, particularly for Metronet. Asset condition and programme information is finally being provided, but the quality of this information is inconsistent. The Infracos and their shareholders are earning significant sums through the PPP, but the volume of real work out on the railway is not consistent with the payments being made. (TfL, 2005a: 4)

Already a consensus is emerging on both sides of the contracts that it will soon be sensible to renegotiate some of their terms. Several consortium members have run into serious financial difficulties (for reasons not all to do with the Underground PPP): Amey has been taken over by a Spanish company, and in December 2004 Jarvis sold its interest to the same company.

Announced in 1998 and completed five years later, the PPP was forced through by two Labour administrations in the face of several sceptical assessments by the House of Commons Transport Select Committee, one from the Treasury Select Committee, one from the NAO (plus two post-completion) and a steady stream of critical assessments from independent bodies. They culminated in a critical report from the House of Commons Public Accounts Committee in March 2005 which found that the PPP had caused years of avoidable delay and that the procurement alone had cost the taxpayer £900 million, about half in fees to advisers and consultants to the various parties, and half in higher borrowing costs than an alternative promoted by the Mayor.

The advent of the Treasury's prudential borrowing regime from April 2004, together with the outcome of its Spending Review in July 2004, represent a marked change of policy towards local authority borrowing. Ironically, after such a bitter refusal to countenance the raising of bonds to finance the London Underground or National Air Traffic Services, the government granted TfL permission to issue £3.3 billion in bonds over five years. TfL successfully made its second issue in March 2006, which brought the total to £400 million. TfL was granted an AA investment grade rating by the rating agencies, the issue was over-subscribed and the cost of the borrowing was only slightly higher than that which the government achieves for its direct, government-guaranteed borrowing. The debt created under the PPP has now been classified as on the public balance sheet. Further, the government has actively encouraged Network Rail to use what are effectively revenue bonds to raise the long-term borrowing it needs, even though it remains determined to keep Network Rail's debt off the public balance sheet (NAO, 2004, paragraph 3.18).

These experiences with the national railway and with London Underground raise the fundamental question of the circumstances under which competition for large, long-lived contracts for the provision of public services can, in view of the inevitable political interference, be expected to produce the kind of value for money outcomes normally expected from the classical models of competition for contracts.

Chapter 8

Paying for Transport: Appraisal and Economic Issues

For many years transport policy in Britain has been exploring how best to harness market forces to the delivery of best value-for-money, whether within the public sector or, more recently, in partnership with the private sector. Competition has been encouraged in or for the provision of services. Most of the transport industries, many of them formerly owned by the government, have been returned to the private sector. But the government remains an important provider of resources, both for capital investment in roads and in public transport infrastructure, and as an additional source of finance, alongside the fare-box, under those contracts which guarantee payments in return for the provision of services. This chapter analyses recent levels of government spending on transport, and discusses sources of funding and methods of financing. It discusses existing and alternative sources of national and local taxation, including road user charging. It also concerns the role of central and local government in appraising investment proposals and determining physical investment, as well as setting transport prices and determining levels of service.

There are many reasons why a government might wish to keep charges for services or infrastructure low (in the British case most roads are free apart from the duty paid on fuel) but, if transport is under-priced, then unless it has a generous and reliable source of funding from local or national taxpayers it will be condemned to provide inadequate services. Where capacity is limited in relation to the level of demand, there will be crowding, congestion and unreliable service. In such circumstances increasing charges will reduce demand and increase the quality of service enjoyed by the remaining users. This method is likely to be more efficient than rationing capacity through queuing or congestion, because raising the price will increase the average value of the facility to those that continue to use it, whilst offering the opportunity to make most people better off, providing that a suitable mechanism can be implemented to compensate the losers out of the extra revenues. The London congestion charge has shown how this can work: the price reduced demand, congestion was relieved to the benefit of the remaining users, and at least some of the losers saw compensation in the form of improved bus services. A final section of this chapter considers whether a similar approach might apply to national road user charging.

Government spending on transport

In the public spending crises that recurred during the post-war period transport was always one of the main targets for cuts. Figure 8.1 displays government expenditure on transport as a proportion of Gross Domestic Product (GDP). Public expenditure on transport (in 2001–02 prices) declined from £15.8 billion to £9.0 billion between 1992–93 and 1999–2000. It subsequently increased, though to figures well below those of the mid-1990s. As a proportion of GDP, transport spending was halved in the short period

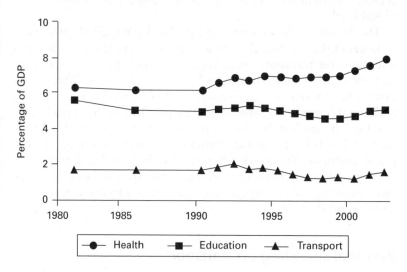

FIGURE 8.1 *Public expenditure on transport as a proportion of GDP*

Note: Figures are for total managed expenditure on health, education and transport.

Source: Data from HM Treasury, *Public Expenditure Statistical Analyses*.

from 1992–93 to 1998–99 and has only marginally recovered in the most recent period. Although transport spending has become more substantial since 2000–01, the government has increased public expenditure on health and education more strongly, both absolutely and as a proportion of GDP.

However, the importance of the *10 Year Plan* (DETR, 2000) should not be under-estimated. Although it had fundamental flaws it was a ten-year expenditure plan with a firm commitment from the Treasury: something that had very rarely been achieved before. It also represented a worthwhile increase in the public funds to be made available (see Glaister, 2002 for more detail). It took a strong line in favouring investment in rail infrastructure over investment in roads, despite the much higher modal share of roads: only 6 per cent of UK passenger-kilometres is by rail, and the Strategic Rail Authority (2003) noted that more than half the population uses a train less than once a year. Buses account for 6 per cent and cars for 85 per cent of all passenger-kilometres (excluding walking). Rail now carries 8 per cent of freight tonne-kilometres. Unfortunately the intentions in the 10 Year Plan were quickly thwarted by a series of events, particularly the fuel price protests and the Hatfield rail accident (both in autumn 2000) and the subsequent administration of Railtrack.

The Transport White Paper of July 2004 (DfT, 2004) gives very little detail, but it does display a chart showing the government's intentions on transport spending up to 2014–15. It indicates an increase of funding above the 10 Year Plan figures for 2005–06 to 2007–08, granted in the Treasury's 2004 Spending Review, and additional funds in the form of a 'Transport Innovation Fund'. This Fund will be small in 2008–09 but is to increase to over £2 billion a year by 2014–15. Local authorities are being encouraged in their Local Transport Plans (see Chapter 3) to bid for Fund awards to develop road user charging schemes, higher-quality bus services or other projects that encourage people to use cars less or will enhance national productivity.

Personal spending on transport

Transport makes up a high and increasing proportion of household budgets. The annual Family Expenditure Survey reveals that, in 1962, households allocated about 9 per cent of their expenditure to transport and 33 per cent to food, alcohol and tobacco. Real

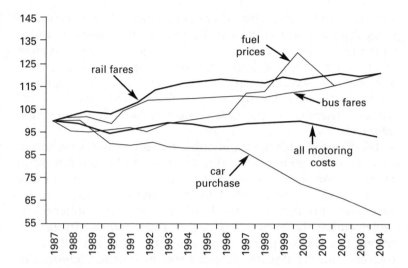

FIGURE 8.2 *Transport prices relative to retail prices*
Note: Prices for each component of transport costs are given relative to general retail prices, each indexed to 1987 = 100.
Source: Data from Office of National Statistics, *Monthly Digest of Statistics*.

income is now well over twice as high as in 1962. Transport at 15 per cent is second only to expenditure on housing and utilities at 18 per cent, while food, alcohol and tobacco now account for only 13 per cent. Most of this vastly increased transport spending is on owning and running private vehicles. While car ownership is certainly not universal, it is far more common than it used to be. This change has been the result of growth in real incomes, demographic changes, stable real costs of motoring (see Figure 8.2) and spectacular improvements in the quality of the used vehicles that can be purchased for a modest sum. Meanwhile, public transport has become much less relevant with the exception of some special markets such as commuting into London.

The distinction between specification and provision

As the examples in the previous chapter illustrated, there is a distinction between the body that specifies the service that is to be provided and the body that actually provides the service. But if the provider is to be something other than an integral part of national or local government then careful attention must be given to the arrangements that seek to ensure that the agent (provider) is given effective incentives to deliver what the principal (government) has specified and paid for. These arrangements can include statutory regulations, supervision by an independent regulatory body and financial incentives in payment regimes embodied in commercial contracts.

If there is to be borrowing in order to finance capital investment it can be either conventional direct borrowing by government or indirect borrowing by private bodies on behalf of government. The Private Finance Initiative (PFI) and PPP have continued to evolve since their introduction in the 1990s as a way of simultaneously implementing the principal–agent split and the substitution of private finance for public borrowing. PFI is described by the Treasury and the Private Finance Panel in *Private Opportunity, Public Benefit* (HM Treasury, 1995), and its more recent evolution is discussed in *PFI: Meeting the Investment Challenge* (HM Treasury, 2003). Rather than government specifying what it wants, how it is to be provided and then providing it 'in house', government specifies the outcomes it wants and then holds a competition amongst private-sector providers for a commercially-binding, 20- or 30-year contract for the right to provide the outcomes in return for an annual fee. The magnitude of the fee paid will depend on the extent to which the promised output targets are met according to a schedule specified in the contract. The objective is to create incentives to good performance by transferring the risk of inadequate performance to the private-sector providers and by rewarding over-performance. Contractors are free to choose their own technical solutions and to employ their own staff on their own terms of employment for design, construction and subsequent operation. If, as is often the case, initial capital investment is required, then the necessary funds will be raised by the private-sector contractor from its own lenders and shareholders. This has the effect of converting what would, conventionally, have been capital purchases, funded out of either current taxation or public borrowing, into private borrowing to be repaid from future taxation spread over many years to come.

Whatever the institutional detail, government must be in charge of specification, must manage and enforce the contracts and must take responsibility for raising such tax funding as will be necessary sooner or later.

National taxation

In setting taxes affecting transport the Chancellor of the Exchequer has to balance a great variety of policy considerations, such as reducing the demand for both private and public transport, reducing carbon emissions and air pollution, encouraging sales of British-made vehicles and assisting the competitiveness of British business by keeping down transport costs. The tax-gathering departments which include HM Revenue & Customs and the Department of Social Security prefer tax regimes that are easy to administer. Many decisions about taxation are so sensitive that the Chancellor has to take them under conditions of the tightest security within the very small circle of advisers who prepare the budget. This regime of budget secrecy makes it almost impossible to conduct an open interdepartmental debate about the impact of taxation policy on transport (see Chapter 2).

Vehicle excise duty (the annual 'tax disc') raised £4.6 billion in Great Britain in 2002/03. Fuel tax is a larger source of revenue, raising £22 billion. Despite the claims of some who participated in the demonstrations of autumn 2000, the real index of all motoring costs was stable between 1987 and 2005, as Figure 8.2 illustrates, while bus fares rose on average by 24 per cent more than retail prices, and rail fares rose 33 per cent more than retail prices. After the 1992 Earth Summit in Rio de Janeiro, fuel duties were raised every year under the Conservative government by at least 5 per cent more than the rate of inflation. Under Labour after 1997 this was increased to 6 per cent as a measure intended to reduce emissions of carbon dioxide, the main greenhouse gas. However, in 2000 the routine fuel-tax increase compounded the effect of an increase in the world price of oil to create the peak in July shown in Figure 8.2. It precipitated the fuel price protests of that autumn. The government responded by abandoning the policy of increasing fuel taxes, thus destroying one of the foundations upon which the 1998 Transport White Paper was built.

Local forms of taxation

Borrowing is a mechanism for changing the timing of the required tax payments (financing), but taxpayer funding is inevitable sooner or later; and if it is not to be national tax, then it must be a local tax of some form. The economic arguments underlying the leading contenders are outlined here (their characteristics from the perspective of local government's role as transport provider are described in Chapter 3).

Land value capture

New roads and railways create new value by making particular locations quicker and easier to reach. That new value will either be abstracted from passengers in the form of increased charge revenues or, providing the land and rental markets are working reasonably well, it will appear in the form of increased land values. A classic way of funding new railways serving 'green field' sites was to purchase undeveloped land, build a railway and then sell the land on at an increased price to reflect the improved accessibility. But in the UK there is no systematic tax regime to take full account of the benefit that will accidentally accrue to those who already own and occupy property close to infrastructure developments. In a couple of cases there have been single, large beneficiaries of improvements (extensions and improvements to the Docklands Light Railway and the extension of the Jubilee Line) where contributions have been negotiated, but these mechanisms do not help much with funding improvements to an existing system.

The uniform national non-domestic rate (NNDR)

The current system of tax on commercial property was introduced in 1990 by the Thatcher Government as part of the attempt to reform the then system of local property taxes known as domestic and non-domestic rates (see Chapter 3). Every five years, each commercial property is assessed to estimate the annual rental it could command on the open market: the rateable value. A tax rate uniform across the country – the poundage or multiplier – is then applied and the yield is collected into a central pool. At the time of the introduction of the system the government made a commitment that the total yield would change by no more than the Retail Prices Index. The multiplier is adjusted each year accordingly. The yield is distributed back to local authorities in direct proportion to their resident population. An area in which commercial property values are rising faster than the average will end up paying a larger proportion of the fixed real total. Any increased taxes paid by property owners in an area in which infrastructure has been improved are blindly redistributed to other areas. The tax rate increases when the general property market falls, and it decreases in a buoyant market. A local authority gains little in financial terms if business development takes place in its area. Since new developments generally impose additional servicing costs on local authorities, there is a perverse incentive for them to suppress commercial development. Above all, the system prevents the government from collecting any net national increase in real values as a contribution towards funding the infrastructure that promotes higher real property values. The cash increase in the yield of the national non-domestic rate in England in the period since the last major reform of local government finance in 1993–94 has been 44 per cent, compared with 87 per cent for council tax (ODPM, 2003).

Increase in domestic and non-domestic rate yields

Domestic property owners usually benefit from an increase in property values if local transport infrastructure is improved. One mechanism would be to increase the tax taken from domestic households under the council tax system and, in principle, there is no reason that domestic property owners should not be asked to make an extra contribution. However, given the other pressures on the domestic council tax and its extreme political sensitivity, it is unlikely to prove a buoyant source of new transport funding. Another, more promising possibility would be to relax the rule that the total take from the NNDR is to be kept constant in real terms. It would be administratively simple to increase the NNDR multiplier in order to create funds for a new (and genuinely additional) national transport infrastructure fund.

A local non-domestic rate levy

Alternatively, it would be possible to raise the existing NNDR multiplier within a defined zone so as to raise additional resources for infrastructure projects (Glaister and Travers, 1994). A supplementary levy could operate either across a whole city or within smaller areas. Payments would be based upon an additional rate-in-the-pound, to be paid by all NNDR payers within the area, and would be ring-fenced or 'hypothecated' to a particular project or projects. The smaller the area within which the levy operated, the more precise would be the link between levy and benefit. It would be possible to hold a vote to test opinion among the businesses that would pay the levy. A levy based on a business plan and a vote among local taxpayers would be very similar to the Business Improvement Districts that operate in many US and Canadian cities (see below). The great certainty associated with the NNDR yield would make any money raised from it (including as an income flow to finance NNDR-backed borrowing) highly predictable.

Tax Increment Finance (TIF)

Tax Increment Finance was proposed by Lord Rogers's Urban Task Force (DETR, 1999b) as a possible method for urban areas to re-invest in their physical assets. The Task Force had found such mechanisms in use in North America and believed they could play a part in the 'urban renaissance' that Lord Rogers hoped to kick-start within Britain. Tax Increment Finance works by capturing part of the gain generated by rising land values in the immediate vicinity of a major infrastructure development. The value of properties within a zone around a new railway line, road or other asset would be monitored, so as to make it possible to compare changes within the zone with those outside. Insofar as values within the zone rose more quickly than values outside, the difference would be attributed to economic benefits of the new infrastructure. This margin of difference could then be subject to a tax rate-in-the-pound. The non-domestic rate multiplier would be the same for businesses inside and outside the TIF zone but, within the zone, part of the yield would be attributed to the project that created value up-lift and collected into a separate account. It would be possible to have a more sophisticated scheme, perhaps with graduated zones stepping away from new infrastructure. Compared with Tax Increment Finance, the NNDR would be likely to produce a larger and more certain yield: it is, in effect, a general infrastructure levy and would not tie benefits directly to location (see Glaister *et al.*, 2004, for estimates in the case of London).

Business Improvement Districts (BIDs)

BIDs were originally created in the United States and Canada to allow small areas of towns and cities to create new micro-government institutions that could raise resources from the property tax paid by businesses. A study of BIDs in New York (Travers and Weimar, 1996) made the case for a possible experiment in London and elsewhere in Britain. BIDs would operate where businesses within an area saw the need, created a business plan and then held a vote among businesses within a designated zone. If there were a vote in favour of the BID the new entity would be formed and would have the power to levy a supplementary non-domestic rate within its area. Such mechanisms are not designed to be used to fund infrastructure: they are explicitly intended to provide day-to-day 'clean and safe' services funded from revenue expenditure rather than capital investment. Having said that, in at least one of the New York BIDs (Grand Central Partnership), capital works were undertaken to renew pavements, lighting and street furniture.

Planning gain

Powers were given to local authorities under Section 106 of the Town and Country Planning Act 1990 to allow them to negotiate capital expenditure contributions as part of their decision to grant planning permission for larger developments. Inevitably, such powers work far more effectively in London than in other parts of the country: high demand for housing coupled with high land values in the capital has made it possible for London boroughs to negotiate greater totals of Section 106 contributions than have authorities elsewhere. For their part, developers complain that there is only so much to be squeezed from each particular site and development. Expecting developers to include about 35–50 per cent affordable housing within a particular housing development, plus transport infrastructure, plus schools and hospitals, is likely to deter investment.

Local sales or employment taxes

Many other countries use supplementary taxes to fund transport. In France a supplementary payroll tax on employers, *Le Versement Transport*, is used to fund a large share of the transport costs. In Australia a development levy was recently used in Sydney to build the central railway station. In the USA dedicated mortgage recording taxes, in addition to local corporate and certain sales, fuel, and service taxes, are used to fund infrastructure.

Workplace parking charges

The road charging options for London study (Government Office for London, 2000) found that a levy of £3,000 per space for employer-provided workplace parking spaces could yield £100 million a year in an extended central London area. Imposing the levy might reduce overall traffic-related congestion but the challenge of implementing and enforcing the levy remains to be investigated fully. Workplace-parking charging has been successfully implemented in Sydney and Perth. In the UK the Government's *10 Year Plan* (DETR, 2000) estimated that 12 cities would use workplace parking levies by 2010 (in addition to expecting eight of the largest cities to introduce congestion charging schemes). However, although some cities have studied the idea, they are not currently developing plans for imposing a levy.

Borrowing

If the full capital sum for new infrastructure cannot be found out of current taxation then borrowing is necessary. In order for the capital markets to continue to have confidence in lending, prudence and some kind of discipline is necessary to ensure that servicing the borrowing does not become an unreasonable burden on future taxpayers and that the borrowing can eventually be repaid. Under the Labour government, Gordon Brown as Chancellor of the Exchequer sought to rationalize revenue and capital controls at the national level: his 'golden rule' said that the government can – over the economic cycle – borrow only to fund its investment during that cycle. The 'sustainable investment rule' says that, again over the economic cycle, public debt should be kept below 40 per cent of GDP.

The Private Finance Initiative and Public–Private Partnerships

The demand for more investment in transport infrastructure at a time when governments have been trying to reduce public expenditure and borrowing has led to much debate about ways of involving the private sector more fully. A number of creative ideas were put forward in the 1980s and early 1990s. By 1995 Treasury ministers had evolved a firm policy towards the replacement of conventional public sector funding by private finance, encapsulated in the PFI. Kenneth Clarke, Chancellor of the Exchequer, published an important consultation document, *Breaking New Ground: The Private Finance Initiative* (HM Treasury, 1993):

We aim to promote efficiency, to improve services and to stimulate fresh flows of investment. We want to harness the private
sector's efficiency and management expertise, just as much as its
resources, bringing a new approach to investment in a whole
range of activities and services traditionally regarded as the
exclusive domain of the public sector.

Labour politicians – including, significantly, John Prescott
(later to become Secretary of State for Transport) – had already
identified the scope that leasing and franchising arrangements
might offer to increase investment in transport infrastructure
without immediately increasing public expenditure. These
concepts, given the new name of Public–Private Partnerships (see
Corry, Le Grand and Radcliffe, 1997), were positively embraced
and further developed by the new Labour government of 1997. In
fact, officials in education, the health service and both national
and local transport administrations came to believe that the
Treasury would approve capital expenditures only if they were
PFI or PPP projects.

Risk transfer is a crucial part of the concept. At least some of the
risk must be transferred, otherwise there would be no incentive for
the private sector to increase efficiency in order to reduce the risk to
its profits or to mitigate its consequences. Many risks will be
present under both conventional public-financing and private-
financing systems, but the costs associated with the risks are often
greater if they are borne by the private sector, and this greater risk
will be reflected in a higher cost of borrowing. While government
can raise money relatively cheaply because it is a large low-risk
borrower, account must be taken of the benefits that tend to go with
private finance and management, such as improved efficiency,
lower costs, and a reduction in the risks falling on the taxpayer.
There is, therefore, a trade-off between shifting risk on to the
private sector to sharpen the incentives to mitigate risk, and retain-
ing it in the public sector to reduce its social cost. This tension was
particularly clear in the debate on the PPP for the London
Underground.

The use of PFI and PPP has been increasingly favoured by the
Treasury in many fields of public procurement, notably in health,
education and the prison service. One reason may be that Whitehall
government no longer trusts local government or other public
bodies to procure and manage projects efficiently. It knows the
Treasury will ultimately bear the financial consequences of any

decision: under the centralized system of government, over-runs and excessive costs will eventually fall back on central government. At the same time, the Treasury recognizes that the Whitehall civil service is rarely the right body for sponsoring and delivering projects. One solution has been to insist that projects be procured from the private sector on tightly specified and commercially-binding contracts. Hence there has been an emphasis on PFI and PPP deals which devolve the raising of capital and project design and procurement to the private sector, thereby fettering the ability of public authorities to intervene.

This strategy has worked much better in some cases than in others. One difficulty that has emerged is that it can be hard or impossible to codify some public procurements into single contracts. Another is that these contracts have to be very long term in order to make the financing work, and in practice it is often found to be difficult to enforce or terminate a failing contract. Furthermore, it is no more likely that weak public bodies would be able to manage contracts with the private sector successfully than that they would be to carry out the work on their own account. The consequence is that the incentives towards efficiency generated by risk transfer can be undermined.

Governments feel the need to keep service delivery working seamlessly whether or not there is a formal public service obligation, so they are reluctant to allow service providers to fail. In other words, in the end, risk transfer may not be achieved in practice. This effect has been illustrated by the rescue of failing Train Operating Companies and of the National Air Traffic Services PPP, and is identified as a problem with the London Underground PPP by many authors including the Public Accounts Committee (2005) of the House of Commons. While the Private Finance Initiative and Public–Private Partnerships may have merits in some circumstances, they represent only one of many available techniques for public procurement and borrowing. As HM Treasury has emphasized (2003, paras 2.8 and 2.9), PFI is actually a small part of current activity.

PFI and PPP will clearly continue to have a role but it may be a minor one in future. PFI and PPP are just particular mechanisms for procuring services from the private sector. They bundle together the raising of finance and the contracting for the actual services. Conventional procurement keeps the two separate and therefore needs to make alternative arrangements for finance.

Debt and prudential borrowing

Any well-managed enterprise should have a plan for its capital assets on a horizon commensurate with the lifetime of those assets. This principle applies also to a public authority responsible for transport infrastructure. It enforces transparency of the public planning process and provides a degree of insulation against short-term political whim. Indeed, it provides a strict discipline in that, in order to preserve the trust of investors (and thereby retain the ability to borrow in the future), each administration must honour the commitments made by itself or by others in the past.

Bonds

Any income stream, if it is reasonably secure, may be converted into a capital sum. As an illustration, if the income stream were certain and available in perpetuity and the interest rate were expected to be always 10 per cent, then £1 per annum would equate to a capital sum of £10. Lower interest rates would lead to a larger capital sum. A nearer horizon would lead to a smaller capital sum. 'Securitizing' future cash flows as capital sums by selling bonds in the general capital markets is commonplace with local authorities throughout the world. It used to be so in the UK. The capital for many local authority projects was raised in this way and local authority debt was routinely traded on the financial markets. Interest rates were typically low because the market regarded local authorities as excellent risks, although central government concern because of the magnitude of local authority spending financed by borrowing eventually led to severe restrictions.

Bonds secured on future revenues have received much attention as a possible means of raising resources for public transport and other major infrastructure projects in London. The advantage of bonds of this kind is that they are a cheap, tradable, way of borrowing. In many American states, a referendum is held when it is proposed to issue a bond to finance a particular package of infrastructure investments. Thus the public must assent to the long-term cost of projects. Bonds offer a number of potential advantages. In particular, they allow bond holders to assure themselves that their lending is part of a coherent capital spending plan that is being prudently managed and regulated. With a new 'Prudential Borrowing Framework' for capital finance under the Local Government Act 2003, an English local authority is now able to borrow for any purpose relevant to its functions up to the borrowing limit it judges to be affordable (or any lower limit set by the Secretary of State). As noted in Chapter 7, Transport for London (part of the Greater London Authority) successfully issued its second £200 million of debt in March 2006. Crucially, the local authority must determine and keep under review how much money it can afford to borrow having regard to the *Prudential Code for Capital Finance* published by the Chartered Institute of Public Finance and Accountancy (CIPFA). Over the medium term, net borrowing should be only for capital purposes. This mirrors the Chancellor's own 'golden rule'. The extent to which this new regime gives greater freedom clearly depends upon whether or not Secretaries of State exercise their powers to set over-riding limits. In practice, this central regulation restricts the freedom that 'prudential borrowing' might otherwise have provided. In any case this new borrowing regime is only useful insofar as there is a stream of income available to service the debts.

Transport project appraisal, financing and pricing

The Exchequer funds UK trunk roads, motorways and many local roads, and makes major financial contributions to the rail and bus industries; the Treasury therefore has a direct interest in securing value for money. However, to be useful, a technique for evaluating or appraising the value of a transport project must gain the acceptance of those that will have to be influenced by it, perhaps against their instinctive judgement. New construction is controversial because there are direct conflicts of interest between individuals who would benefit (typically many and geographically dispersed) and those who would be disadvantaged (often few and located close to the scheme). Some of the disadvantaged individuals will have their property and other rights affected, while others will suffer external effects of various kinds. The problem has to be seen in the broader context of a need for a mechanism to assist the management of a complete public spending programme.

In response to these needs, the Treasury in the 1960s encouraged the Transport Department to develop standardized economic appraisal techniques for trunk road proposals. Nobody claimed that they were perfect, but they were as good as those in routine use in any government department world-wide and better than most. COBA is an appraisal routine (codified in a computer program) first developed by the Road Research Laboratory and refined since. It compares the costs of constructing and maintaining a road scheme for 30 years with the benefits gained by road users and others, all against a do-nothing or do-minimum proposal. Benefits are calculated in money terms from the expected changes to traffic volumes and traffic conditions, both on the new or improved road itself and on the network of roads nearby. COBA estimates the money values of the savings in vehicle operating costs, savings in journey times and reductions in the number and severity of accidents, and balances them against construction and maintenance costs. Whilst the techniques were first put into routine use in the context of the national roads programme, they are equally applicable in other areas. Two of the best known early applications were on the Victoria Line on the London Underground (Beesley and Foster, 1963), and the Roskill Inquiry on the Third London Airport (Abelson and Flowerdew, 1972).

The principles behind cost-benefit analysis and some of the empirical evidence are set out in detail in Layard and Glaister (1994) and current official values are published on the Internet at www.webtag.org.uk. The basis for calculating a benefit is the price people would be willing to pay for that benefit. The valuation of a saving in journey time depends upon whether the subject is travelling on business or for leisure. Working time is valued at the cost to the employer including income tax and the overhead costs of an employee. Leisure and shopping trips and other personal journeys are regarded as 'non-working time' and valued on the basis of empirical estimates of the willingness of these travellers to pay to save time. Accident costs are mostly valued as the medical, police and material damage caused, the loss of output from people injured, and includes an element for 'pain, grief and suffering'. The valuation of a life saved is estimated on the basis of willingness to pay for a reduction in the risk of death. Vehicle operating costs are the direct costs to road users.

Another strand of appraisal of a project is a non-quantitative assessment of its impact on the environment, both positive (such as the removal of heavy vehicles from the proximity of mediaeval foundations) and negative (such as the destruction of rare types of natural habitat), and the costs of mitigating adverse effects. The 'environment' here includes the landscape, nature conservation, buildings/townscapes and air quality. The Standing Advisory Committee on Trunk Road Assessment (SACTRA, known originally as the Leitch Committee) was set up in the mid-1970s to carry out an independent review of these road appraisal methods. Leitch found that the methods of economic cost-benefit analysis are essentially sound but that they needed to be put into a broader framework of appraisal. His report recognized that considerations incapable of monetary valuation or that could not be quantified should be given equal attention. Moreover, projects typically pose significant issues arising from the different incidences of costs and benefits on groups of individuals. The Leitch 'framework' was proposed as a way of putting economic cost-benefit analysis into an appropriate wider context.

Environmental appraisal had been a part of the Transport Department's procedures since the mid-1970s. The EU Environmental Impact Assessment Directive 85/337 extended principles already generally adopted for roads in the UK. Large projects may now come to the attention of the European Commission and the European Court of Justice. The procedures set out in the directive must be applied to all motorways and to most other transport projects if they are likely to have significant effects on the environment. Lines for long-distance rail traffic are also required to have an environmental appraisal.

The department published a Manual of Environmental Appraisal in 1983, and an updated volume was issued in July 1993; the Scottish Office issued the similar Scottish Traffic and Environmental Appraisal Manual in 1986. The methods were originally developed for inter-urban routes and adapted for urban roads from 1987 on the basis of advice from SACTRA. The techniques set out in the manual assist department officials to assess in a structured way the impact of changes in traffic noise, visual intrusion, accidents, effects on the ecology, development potential and conservation areas. Traffic flow data is used in the assessment of road safety, driver stress, pedestrian delay, traffic noise and pollution caused by vehicles. The DoT accepted in 1992 SACTRA's recommendation to add water quality and drainage, vibration, night-time noise and the effects of blight. SACTRA's examination of the DoT's procedures for assessing environmental impact recommended that the DoT improve its environmental assessment by putting monetary value on those environmental effects which could be so valued, and that the government should carry out research and tests to this end. In addition, 'the value judgements and technical assumptions made, and the methods used, should be explicit, open to scrutiny, challenge and possible revision'. There has been considerable progress in recent years in estimating the costs of noise, air pollution and carbon emissions. Sansom *et al.* (2001) give a good summary.

After the General Election of 1997 the new Labour government undertook a series of reviews of economic appraisal methods in general, and the way it appraises transport proposals in particular. In transport the objective was to ensure that transport appraisals are 'even handed across modes (e.g. rail, road, cycling, walking, etc.) and take account of all effects (not only direct transport effects)'. The general review culminated in the publication by the Treasury in 2003 of a new edition of the 'Green Book', *Appraisal and Evaluation in Central Government* (HM Treasury, 2003a). Since 2004 the procedures in relation to road and other transport schemes have been helpfully set out in considerable technical detail on the Internet site, www.webtag.org.uk. There is *An Introduction to Transport Analysis* at www.dft.gov.uk. This includes and updates the material originally issued as official *Guidance on the Methodology for Multimodal Studies* (GOMMS), which was the primary guidance document on the multi-modal New Approach to Appraisal (NATA), first introduced in the 'Integrated Transport' White Paper (DETR, 1998). There had been a change in transport policy involving 'reducing dependency on the car', and the change in appraisal techniques and the roads programme was a reflection of this.

In a spirit of continuing to develop the Leitch Committee's 'framework approach', the 'hard' economic benefits and other cost-benefit techniques were placed in a context with other considerations. *An Introduction to Transport Analysis* states the following:

> The NATA process requires a number of steps to be taken prior to the formal appraisal process. These steps are usually defined as a 'transport study' . . .
>
> Throughout the NATA process five objectives for transport as outlined in the White Paper are central: Environmental impact . . . Safety . . . Economy . . . Accessibility . . . Integration . . .
>
> The appraisal output in NATA is made up of four distinct parts: [a one page] Appraisal Summary Table [AST] (Achievement of Government objectives); Achievement of regional and local objectives; Effectiveness of problem solving; Supporting analyses. These four strands when considered together provide the decision-maker with the information needed to reach a considered judgment on the worth of a project . . .
>
> As part of the process, specific regional and local objectives

will be set . . . The results of this analysis should be summarised in a form similar to the AST, showing how each option has fared against particular regional and local objectives . . .

Supporting analyses cover three additional groups of issues: distribution and equity . . . affordability and financial sustainability . . . practicality and public acceptability.

The NATA goes as far as it is sensible to go towards implementing multi-criteria analysis. It is clear that there are several criteria and sub-criteria that might be applied, some involving characteristics that cannot be quantified. The NATA suggests describing most effects that cannot yet be quantified on a seven-point scale. But these are to be verbal descriptions and are not to be represented numerically. This usefully clarifies that this is not to be taken as far as a 'scoring and weighting' scheme. Whilst such schemes can be useful in some situations they are largely an illusion: if something cannot be quantified, then that should be accepted. To give a numerical score to more than one characteristic and then to trade one against the other (or against some cardinal quantity), on the basis of these numerical scores, with or without explicitly giving them weights, is to pretend that what was assumed to be unquantified is, in fact, capable of cardinal measurement. That would not be consistent and the trap is successfully avoided in the NATA.

Conventional cost-benefit appraisal of projects does not normally include any explicit element for gains made to individual regions, industries, firms or people. However, the DfT is consulting on how these issues might be incorporated in future (see, for instance, 'Transport, wider economic benefits, and impacts on GDP', at www.dft.gov.uk).

The strategic roads programme

When in 1998 the new Labour government first published its proposals on the NATA it also published an economic appraisal of a number of schemes in its current portfolio of proposals. As Figure 8.3 indicates, the benefits of most of these were assessed as being higher than the costs, and in many cases they were very much higher. None the less, the government decided to delete those to the left of the vertical line in Figure 8.3 from the programme. The average ratio of benefit to cost of those deleted was 4.25:1, somewhat better than the average for those that were to survive at 3:1.

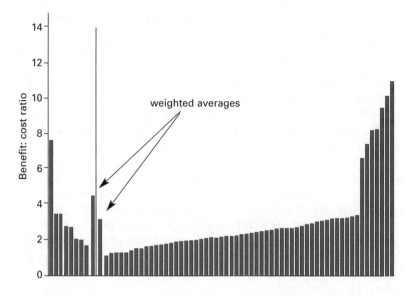

FIGURE 8.3 *Road schemes appraised by NATA in 1998*
Source: Data from DETR, *Understanding the New Approach to Appraisal* (DETR, 1998).

This action was consonant with the policy of the day which was greatly to reduce investment in new road building: essentially a continuation of the trend set under the latter years of the previous government. But the policy was somewhat modified in the *10 Year Plan* (DETR, 2000) which, as Figure 8.4 shows, anticipated a return to the rate of spend typical of the early 1990s. As the realization came that investment in public transport was never going to be able to stop the growth in traffic, and many people wanted more roads, such as local bypasses, the Labour government changed its position and started to reinstate some of the schemes that had been withdrawn in its early days. The 2004 White Paper, *The Future of Transport,* goes further and feels able to claim that:

> Over the past six years we have made real progress in developing a programme which will deliver significant improvements to both the strategic and local road networks. The Highways Agency has a programme of major projects which include:
> - widening of the M25 – six schemes;
> - widening and improvement of the M1 – four schemes; and

- the A14 connecting the East Coast ports with the Midlands – three schemes.

The Highways Agency has completed 20 major schemes since 2002, plus the M6 Toll, which is now producing improved traffic flows on the strategic road network around Birmingham. The Highways Agency is also taking forward a programme of smaller schemes which will help to make best use of the strategic road network by tackling local bottlenecks, improving junctions and addressing safety issues. (DfT, 2004: para. 3.9)

This language could not have found its way into an official policy document in the early years of the 1997 Labour government. Even so, the rate of investment in new road capacity is bound to continue to fall behind the growth of traffic on current policies. It seems inevitable that the principle of using road user charges to manage demand and to achieve a better use of the limited available capacity will become more attractive to future governments. We return to road pricing below.

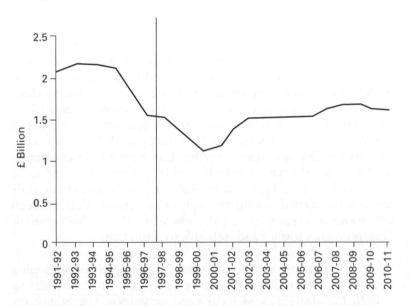

FIGURE 8.4   *Planned public expenditure on strategic roads (1999–2000 prices)*

Source: Data from DETR, *Transport 2010: The 10 Year Plan* (TSO, 2000).

Private-sector financing of toll motorways

The direct approach to using private-sector funding to build transport infrastructure is to encourage private companies to design, build, finance, and operate (DBFO) routes themselves. In 1990 central government named several toll road schemes but there was not much enthusiasm. Two toll bridges have been built (Dartford Crossing and the second Severn Bridge) and the first wholly privately-funded and operated overland motorway in the UK was the Birmingham Northern Relief Road, for which a 53-year concession was granted in 1992; it opened in 2004.

Until 1993 the government had rejected the road construction industry's proposals to use 'shadow tolls' – in which contractors are paid in proportion to traffic flows – as distinct from real tolls. Then the Treasury issued a statement in which the government recognized the potential offered by shadow tolls: 'Promoters will receive payments from the government in relation to the level of traffic using roads constructed or improved in this way . . . The aim will be to secure substantial transfer of risk to the private sector' (HM Treasury, 1993).

A Highways Agency and Private Finance Panel case study of March 1997 notes that 'One of the objectives of the DBFO programme was to foster a private sector, domestic road operating industry' (DoT, 1997: ch. 6). There is now considerable flexibility evident in the arrangements for privately-funded road schemes. Public expenditure was reduced in the short term. The shadow toll system was seen as successful in bringing the perceived benefits of private sector involvement. The Highways Agency claimed that the first eight DBFO contracts have beaten 'the public sector comparator by an average value of 15%' (DoT, 1997: foreword). The 10 Year Plan expected 'that around 25% by value of current and new major schemes will be procured using private finance contracts', including DBFO (DETR, 2000: 53), yet in practice few new DBFO deals for roads have been completed since 1997 and, whilst there has been talk of a tolled extension to one or two motorways, there are no firm plans for new tolled roads.

Road pricing

There are at present no explicit charges for the use of the road system, although the heavy duty on fuels could be regarded as a surrogate. Road pricing or road user charging is the charging of individuals for their use of roads at rates that vary by time of day and by place. Its constructive use could introduce a valuable new dimension to transport policy. It could achieve more efficient use of the existing transport infrastructures, help manage traffic growth and offer the right signals about when, where and to what extent it would be worthwhile investing in new capacity.

The successful implementation of the London congestion charging scheme of February 2003 (see Chapter 3) has stimulated the first serious investigation by senior UK politicians of the feasibility of introducing a national scheme (DfT, 2004h). The fact that the government has been willing to lead a new debate on the subject is, in itself, a remarkable development, made possible only by the success of the London scheme. Both Labour and Liberal Democrat *Manifestos* for the 2005 General Election contained long-term commitments towards this policy.

The principles behind road user charging

The economic principles underlying road user charging are essentially those underlying any Pigouvian tax intended to internalize such external effects as congestion, noise and accident risk. The theory was completely specified in Alan Walters' (1961) seminal article which illustrated it with an application to Manhattan Island.

An official UK committee under the chairmanship of Ruben Smeed (1964) thought road pricing both timely and technologically practicable. Colin Buchanan correctly and far-sightedly diagnosed the traffic growth problem in his influential *Traffic in Towns* (1963), but he did not embrace pricing as a possible solution. In passing he did mention 'a system of pricing the use of road space' as one of four options but then said no more about it. Since then several authors have articulated the case for road user charging (for example, Hibbs and Roth, 1992; Hibbs, 1993; Roth, 1995). There was an experimental electronic scheme in Hong Kong and a long-standing, paper-based scheme in Singapore (now converted to an electronic system). Small-scale bridge and individual highway tolling systems have worked without difficulty and several Scandinavian towns are operating charges for crossing a town boundary, often as a revenue-raising rather than as a congestion-reducing measure.

However, at the national level there are several obstacles to universal road user charging. The situation is set out in the *Road*

Pricing Feasibility Study (DfT, 2004h). First, the DfT has accepted that the methods likely to be feasible within the next few years would consist of equipment in fixed roadside locations that would interact with vehicles. Given the dense network of roads in the UK and the high proportion of motorized trips that are for short distances, the implication is that electronic charging would be sensible only on a minority of specialized roads. Glaister and Graham (2004) suggest the outline of a national scheme and discuss some of the issues that would have to be resolved. The White Paper, *The Future of Transport* (DfT, 2004), accepted the case, in principle, for road pricing. Douglas Alexander, in his first public speech as Transport Secretary, reiterated the government's willingness to fund technological development and pilot schemes by local authorities (*Financial Times*, 11 May 2006).

From 2002 the Treasury issued a series of 'discussion papers' and 'progress reports' on *Modernising the Taxation of the Road Haulage Industry – Lorry Road-user Charging* (April 2002, May 2003, January 2005, March 2005, see www.hm-treasury.gov.uk). In 2004 the government issued an invitation to tender to provide the equipment and systems to implement distance-based charging for lorries by 2007. This policy was a response to complaints from the UK road haulage industry about the high UK rates of duty on fuel and demands to equalize the competition with carriers who can buy cheaper fuel before they cross the English Channel or the Irish border. The government pledged that the new system would be revenue neutral: that is, the rates of charge would be adjusted so as to keep the total yield the same as it would have been if lorries had continued to pay the same fuel duties as other road users. However, as the practical complexities and the potential inconsistencies with national road user charging for all users became apparent, the Secretary of State for Transport abandoned the scheme in 2005.

For the generality of vehicles there may well be a case for considering a scheme that does not attempt to cover the whole country. The issue of initial investment and ongoing administration costs is crucial, as illustrated by the experience with the congestion charge scheme introduced in London where a substantial part of the gross revenue is consumed by the capital and operating costs of the scheme. Research for the *Road Pricing Feasibility Study* (DfT, 2004h) indicated that costs could be prohibitive. Consideration would have to be given to how best to deal with the monumental administrative tasks. Even in the relatively small London scheme, over 100,000 payments are made each day and more than 900,000

Penalty Charge Notices were issued in the first eight months of operation. Further, the capabilities of the vehicle registration system would have to be confirmed to be adequate.

The additional cost could be reduced by exploiting initiatives that are going to happen in any case. Car manufacturers are installing navigation facilities in new vehicles as a matter of routine, and important commercial opportunities will be created by time and position information: for instance, in matching insurance charges to risk exposure. If the EU's new Galileo system of satellites is operational by 2008 as planned, it will widen the options for charging based on geographical positioning systems. The technical appraisal and costing of the technologies and administration depend upon a clear specification of the content of the policy.

A careful analysis is needed of the incidence of the proposed policies on different groups. In particular, assessment will be needed to assess the familiar proposition that user charging would disadvantage the low-income motorist. The answer on this point will depend, in part, on the magnitude of the net revenues, and how and where they would be spent. If revenues were used to reduce fuel taxes and vehicle ownership taxes, there might be a benefit to the substantial number of lower-income private-car users to be found in rural areas who have no realistic public transport alternative. In urban areas the relationships between gainers, losers and income will depend crucially on where different income groups live in relation to the charging areas. This will vary from place to place (see Santos and Newbery, 2002, and other work by these authors). Similarly, there are issues concerning the likely impact on business and commerce, and the impact on freight service providers relative to that on private vehicles and buses. Linked to the question of incidence on particular groups is the thorny question of what discounts and concessions would be granted. The basic principle is that where road users are causing environmental damage and consuming valuable road space, they should pay for it. Any need to compensate particular groups for social or political reasons can and should be dealt with in ways other than by granting exemptions. Too many exemptions would fatally blunt the effectiveness of the policy.

It is clear that there will always be important considerations that must be dealt with in other ways. Some of the most important of these are aspects of land-use policy; current land-use policies may to some extent be a surrogate for proper road user charging. It would be useful to be able to make more definitive predictions than seems to be possible at the moment on the long-term impact that charging would have on the densities and economic vitality of cities.

Governments find it tempting to promise that a new system of road charges would be 'revenue neutral' as the proposed distance-based taxation for commercial vehicles seemed likely to be. However, a policy of revenue neutrality at the national level creates difficulties. Whilst it may be neutral for road users as whole it will not be neutral from the perspective of most individuals. Further, there would be no revenue available to pay for the costs of collection or for 'complementary measures' such as road or public transport improvements local to the charged areas, which would make it difficult to present the policy attractively to the general public. No doubt the Treasury would want any scheme to provide at least sufficient net revenue to pay for additional public transport costs. It might go further, and look for a contribution towards the present, spiralling costs of both buses and railways. Whatever policy is adopted on revenue neutrality at the national level it seems likely that road user charging will create pressure for an adjustment to the flows of cash caused by the present local government finance regime in order to mitigate the opposition from communities that would otherwise lose out.

Roads, arguably, constitute a utility like the electricity, gas and telecommunications networks. As those industries were privatized and economic regulation was developed, important questions were asked about the parts of the industry that formed a natural monopoly. Efforts were made to isolate the natural monopoly element for special treatment by a regulator. Similar issues apply with the road systems and road charging technology. Road users would want to know who would set the charges and by what objective criteria, who was accountable for the money collected and for decisions on how that money would be spent. In the case of the London scheme this issue was explicitly dealt with by making the new Mayor accountable and by making it a legal requirement that all charging revenues be spent on local transport. Similar charging powers were given to other UK local authorities under the Transport Act 2000. Some have shown interest, especially in the Local Transport Plans they are developing for 2006–10, but so far none has adopted them (except for a very small scheme to deal with a special problem in Durham). In any case, some of the nation's congestion problems occur on long-distance motorways and strategic roads that do not naturally fall within the jurisdiction of any local authority. These are some of the reasons for considering a national scheme of road user charging.

However, a new national scheme would require some kind of national body to be accountable. The concept of a new, independent body operating under clearly-defined rules and objectives could be attractive. The tried and tested concept of a public trust has much more to offer. It has a long and successful history in the ownership and administration of roads and other transport infrastructure in the UK and in North America. Inevitably this issue becomes entangled in the debate on the current powers, or lack of them, enjoyed by local authorities and the devolution debate. Transport problems are mainly local and are arguably best left to local authorities to deal with. Further, the potential scale of the administrative operation that might be implied by a national scheme is alarming, and it is yet to be established that there would be sufficient scale economies from operating a larger administrative scheme.

If national charging is to become a reality then central government will have to take a clear lead; it must decide and clearly state what the policy is to be, in terms of the governance arrangements, the level of charge, the nature of any concessions, how the revenues will be spent and the role of local administrations. Once these decisions are made then policy can be sensibly debated and the search for an affordable technology can begin.

Chapter 9

Conclusions

This book has explored the financial and economic constraints within which British transport policy is made (Chapters 7 and 8), as well as the planning systems at local and national level which allow both environmental and economic considerations to be assessed and given proper weight in the taking of decisions about particular schemes (Chapters 3 and 5). The networks of policy-makers at local, national and supranational levels of government have been identified in Chapters 2 to 4, and the influence of a wide range of interest groups has been discussed in Chapter 6. These structures, networks and institutional arrangements reflect the complexity of the pressures and influences which have to be reconciled in the formulation of transport policy. Having marked out the pitch, explained the rules of the game and provided notes on the players, it is now time to return to a review of the key issues and policy options which need to be addressed as transport policy, shaped by these players and limited by these constraints, moves into a third millennium in which more people and more goods will want to travel further and faster than ever before.

Two major changes

For two centuries transport policy in Britain developed largely as a pragmatic, evolutionary response to the need for government intervention to direct and facilitate supply, notably through the planning system, and to safeguard the public interest by regulating for safety and for the provision of services at a reasonable price. Over the years the latter has been achieved so far as possible by means of competition, or failing that by direct intervention to control market access or fares. Governments from the Left of the political spectrum might have been more inclined to favour intervention, whilst governments from the Right might have been more inclined to rely on market forces, but there was in practice much common ground in the provision of a framework of necessary infrastructure in the public sector (notably roads), whilst allowing transport operators as much freedom as possible to develop their services within such constraints as might be thought necessary in the public interest.

Since 1979 British transport policy has been particularly interesting on account of two major changes. The first is the privatization of the transport industries and the consequent redesign of their relations with government. The second is the emergence of environmental concerns as a major factor in transport policy and the attempt of the British government to devise and put into effect an environmentally sustainable transport policy.

Government relations with a privatized transport industry

Britain has experimented more extensively than any other country (except possibly the United States) with reliance on the private sector to deliver public services. There are particular reasons for this state of affairs, the most obvious being the ideological commitment of Conservative governments between 1979 and 1997 to rolling back the frontiers of the state. This policy paradigm applied with particular force to economic activities including transport, where it was felt that the skills and incentives of the private sector could be relied on to deliver better services at lower cost than management by government-directed bureaucracies. The underlying convictions may have waned somewhat by the time John Major succeeded Margaret Thatcher as Prime Minister in 1990, but the Major government continued to regard privatization as a winning formula, pressing ahead with an exceptionally radical privatization of British Rail, and promising the privatizations of both the National Air Traffic Services and the London Underground, which were to be taken up by Labour governments after 1997.

The second reason for such an exceptionally thoroughgoing commitment to the private sector is more specific to the British system of government. The widely attested power of the Treasury within the British government, which reaches back to Gladstone's Treasury (Heclo and Wildavsky, 1981), has its roots in the firm control of all government expenditure. Transport rarely has the political clout to extract from the Treasury the public resources which are needed to finance major infrastructure projects in the public sector. Consequently, transport ministers, even if they might have doubts about the capacity of the private sector to deliver a better transport service, are driven towards solutions relying on the private sector in the expectation that they will at least deliver the investment they know they will never extract from the Treasury in the face of more urgent or more attractive bids for hospitals, schools and prisons, not to mention aircraft carriers and missile systems. Release from Treasury control is complete only if the industry needs no further financial support from government but, even where this is not the case, a legally binding contract that may have a life of up to 30 years appears to offer more certainty and continuity than the biennial round of public expenditure negotiations with the Treasury.

Whatever the reasons, the delivery of transport policy in Britain now relies more heavily on the private sector than is the case in any other European country. In many instances the results have been very encouraging, and the relationship between government and the transport industries has been established on a much more businesslike foundation (Chapter 2). However, Chapter 7 draws attention to serious problems which have been encountered already, or are building up, notably in the debt burden of Network Rail and in the contracts between Transport for London and the two companies responsible for maintenance and renewal of London Underground's infrastructure. The competitive pressures which operate within the private sector may be a powerful ally in the delivery of value for money, as has been demonstrated in the bus industry and in the vigour of the competition for bus and rail franchises; yet the efficacy of competition is much diminished if no competitor is able and willing to take over when a franchisee fails to deliver its contractual obligations. The government, or its agent as the procurer of services under contract, does not really have the option of terminating the contract, since such a course of action would precipitate a period of chaotic disruption which few ministers would be prepared to risk (for the very good reason that they would be blamed by the public). Putting Railtrack into administration avoided this trap, but even this procedure led to an extended period of management hiatus. During this time the company in administration built up debts which may yet cripple its successor, or force the government to bail it out, as it was earlier forced to bail out a number of train operating companies which similarly failed to meet their financial obligations (Chapter 7).

By contrast, it should be remembered that the privatizations of British Airways, ports and airports, coach and bus services have all been very largely successful. Even on the railways there is much to celebrate, notably in the renewal of rolling stock at no direct cost to the government's balance sheet, in a more innovative approach to service provision, and above all in the reversal of 40 years of declining patronage. Any government thinking about making more use of the private sector in the provision of public transport services would have much to learn from studying the successes as well as the failures of British transport policy over the past 25 years.

Reconciling policies for transport and the environment

Included within Chapter 1 was an account of the public debate about transport and the environment which followed publication of the White Paper, *Roads for Prosperity* (DoT, 1989), and continued through the remaining years of Conservative governments, culminating in what Brian Mawhinney called a national transport policy debate. It culminated in *Transport: The Way Forward* (DoT, 1996), a disappointingly inconclusive Green Paper, but the Labour government which took office in 1997 brought transport and the environment together in a single department, and set out with the declared intention of getting people to make more use of public transport and less use of their cars. A year later, the White Paper *A New Deal for Transport* (DETR, 1998) advocated a sustainable and integrated transport policy, which disparaged the building of more roads, and called for new powers to impose congestion charging in cities, to tax workplace parking and to introduce road charging.

However, by the time these powers finally reached the statute book in the autumn of 2000, the DETR and its policies were already in terminal disarray (Chapter 1). By 2002 the department itself had been dismembered, and the direction of transport policy, unfettered by other considerations, transferred to a Secretary of State who was content to respond to pressures from the business community and public opinion for the construction of more roads and a massive expansion of airport capacity. Road charging was still on the agenda, but not before 2014, and its early application to heavy goods vehicles had been withdrawn. This had been seen as the environmentally sustainable part of a package of measures responding to the fuel price protests of 2000, but in the event there was no environmental quid pro quo for the concessions which were made in the form of substantial reductions to the licence fees for heavy goods vehicles, and the abandonment of automatic higher-than-inflation increases in fuel duty. The legacy of the DETR lingers on in the environmental considerations built into NATA, the New Approach to Appraisal (Chapter 8), but ministers do not have to follow the environmental rankings when they select road projects for implementation. Those schemes which have attracted a lot of attention on environmental grounds (for example, the A303 at Stonehenge) may well be treated sensitively, but others may slip through the net. The scale of the roads programme has been restored, and the real-terms cost of motoring has continued to decline, making it unlikely that transport emissions will fall, as they would have needed to do in order to meet the national targets (more stringent than the formal international obligations), which the Labour government had set for Britain. In short it is difficult to avoid the conclusion that, despite fine words – for example, in the Prime Minister's Foreword to the White Paper *The Future of Transport* (DfT, 2004) – the pursuit of an environmentally sustainable transport policy has slipped quite a long way down the Transport Department's list of priorities. In any case, the 'balanced approach' to which the Prime Minister referred leaves the government with ample discretion to strike the balance between economic and environmental considerations wherever political considerations dictate.

Some theoretical reflections

Observation of the forces that have shaped transport policy, particularly since 1979, prompts some theoretical reflections which may also be relevant to the likely future course of policy. Why did a Labour government which, in opposition, had resisted the privatization of British Rail, work so hard in government to find imaginative new ways to make the privatized railway work in the public interest, rather than seeking to reverse the policy? Why did it proceed with the privatizations of air traffic services and the London Underground that it had likewise resisted in opposition? What lies behind the rise and fall of a sustainable integrated transport policy? We have noted the immediate causes and particular events which triggered policy change, but are these a sufficient explanation or do they point to powerful underlying forces which drive policy inexorably in certain directions, in much the same way as earthquakes are symptomatic of the movement of tectonic plates deep below the surface?

There have been many attempts to explain the complex processes by which policy is made. John Kingdon (1984) constructed a useful model in which three independent streams of problems, policies and politics come together in windows of policy-making opportunity. Stevens (2004) adapts this framework to a more European (and British) policy-making environment by proposing a four-dimensional model in which policy preferences are shaped within the practical environment, the organizational environment and the political environment, evolving independently within each of these three dimensions over time, which is seen as the fourth dimension. If policy is pulled in different directions within each distinct environment, the ensuing debate may not reach a sufficient consensus for policy to be changed, or it may be adjusted only marginally, but from time to time, when conditions are more favourable, there may open – in Kingdon's term – a window of opportunity, and policy will change direction much more significantly.

Applying this model to transport policy, we find that the first dimension of policy-making, the practical dimension, tends to favour the use of the best available technology to get people about as safely, quickly and conveniently as possible at the lowest possible cost. Other things being equal, a new mode of travel that offers a better combination of speed, comfort and convenience than the existing service will drive its predecessor out of business. The horse and cart, or the canal barge, could not compete against the railway, just as the railway could not compete against the lorry or the car. But safety and cost also enter into the equation. Concorde, the Anglo–French supersonic airliner, is a good example of a wonderfully fast and convenient way of crossing the Atlantic which could never command more than a tiny share of the market because the cost was so high. After an aircraft crashed shortly after take-off from Paris in July 2000, extensive safety modifications were undertaken and flights were eventually resumed, but the market never recovered from the damage to Concorde's safety record; flights were suspended in October 2003.

The trade-offs between speed of travel, cost, safety and convenience are complex, and every passenger or logistics manager strikes his or her own balance in the light of circumstances and priorities. This multiplicity of practical considerations explains the survival of extensive inter-modal competition (for example, between London and Glasgow, where there is a choice of air, rail and road services) offering very different standards of service at a wide range of different prices. On the other hand, air transport has driven oceanic passenger services almost completely out of all but the holiday cruise market, just as the car and the lorry have led to the closure of thousands of miles of rural railway lines. The practical dimension of transport policy-making can accommodate a wide range of competing services, but those which fail the unforgiving tests of safety, cost and convenience must eventually give way to those which perform better. The inexorable pressures which operate within the practical dimension can be resisted to some extent by transport operators or governments who may be prepared to subsidize advanced technology (such as high-speed trains in France) or uneconomic services (which includes most rural railway lines), but the cost may be very high. In Britain the acceptable balance between cost and technology, and between public subsidy and public service, tends to be struck at a lower level of technology and public service than is the case in some other European countries; but this result is arguably the consequence of powerful pressures in the political and organizational dimensions of British policy-making where engineers are less highly regarded, and economy in the use of public resources (some would say parsimony) carries more weight than it does elsewhere.

The second dimension of policy-making is institutional or organizational. The institutions of the European Union, the Department for Transport, the Treasury, local authorities, transport providers, unions and pressure groups all have an institutional bias in favour of policies which perpetuate (and, where possible, enhance) their own role. When a plane crashes into a mountainside, and questions are asked about the safety record of the airline concerned, the European Commission seizes the opportunity to advance its proposal for the establishment of an EU blacklist which would ban such airlines from all European airspace, rather than leaving that decision to the discretion of each member state. When railways policy became controversial, the Department for Transport advises ministers to bring the policy-setting functions of the Strategic Rail Authority back into the department. When the Treasury moves from annual expenditure settlements to biennial spending rounds, it compensates for any loss of short-term control by the establishment of Public Service Agreements. To the extent that spending decisions are devolved to local authorities, they are constrained by requirements for the approval by central government of Regional Spatial Strategies and Local Transport Plans. Within a liberal democracy, even the independent pressure groups whose activities were described in Chapter 6 have a legitimate and often an official role to play within networks and policy communities, which enhances their capacity to exercise influence. All these institutions make their distinctive contribution to the policy debate, bringing expertise to bear from their own perspectives.

The third dimension of policy-making is political. The power of ministers within the British system of government is very great, since the executive branch of government normally controls the legislative branch. Since 1979 political direction has been responsible for the privatization of all the transport industries, the application to transport of the Private Finance Initiative and its Labour successor, the Public–Private Partnership, the adaptation of policies to concerns for the environment, and the attempt to devise and implement an integrated transport policy. However, the political dimension is also the most fickle, not least because politicians may be swayed by the changing priorities of a fickle electorate. Even without a change of government, we have seen since 2000 an unobtrusive but unmistakable retreat from an environmentally sustainable transport policy, which was perceived as 'anti-car', and consequently as a political liability (Chapter 1).

The fourth dimension of policy-making is critical to the other three. The political dimension is immensely powerful in the short term. A new government can cancel road projects instantly and switch the emphasis of policy-making to public transport, as the Labour government did in 1997. But political fashions can change, and the same prime minister who brought environment and transport together in one department in 1997 can as easily separate them in 2001. The time-horizon for political decision-making tends to be relatively short, rarely extending beyond the next election. Even when the consequences extend further into the future, today's announcement of a ten-year plan is much more important politically than tomorrow's patient implementation. As a result it is not uncommon, when the political priorities change, for the implementation of one set of plans to be overtaken and quietly set aside by the announcement of another, as *The Future of Transport* (DfT, 2004) succeeded *Transport 2010* (DETR, 2000). Institutions generally have a longer shelf-life than politicians (DETR was an exception as a particular configuration, but its constituent divisions lived on), and if they are part of the policy-making process, or well connected to it, they have the capacity to shape policy in the medium term in the direction of their own agenda. Highway engineers, civil servants and specialized interest groups almost always have projects and proposals that they can bring out of their filing cabinets when ministers need to respond to a particular challenge or opportunity. And finally, the practical dimension is immensely powerful in the longer term. Transport is a severely practical business, moving people and goods safely, conveniently and cheaply from one place to another, and in the end the technologies and institutional arrangements which best serve those practical ends have a habit of imposing themselves on the agenda.

Theory and practice

Observing the application of this model to the privatization of the transport industries since 1979, and the attempt to establish an environmentally sustainable transport policy since 1997, may help us to identify some considerations of relevance to the future direction of transport policy, and in particular to the proposed introduction of road charging from 2014.

The most powerful impetus behind the privatization of the transport industries was political. Privatization was central to the programme of an administration that believed in the virtues of small government, and was more inclined to trust the competitive pressures of the marketplace than the best intentions of civil servants to impose the disciplines that deliver value for money. In addition it was hoped that the sale of shares would shift the political balance towards Conservative values by broadening the base of share ownership. The climate of opinion within the organizational dimension of policy-making was also, on balance, favourable. Within the Department for Transport, ministers and civil servants would have to relinquish a measure of direct control, notably over the appointment of the Chairs and Board members of the nationalized transport industries; but the process of privatization provided an opportunity to review the framework of regulation in the public interest. In any case the Treasury was strongly in favour of a process which promised both short-term gains in the form of privatization receipts, and long-term gains in the form of reduced subsidies. Moreover, in the practical dimension of policy-making, past experience with the relaxation of controls over the road haulage industry in the 1960s had set a favourable precedent, and in the new wave of privatizations success soon followed success as long-distance coach services, the National Freight Corporation, local bus services, British Airways and the British Airports Authority were all privatized in the course of the 1980s (see Chapter 1), followed by British Rail between 1993 and 1996.

If this was a window of opportunity in Kingdon's terms, it was an exceptionally long one. It is easier to regard it as an extended period of time when conditions in all three dimensions of policy-making were favourable to such a transformation. The election of a Labour government in 1997, which had been opposed to privatization in opposition, began to shift the balance, but the institutional pressures emanating from the Treasury, reinforced by the Labour government's political commitment in its first two years to the public expenditure targets of the outgoing Conservative government, were sufficient to carry the process through to the part-privatization of National Air Traffic Services, and the negotiation of Public–Private Partnership contracts for the maintenance and renewal of London Underground's infrastructure.

It was only when a series of railway accidents between 1999 and 2001 raised doubts about the safety of a fragmented and privatized railway, and when subsidy costs began to rise instead of fall, that conditions within the practical and political dimensions of policy-making began to change; but by then the process of privatization was complete. Although there were growing doubts about certain aspects of rail privatization in particular, there was little appetite in any of the policy-making dimensions for anything more than significant (but essentially marginal) incremental adjustments to the existing policy to ameliorate its deficiencies. The government dealt with these pressures by simplifying what was seen as an over-complicated structure of train operating companies, and restructuring the private operation of railway infrastructure under clearer, more direct strategic supervision. These adjustments responded to the pressures in all three dimensions which became intense in the wake of the Hatfield crash in October 2000. There are indications that adjustments of a similar magnitude may be needed in due course in the contractual arrangements for the maintenance and renewal of the London Underground, but there is no sign at this stage of any development which would lead to a reversal of the overall policy for the supervision of the transport industries within the private sector.

The second major policy development of the past 20 years has been the impact on transport policy of growing concerns for the environment. The long-standing concern for the protection of the countryside as well as the built environment had been growing for many years, but the focus was on individual projects (usually roads or airports); in all but the most extreme cases there was usually at least as much support for the new infrastructure from national (and even local) business and industry as there was opposition from organizations committed to environmental protection, acting in support of those people most directly affected. What added significant weight to environmental policy considerations in the 1990s was the growing awareness of the contribution of transport in general and cars in particular to the greenhouse gas emissions which are believed to be responsible for climate change. The government estimates that transport produces about 25 per cent of all UK emissions of carbon dioxide, of which 80 per cent comes from road transport (DfT, 2004: 23), because far more people rely on their cars for most of their journeys than on any other form of transport. Commitments to reduce carbon dioxide emissions are therefore meaningless unless they impact on the motorist. In the past motorists had been prepared to pay an environmental premium to remove lead from exhaust emissions, but it became apparent in the summer of 2000 that they would resist paying ever-higher prices for fuel (increased taxation on top of rapidly-rising world market prices) if the object of government policy was to cut emissions of carbon dioxide by pricing them off the road, at least for their more marginal journeys. The protest movement was led by farmers and truck drivers whose livelihood was most directly affected by increased fuel costs, but it received support from a much wider public, resentful of a tax which hit them in the pocket with enough impact to be perceived as posing a threat to an important aspect of their way of life.

When rising fuel prices coincided with widespread cancellations and delays to railway services, as a result of the imposition of thousands of speed restrictions necessitated by the need to check for cracked rails following the Hatfield derailment, John Prescott's policy of getting people out of their cars and on to public transport was seen to be failing both as a political project, and in practical terms. Even if rising fuel prices could be used to discourage car travel – and there were clearly limits to the political acceptability of that – a key part of the public transport system could not offer a reliable alternative. A transport policy whose strategies relied so heavily on public transport (moving investment from roads to buses and trams as well as to trains) was never very realistic, simply because even very large percentage increases in public transport journeys have only a small effect on the volume of road transport; it took the events of 2000 to make that plain. The realities of the practical dimension of policy-making had made themselves felt, the political dimension had turned against an aggressively environmental policy stance, and the organizational dimension – which had been neutralized while the two other dimensions favoured environmental transport policies – was ready to reassert its traditional support for a substantial roads programme.

Implications for future policy development

If the old politics of 'predict and provide' seems to have gained the upper hand over the new politics of sustainable development since the autumn of 2000, with fuel tax concessions, the restoration of a substantial roads programme and provision for an enormous increase in air travel, the balance within the four-dimensional model of policy-making is finely poised and could shift again, particularly if unforeseeable events were to push the politics of sustainable development back up the agenda. The implications for policy development may be seen first in the evolution of policy towards the privatization of road construction and maintenance, and then more speculatively in the prospects for road charging.

On the basis of a detailed study of the DBFO project to modernize the trunk road between Swindon and Gloucester, Geoffrey Dudley (2004) observes a clash between the political idea of privatization, which led to the seemingly successful contracting-out to the private sector of the reconstruction and subsequent maintenance of the road in return for shadow tolls, and the alternative political idea of sustainable development, which during the 1990s 'had the effect of transforming road building as a policy idea from the principal policy "solution" to a first class policy "problem"'. The construction of the new road was in its own terms a success, completed within budget and nine months ahead of schedule. It included environmental features such as badger runs and an archaeological investigation. But when the road opened, the concrete surface which had been applied to part of it was much noisier than the tarmac alternative, provoking howls of protest from local residents, including Michael Meacher, who as Environment Minister was part of the ministerial team at DETR. In the end the road construction consortium had to pay out £2 million in compensation payments, and DBFO policy suffered a considerable setback while implementation of the policy was reviewed, leading to proposals for the earlier involvement of local community and other environmental stakeholders in the process (Dudley, 2004: 405). Dudley argues that the sustainable transport idea was better at self-propagation than the privatization idea because sustainable development could appeal to a wide public, whereas the virtues of the privatization process could be fully appreciated only within the small and specialized road construction community. This application of the 'enlightenment function' is consistent with our view that the political dimension of policy-making can be very powerful. In this case, the politics of environmental objection led not merely to a substantial compensation payment but to a considerable retreat in private-sector road building. However, the power of the political dimension in policy-making is short term. DBFO survived with some modifications, and three years after the completion of the Swindon–Gloucester road it was still the intention of the Department of Environment and Transport to use DBFO for about 25 per cent of road construction (DETR, 2000c: 53).

Since then, the political fortunes of an environmentally sustainable transport policy have waned, whilst the need to build more roads, and to stretch public expenditure limits by building some of them in the private sector, has re-emerged as an important policy objective. Britain's first modern toll road, relieving pressure on the M6 motorway through Birmingham, opened in December 2003, and proposals were soon made for its northwards extension as an alternative to widening the existing untolled motorway. Certainly the privatization of road construction has encountered some resistance, as Dudley shows, but the signs are that it will continue to make progress, whether by tolls or shadow tolls. Pressures within the practical dimension of policy-making will grow as traffic continues to increase; pressures within the political dimension seem more likely to favour congestion relief than the virtues of sustainable development, at least in the short term; and pressures within the organizational dimension, notably from the Treasury (backed up by its ability to constrain public expenditure), will probably outweigh any reluctance there may be in the DfT and the Highways Agency to relinquish their direct control over the process.

Road charging is a policy idea which has been around for at least 40 years. In that time its elegance as an economically attractive approach to the rationing of a scarce resource (limited road space) has gained substantial support from key organizations within the policy-making community, including the DfT and the Treasury. If it could be made to work, it could have significant attractions in the practical dimension of policy-making (see Chapter 8). It could be used to tackle congestion by encouraging people to travel at less congested times, discouraging marginal journeys altogether, and speeding up those that remain essential, whilst reducing the need for massive, costly and controversial road construction programmes. The relative success and acceptability of the congestion charging scheme for central London has shown that there can be a point where the benefits of congestion relief are sufficient to outweigh the imposition of a new charge. But if a road charging programme had to raise enough money to take the place of other motoring taxes, as well as pay for its own administration and for the public transport improvements needed before people had any real choice of journey modes, charges would have to be set at a level that could spell political suicide for the government that introduced it. That is why ministers are happy to talk enthusiastically about it as a future option, but remain very cautious indeed about any commitment to early implementation (Darling, 2005). It may be necessary to think in terms of the lowest rate of charging that would deliver worthwhile benefits, and in terms of a pilot scheme or schemes that could test both the technology and its effect on travel patterns, before embarking on anything more ambitious.

In the terms of our model, there is already support in the organizational dimension of policy-making, and advances in computer technology are bringing nearer the day when a scheme could be devised which would work in the practical dimension. Our model suggests that it will be important to keep the idea in the public mind, with a focus on the benefits outweighing the costs, and to commit serious resources to working up the details of a scheme which could be implemented successfully, so that if and when the political opportunity arises – for example, as a result of further shocks related to climate change, or when rush-hour road congestion becomes intolerable – the moment can be seized to act decisively while conditions are favourable in all three dimensions.

The key issues

Rising demand

There are those who, seizing enthusiastically on SACTRA's acknowledgement that new roads can generate additional traffic, would like to believe that the problem of rising demand could be solved by consigning all the bulldozers to the scrapyard. However, most commentators accept that rising demand cannot be so airily dismissed. Forecasts have varied since 1989 when the national road traffic forecasts, pointing to an increase of between 87 per cent and 142 per cent by 2025, prompted a serious debate about policies which might reduce such increases. *The Future of Transport* (DfT, 2004: 44) suggested that traffic would increase by only 40 per cent between 2000 and 2025, but still described such an increase as unacceptable. Whether we like it or not, it will be extremely difficult to suppress. The link between economic growth and transport demand is strong and well attested, and there are several other social and economic factors which will continue to drive up traffic levels. As the economy continues to expand, and people have more disposable income, they tend to spend more on travel. As the size of households falls and the number of households increases, people have to travel more to maintain their relationships. People are living longer, and the proportion of older people with a driving licence (especially women) will continue to rise. The opening-up of the British economy to European and global competition has contributed to increased demand for the transport of both goods and services.

Another factor which influences transport demand is the trend towards larger schools and hospitals as well as shops. Larger units are often able to deliver a higher standard of service at an accept-able cost or a competitive price, but a smaller number of larger units serving larger catchment areas must mean that on average both staff and customers have to travel further. There are limits to effi-ciencies of scale, but it is not clear that these have yet been reached in all cases: for example, in the optimum distribution of hospital services, where the rising cost of new specialist technologies makes it expensive and inefficient to provide them at more than a few of the largest hospitals.

There are powerful economic forces at work here, associated with changing lifestyles (Houghton Report, 1994: 16–18), and much as people might like to see a levelling-off in the rate of growth of demand for transport, it is not realistic to plan on the basis that such growth will cease. Even if demand for travel grows no faster than the increase in GDP, there will be important consequences for transport policy. In particular it is no good placing too much reliance on cutting the road-building programme. This strategy was tried after 1997, and was reversed within a few years. In the absence of other policy changes, cutting the roads programme means more congestion and more pollution as stop-start conditions become ever more widespread. What is needed is a clearer focus on the other steps which could be taken to reduce both congestion and pollution on the assumption that transport demand will continue to increase at least in line with growth in GDP.

Safety

Safety is the first of two factors which are likely to make it more expensive to devise an acceptable transport policy for conditions of growing demand and congestion. Public transport operators are expected to make the provision of a safe service their first priority. The government is also expected to give the highest priority to safety in any aspect of transport policy for which it is responsible. Changing technologies, increasing speeds and increasing congestion all carry risks. Many of these are successfully anticipated at the design stage, but centuries of experience suggest that accidents will continue to occur and that many advances in transport safety will flow from their rigorous and impartial investigation and the application by regulators and operators alike of the lessons drawn from them. No one disputes the need to take steps to prevent the recurrence of avoidable accidents, but almost invariably the recommendations which flow from accident inquiries lead to increases in the capital or ongoing costs of transport provision.

Although people are prepared to take calculated risks with their own lives (for example, in crossing the street or in driving too fast on a foggy motorway), they like to regard safety as an absolute requirement when they travel by public transport. But absolute safety is unattainable and the quest for it is unrealistically expensive. For instance, the most sophisticated form of automatic train protection (ATP) could reduce the risk of collisions, but installing it across the whole railway network would imply expenditure in the region of £10 million for every life which might be saved (Evans, 1996), expenditure which would displace or at least delay other projects which could make a more cost-effective contribution to passenger safety. As a result, and following a study of the costs and benefits of different train protection systems, the government decided to accept the lower standard of protection provided by the Train Protection and Warning System, which could be introduced much more quickly and at much lower cost (DETR, 2000: 76). The European Rail Traffic Management System (ERTMS), a higher standard broadly equivalent to ATP, but agreed within the EU, is being applied to all newly-built high speed lines, and will be applied by about 2015 to lines used by trains travelling at more than 100 mph. In future the terms of reference for public inquiries following major transport accidents are likely to be required to take into account the costs as well as the benefits of any new safety measures which may be recommended. There will no doubt be strong pressure to take whatever steps are necessary to prevent the recurrence of accidents on public transport, even if the cost is high, but this proviso should enable a more rational debate to take place.

Environment

The second factor pushing up transport costs is a growing concern for the environment. The impact of transport on the environment takes many forms, and may well have to be countered in a variety of ways. For example, transport contributes significantly to the increasing concentrations in the atmosphere of carbon dioxide which, with other greenhouse gases, is held responsible for global warming. The Prime Minister's foreword to the White Paper, *UK Government Sustainable Development Strategy* (DEFRA, 2005), refers to 'an almost universal consensus that climate change is happening and is the result of human activity'. Under the Kyoto Protocol, the UK is committed to reducing its greenhouse gas emissions by 12.5 per cent from 1990 levels by 2008–12. The government set its own target of a 20 per cent reduction in carbon dioxide emissions by 2010, 'and to putting the UK on a path to reduce total carbon dioxide emissions by some 60 per cent by 2050, with real progress by 2020' (DfT, 2004: 107). However, emissions from road transport are expected to continue growing up to 2010, and reductions thereafter depend on a combination of slower traffic growth and continued fuel efficiency improvements. The continuing and rapid growth of air travel will also add significantly to greenhouse gas emissions, whilst action to reduce such emissions (or example, by including them in an emissions trading scheme) may be delayed by the need to reach agreement on the measures required, within at least the EU, and possibly ICAO. The chapter on protecting the environment in DfT's 2004 White Paper concluded that 'more needs to be done to reduce and mitigate the environmental impact of travel and we will continue to look for new solutions and actions that deliver improvements' (2004: 118).

Carbon dioxide is only one of many transport-related pollutants. Some others have much more immediate effects on the local environment. In 1992 transport (mainly road transport) accounted for 90 per cent of UK carbon monoxide pollution, 57 per cent of nitrogen oxides, 48 per cent of particulates and 38 per cent of volatile organic compounds (Houghton Report, 1994: 21–6). However, since the mid-1990s, emissions of the worst of these pollutants have fallen by 50 per cent as a result of EU Regulations imposing ever-stricter conditions on exhaust emissions from new car models, and this trend is likely to continue (DfT, 2004: 24). Similar considerations apply to much noise pollution both from road vehicles and from aircraft. Pitching the regulatory requirements at the right level is difficult and controversial, and agreement has to be reached within the European Union at least, if British manufacturers and users are not to be placed at a serious competitive disadvantage, but the environmental benefits of less noisy vehicles, lower fuel consumption and less noxious emissions could well justify the initial cost associated with such regulations.

Another major concern is the protection of the urban and rural environment, which is the continuing task of the planning system at both local and national levels (Chapters 3 and 5). It may initially be much easier and cheaper to allow development to take place on greenfield sites, relying on most people to get there by car but, if traffic growth is to be discouraged, it will become increasingly important to site schools, hospitals, leisure centres, shops and offices where a high proportion of staff and customers can use public transport. Judgments will have to continue to be made case by case, but where roads, railways or airports must be built or extended, it seems likely that the conflict between economic necessity and environmental concerns will often have to be resolved by accepting higher costs in the public sector, or by imposing them on the private sector: for example, by requiring more tunnelling, or by making more stringent rules about the need to ensure adequate access by public transport.

The policy options

Technology

Given these inexorable pressures to provide more transport whilst raising safety standards and protecting the environment, the first priority must be to make the best possible use of existing transport infrastructure. On all forms of transport the ingenuity of engineers and computer experts has been widely used to optimize the capacity of the network and to enhance safety, and it is to be expected that further advances in technology will continue to make a helpful contribution. Simple concepts such as longer trains and platforms, as well as more advanced systems such as state-of-the-art signalling, can increase the frequency and capacity of trains on congested commuter networks. The humble traffic light increases the volume of traffic which can negotiate junctions safely, while reserved lanes and transponders on buses can enable public transport to be given priority. Integrated systems can link traffic lights to respond to changing traffic conditions and optimize traffic flows over a large urban area. Similar systems can be used on the motorway network to detect the build-up of congestion and, through variable-message signs, slow traffic down or direct it onto alternative routes. In-car computers linked to networks of roadway sensors can already select the most efficient route according to actual traffic conditions, and their use is spreading as system coverage becomes more complete. Engines that are more efficient and catalytic converters to reduce harmful emissions do not increase the capacity of the network, but they do hold out the prospect of accommodating a significant increase in traffic without making air pollution any worse.

All these measures are worthwhile. Many of them succeed in increasing capacity and improving safety without further damage to the environment but, with the possible exception of the scope for technology to further reduce air pollution, they can make only a small impression on the scale of the problem.

Public transport

When the Deputy Prime Minister, John Prescott, launched his 'integrated transport' review, he vowed that within five years more people would be using public transport and driving their cars less and invited the public to judge him against that commitment (*Independent*, 6 June 1997). Major investments in public transport followed in the context of the 'Integrated Transport' White Paper (DETR, 1998) and the '10 Year Plan' (DETR, 2000). The numbers of people using rail and bus services increased to record levels (Chapter 7) but, since public transport accounts for only 15 per cent of passenger miles travelled, any directly-related reduction in car journeys was more than offset by the increases associated with a growing population and rising incomes. Even the highly-successful Manchester Metrolink caused a reduction of only 4–6 per cent in the number of vehicles entering the city centre on the major routes it served during the morning peak. Some people are driving their cars less, as John Prescott promised, but traffic on the roads has continued to increase. Improvements in public transport make a useful contribution to a sustainable transport policy, but they can have only a very limited effect on road traffic.

Control by regulation or charging

If the 'carrot' of improved public transport is not enough on its own to get people out of their cars, it is hard to resist the conclusion that the 'stick' of more coercive measures may be needed as well, designed either to raise the cost of motoring or to impose restrictions on car use. There is a long and successful history of regulatory controls improving safety in all modes of transport. We all benefit from safer cars and railway carriages, safer road design, traffic lights and railway signals. The most successful regulations are those which are self-enforcing, as is the case with most road engineering, or enforced through the licensing of vehicles and drivers or through controls over manufacturing. New vehicles have to meet the latest regulatory standards; older vehicles have to pass certain basic safety tests in order to be licensed, and such regulations (in Britain at least) are hard to evade. Some European cities have experimented with systems which exclude half the cars every day, but this tends to favour those who can afford two cars, or at least two registration plates. France bans lorries on Sundays; in Britain lorries are banned from some areas during the night. Regulations which depend for their effectiveness on the will and the resources available to the enforcement authorities, and critically on whether there is public support for their enforcement, are less certain to succeed. For example, regulations designed to keep bus lanes clear depend on rigorous enforcement by police and traffic wardens.

The difficulty of enforcing speed limits in particular, and the ambivalence of the public about their enforcement, has provoked considerable controversy. Speed humps and chicanes are an effective way of forcing drivers to slow down in residential areas, but drivers do not necessarily accept that they need to be slowed down at all times of the day, and local residents may also complain about increased noise or cracks to walls and pipes, if a minority of motorists hit the humps too hard or accelerate noisily away from them. The use of cameras to enforce speed limits, as well as traffic lights and bus lanes, is also controversial. There are those who are reluctant to accept that the limits should be rigorously enforced when it might be safe for a careful driver with quick reactions to drive faster. The fines imposed in such circumstances may even be regarded as an unjust and disproportionate tax, and ministers, who are aware that the safety benefits of speed cameras come mainly from drivers slowing down when they see one, have been willing to agree that they should be clearly identified, even if this means that a minority of motorists can get away with slowing down only when passing a camera.

Charging is arguably the more appropriate form of regulation for rationing a scarce resource, such as parking in the high street.

Parking meters, traffic wardens and wheel clamps were all unpopular when first introduced, but the evidence suggests that such measures are effective and in practice widely (if unenthusiastically) accepted as necessary. The Transport Act 2000 made provision for charges to be levied on vehicles entering a congestion zone, and on privately-owned parking spaces at businesses within restricted parking zones; the £5 London congestion charge, introduced in 2003, both reduced congestion and improved the flow of traffic within the zone. Traffic fell by about 15 per cent, delays caused by congestion were reduced by 30 per cent, and bus delays were halved (Chapter 3). The charge was raised to £8 in 2005, and plans have been announced for the zone to be extended to further areas of central London. Yet Durham (which introduced a very small scheme in the city centre) is so far the only other town to have introduced a congestion charge. There have been no experiments with charging for privately-owned parking spaces. However, the government has established a substantial Transport Innovation Fund (DfT, 2004: 134), which is being used to encourage local authorities, through their Local Transport Plans, to introduce innovative measures, including road charging, designed to encourage modal shift (Chapter 3).

In the case of company cars, the taxation system used to be perverse from an environmental policy perspective in the sense that it encouraged car use, but such incentives have been substantially reduced in recent budgets. On the other hand, the attempt to use increases in fuel taxation to reduce consumption and thereby to cut greenhouse gas emissions has been abandoned in the face of popular resistance. The Royal Commission on Environmental Pollution (Houghton Report, 1994: 114) recommended that fuel taxes should be used to double the price of fuel relative to other goods over the decade to 2005, and for some years fuel taxes were increased by as much as 6 per cent more than inflation. However, the tax increases were abandoned in the face of the fuel tax protests of September 2000, and this fiscal change, together with reductions in the prices of new and used cars, has meant that the real cost of motoring – which rose gently during the 1990s – has fallen since 2000, and is now less than it was in 1985 (Chapter 8). It would seem that whilst a fundamentally law-abiding public is reasonably tolerant of both charges and regulations, there are limits beyond which it cannot easily be pushed.

A key role in regulation is played by decisions not about transport itself, but about land use. Developers may have to be refused

permission to build facilities which generate large amounts of traffic at locations which cannot be well served by public transport,
and such restrictions may have to apply to the siting of new schools
and hospitals as well as shops and offices. But many of these decisions have to be taken at local level. Acquiring an adequate site
convenient to public transport may be much more expensive than
approving a planning application for a spacious greenfield site on
the edge of town that most people will have to reach by car. Where
private-sector development is concerned, acute financial pressures
may lead a council to make concessions to developers in exchange
for contributions to much-needed community projects. It is tempting to approve the construction of an attractive and lucrative out-
of-town shopping complex on the derelict industrial site beside the
ring road if much of the business will be attracted away from neighbouring town centres which are not your responsibility, and the
developer is offering to contribute to the cost of the leisure centre
you cannot otherwise afford. A hard-pressed council is even more
likely to grant permission if it has reason to believe that development will be allowed by another council nearby, or by the Secretary
of State on appeal.

How far governments are prepared to go in imposing regulations
is a politically controversial matter. Traditionally governments of
the Left have been more willing to impose regulations than Right-
wing governments. For example, it was a Labour government
which in 1968 made the fitting of seat-belts compulsory and introduced breath tests for alcohol. The main alternative to administrative regulation is regulation by price and market forces. This
approach is usually associated with Right-wing governments,
which like to emphasize the benefits of competition in the provision
of public services and maximum freedom of choice for the
customer. These considerations tend to favour methods of control
which rely on pricing signals, such as parking charges or tolling and
road charging, which may be at least as effective as administrative
regulation, but a less comfortable instrument of policy for a government which wants its transport policy to reduce social exclusion.
Regulation by price restricts peoples' choice of transport and travel
to what they can afford.

In practice, once the public has got used to being regulated, Right-
wing governments seldom rush to remove those regulations that are
seen to serve a useful function; and similarly once people have got
used to paying, Left-wing governments can seldom afford to abolish
the charges. Indeed, given tight constraints on public expenditure

and the reluctance of any government to increase direct taxation, the money-raising capacity of road charging may well make it attractive to any government as an alternative to more regulation.

Targets

The government has had a road safety target since 1987, that of reducing road casualties by one-third of the levels of the early 1980s. This goal was achieved within a decade (DETR, 1998: 82) and a new target was set, to reduce the number of people killed or seriously injured by a further 40 per cent (50 per cent for children) by 2010 compared with the average for 1994–98. These targets may have played their part in giving the UK one of the lowest death and serious accident rates in Europe. The Royal Commission on Environmental Pollution recommended additional targets on noise, exhaust emissions, fuel efficiency, the shares of passengers and freight to be carried by public transport, and the proportion of urban journeys to be undertaken by car and by cycle. Targets in general, and the Royal Commission's targets for passenger travel in particular, were rejected by the Conservative government in *Transport: The Way Forward* on the grounds that it was not clear how they could be achieved, or at what cost, or how effective they would be in reducing traffic (DoT, 1996: 87–92). However the Labour government's *A New Deal for Transport* (DETR: 1998) promised a range of new targets – for example, for promoting the use of public transport – and these have become central to the department's Public Service Agreements (DfT, 2004: 135–6; and Chapter 2), covering not only road safety but also the use of public transport, its punctuality and reliability, as well as measures of air quality and greenhouse gas emissions.

Devolution

There is a continuous tension between the desire of a strong central government to direct transport policy strategically and the need for many decisions about transport to be taken close to the communities that will be directly affected by them. In Britain this is managed through the hierarchy of national strategic policy direction, Regional Spatial Strategies, which link together policies and priorities for housing, transport, the environment and economic regeneration, and Local Transport Plans which are subject to close scrutiny in Government Offices for the Regions, and Whitehall. At their best these arrangements facilitate a constructive partnership, but the tension between the centre and the periphery is particularly apparent in the funding arrangements. Much expenditure on local roads and local public transport is funded through block allocations to local authorities, but the planned growth of the Transport Innovation Fund will give DfT and the Treasury ample scope to influence local decision-making. This arrangement has the distinct advantage for central government of allowing local politicians to take the blame if things go wrong, whilst ministers can claim much of the credit if the innovations which they have helped to finance prove successful.

Finding the money

If travel demand continues to grow, and safety and environmental pressures increase the costs of building and operating the transport system needed to relieve the resulting congestion, it will be necessary to consider where the resources will come from. Since there is unlikely to be any easing of those pressures to reduce public expenditure which led to the emphasis on private sources of finance (Chapter 8), it seems prudent to assume that public expenditure will continue to be tightly constrained, and when difficult choices have to be made, capital expenditure on transport will not have a particularly high priority in government expenditure programmes.

The 10 Year Plan envisaged substantial capital investment, but the planned expenditure, particularly for public transport, was heavily dependent on private finance which may not be easy to attract. Major ventures, such as the Channel Tunnel and Network Rail, are burdened with debts which will be difficult to repay, and capital investment in the London Underground under the terms of the Public–Private Partnership is falling seriously behind schedule (Chapter 7). In the roads sector, it remains difficult to justify or pay for the scale of construction thought necessary to relieve congestion, whilst the political limits of fuel tax increases have probably been reached, particularly if world fuel prices remain high. Hence the attractions of road charging (Chapter 8), which could conceivably relieve congestion by spreading demand, and raise at least some money for public transport alternatives. However, a new tax is never easy to sell, and ministers will need to be ready to seize the opportunity if and when conditions in the practical, political and organizational dimensions of policy-making finally make such a policy feasible.

Conclusion

There are no easy answers. For 18 years Conservative governments were markedly successful in improving the efficiency of Britain's transport industries in the narrow sense of reducing unit costs; but they chose to take virtually all the benefit in the form of reduced public expenditure. With the final round of privatizations completed under Labour after 1997, Britain now has a structure of transport industries in the private sector that is probably healthier and less subject to direct government control than at any time since the First World War. There is more competition between air and sea, rail, coach and bus travel in a range of different markets than there has ever been.

This transformation has changed the relationship between the British government and the transport industries, but the disengagement has not been quite as far-reaching as the most ambitious Conservative politicians of the Thatcher era might have hoped, and there are some signs that the pendulum is beginning to swing back towards more intervention. Some of the private train operating companies have been bailed out, and the original infrastructure company has been wound up and replaced by a new company operating under closer government supervision. Public opinion is torn between an urge to build more roads, born of impatience with the daily experience of traffic congestion, and a realization that there are limits to how much traffic can be accommodated without unacceptable damage to the environment. There is a greater understanding of the problems posed by the increase in car travel, which suggests that there may be room for some adjustment to the balance between market determination and public regulation.

Meanwhile, much decision-making has been devolved to different levels of government at national, regional and local levels. Each town and city will have to find its own solution within the broad framework of policies and resources determined centrally, but the government must play its part, too, in carrying any necessary legislation through Parliament, in determining the level of resources to be provided, in setting and using the regulatory framework within which public transport operates, and in carrying out its own direct responsibilities for the national networks.

Since 1997 we have seen the rise and fall of a first attempt to construct an environmentally sustainable transport policy. Since the fuel tax protest of 2000, there has been a regression to more familiar policies of 'predict and provide', but it is difficult to suppose that such policies will be sufficient to meet the challenges of the twenty-first century. Given the conflicting pressures arising from growing demand, tight resource constraints and the requirements of both safety and the environment, together with the direct impact which transport policy decisions have on the quality of life, there can be little doubt that transport policy in Britain will continue to be vigorously debated. Elsewhere, especially among our neighbours in Europe, the British experience of managing the provision of a public service almost entirely within the private sector will be critically observed, and keenly compared with the safety, cost and convenience of arrangements which depend much more heavily on the provision of services within the public sector.

Further Reading

Each chapter in the book has references to works that will be useful for following up an issue. Here we suggest a few texts for each chapter that we think are especially helpful on the topic of that chapter, whether by providing more background, or in giving more detail. However, we start with a list of official reports – not all produced by the government – that are relevant to the debate underlying the whole book and especially to its first and last chapters.

Official reports (in date order)

Department of the Environment (1990) *This Common Inheritance: Britain's Environmental Strategy*, Cm 1200 (London: Her Majesty's Stationery Office).

SACTRA (1994) *Trunk Roads and the Generation of Traffic* (London: Her Majesty's Stationery Office).

Houghton Report (1994) 18th Report by the Royal Commission on Environmental Pollution, *Transport and the Environment*, Cm 2674 (London: Her Majesty's Stationery Office).

Department of the Environment, Transport and the Regions (DETR) (1998) *A New Deal for Transport: Better for Everyone*, Cm 3950 (London: Her Majesty's Stationery Office).

DETR (2000) *Transport 2010: The 10 Year Plan* (London: The Stationery Office).

Department for Transport (DfT) (2004) *The Future of Transport: A Network for 2030*, Cm 6234 (London: The Stationery Office).

Department of Environment, Food and Rural Affairs (DEFRA) (2005) *Securing the Future: UK Government Sustainable Development Strategy*, Cm 6467 (London: The Stationery Office).

1   The Historical Context (in date order)

Royal Commission on Transport (1930) *Final Report*, Cmnd 3751 (London: Her Majesty's Stationery Office).

British Railways Board (1963) *The Reshaping of British Railways* [the Beeching Report] (London: Her Majesty's Stationery Office).

Buchanan, C. (1963) *Traffic in Towns: Reports of Steering Group and Working Group* (London: Department of Transport).

271

Gwilliam, K. M. (1964) *Transport and Public Policy* (London: George Allen & Unwin).

Savage, C. (1966) *An Economic History of Transport*, 2nd edn (London: Hutchinson, 1966).

Beesley, M. E. (1997) *Privatisation, Regulation and Deregulation*, 2nd edn (London: Routledge).

Glaister, S. (2002), 'UK Transport Policy 1997–2001', *Oxford Review of Economic Policy*, 18/2, 154–86.

2   The Role of Central Government

Cabinet Office (various years), *Civil Service Yearbook* (London: The Stationery Office), or see 'Guide to Departments' on www.civilservice.gov.uk under the topic: 'The UK Civil Service'.

Coxall, B., Robins, L. and Leach, R. (2003) *Contemporary British Politics* (Basingstoke: Palgrave Macmillan).

DfT (various years) *Annual Report* (London: The Stationery Office), or see www.dft.gov.uk.

Dudley, G. and Richardson, J. (2001) *Why Does Policy Change? Lessons from British Transport Policy 1945–99* (London: Routledge).

For the role of the Welsh Assembly, see www.wales.gov.uk.

For the role of the Scottish Executive, see www.scottishexecutive.gov.uk.

3   Local Government and Urban Transport

DfT, *Guidance on Local Transport Plans*, and other documents on www.dft.gov.uk under 'Regional and Local Transport'.

ODPM, *PPS12: Local Development Frameworks* and *PPS13: Transport* (London: The Stationery Office); and see the planning section of the Department for Communities and Local Government's website.

Wilson, D. and Game, C. (2002) *Local Government in the United Kingdom* (Basingstoke: Palgrave Macmillan).

On transport in London:

Burnham, J. (2006) 'The Governance of Transport in London Then and Now', *Local Government Studies*, Spring 2006.

Greater London Authority (2001) *The Mayor's Transport Strategy* (London: GLA).

Transport for London (2005) *Central London Congestion Charging: Impacts Monitoring: Third Annual Report* (London: TfL), and see www.cclondon.com

Travers, T. (2003) *The Politics of London: Governing an Ungovernable City* (Palgrave Macmillan).

On other metropolitan areas, see the web-site of the PTE association: www.pteg.net

4 The European Union and United Kingdom Transport Policy

European Commission (2001) White Paper: *European Transport Policy for 2010: Time to Decide*, COM (2001) 370 (Brussels).
On EU transport policies:
Despicht, N. S. (1964) *Policies for Transport in the Common Market* (Sidcup: Lambarde Press).
Stevens, H. M. G. (2004) *Transport Policy in the European Union* (Basingstoke: Palgrave Macmillan).

On the implementation of EU transport policies:
Héritier, A. et al. (eds) (2001) *Differential Europe: The European Union Impact on National Policymaking* (Lanham, MD: Rowman & Littlefield).

On EU policy-making:
Nugent, N. (2003) *The Government and Politics of the European Union*, 5th edn (London: Palgrave Macmillan).
Wallace, H. and Wallace, W. (2000) *Policy-Making in the European Union*, 4th edn (Oxford: Oxford University Press).

5 Planning

Banister, D. (2002) *Transport Planning in the UK, USA and Europe* (London: Spon).
Bryant, B. (1996) *Twyford Down: Roads, Campaigning and Environmental Law* (London: Spon).
Rydin, Y. (2003) *Urban and Environmental Planning in the UK*, 2nd edn (Palgrave Macmillan).
Steer Davies Gleave (1995) *Alternatives to Traffic Growth: The Role of Public Transport and the Future for Freight* (London: Transport 2000).
White, P. (2002) *Public Transport: Its Planning, Management and Operation* (Spon).

See the critiques of parliamentary committees (www.parliament.uk), including:
Transport, Local Government and the Regions Committee (2002), *Planning Green Paper*, HC 476 (London: The Stationery Office).

Transport Committee (2002), *10 Year Plan for Transport*, HC 558 (London: The Stationery Office).
Transport Committee (2003) *Ports*, HC 783 (London: The Stationery Office).
Transport Committee (2004) *The Future of the Railway*, HC145 (London: The Stationery Office).

6 Influencing Transport Policy

On the place of interest groups in policy-making:
Grant, W. (2000) *Pressure Groups and British Politics* (Basingstoke: Palgrave Macmillan).
Lukes, S. (1974) *Power: A Radical View* (London: Macmillan).
Marsh, D. and Rhodes, R. A. W. (1992) *Policy Networks in British Government* (Oxford: Oxford University Press).
Vigar, G. (2002) *The Politics of Mobility* (London: Spon).

On transport interest groups:
Bryant, B. (1996) *Twyford Down: Roads, Campaigning and Environmental Law* (London: Spon): an informed, clear analysis of how a road project was decided.
Dudley, G. and Richardson, J. (2001) *Why Does Policy Change? Lessons from British Transport Policy 1945–99* (London: Routledge).
Hamer, M. (1987) *Wheels within Wheels* (London: Routledge & Kegan Paul): a polemical account of the pro-roads lobby.

7 Engaging the Private Sector

Beesley, M. E. (1997) *Privatisation, Regulation and Deregulation*, 2nd edn (London: Routledge).
Evans, A. W. (1990) 'Bus Competition: Economic Theories and Empirical Evidence', in D. Hensher (ed.), *Transportation Planning and Technology* (London: Gordon & Breach).
Glaister, S. (2005) *Competition Destroyed by Politics: British Rail Privatisation* (London: Centre for Regulated Industries).
National Audit Office (2004) *Network Rail: Making a Fresh Start*, HC 532 (London: The Stationery Office).
National Audit Office (2004), *London Underground: Are the Public Private Partnerships Likely to Work Successfully?*, HC 644 (London: The Stationery Office).
National Audit Office (2004) *London Underground PPP: Were they Good Deals?*, HC 645 (London: The Stationery Office).

8 Paying for Transport: Appraisal and Economic Issues

Beesley, M. E. (1997) *Privatisation, Regulation and Deregulation*, 2nd edn (London: Routledge).
DfT (2004) *Road Pricing Feasibility Study* (London: DfT).
Glaister, S. and Graham, D. (2004) *Pricing our Roads: Vision and Reality* (London: Institute of Economic Affairs).
Glaister, S. and Graham, D. (2005) 'An evaluation of national road user charging in England', *Transportation Research*, Part A, 39, 632–50.
HM Treasury (2003) *PFI: Meeting the Investment Challenge* (London: HM Treasury).
Sansom, T., Nash, C., Mackie, P. and Shires, J. (2001) *Surface Transport Costs and Charges* (Leeds: Institute of Transport Studies, Leeds, and AEA Technology Environment).

For official transport analysis and appraisal methodologies, see www.webtag.org.uk.

Bibliography

Abelson, P. and Flowerdew, A. D. J. (1972) 'Roskill's successful recommendation', *Journal of the Royal Statistical Society*, Series A, 135.

Alderman, G. (1984) *Pressure Groups and Government in Britain* (Harlow: Longman).

Audit Commission (2004) *Initial Performance Assessment: Transport for London* (Audit Commission).

Bachrach, P. and Baratz, M.S. (1962) 'Two faces of power', *American Political Science Review*, 56, 949–52.

BALPA (2004) *What next for BALPA?* (www.balpa.org.uk).

Banister, D. J. (1994) *Transport Planning in the UK, USA and Europe* (London: Spon).

Beesley, M. E. (1985) 'Deregulating the bus industry in Britain: A Reply', *Transport Reviews*, 5/3, 223–4.

Beesley, M. E. (1997) *Privatisation, Regulation and Deregulation*, 2nd edn (London: Routledge).

Beesley, M. E., and Foster, C. D. (1963) 'Estimating the social benefit of constructing an Underground railway in London', *Journal of the Royal Statistical Society*, Series A, 126.

Bishop, M., Kay, J. and Mayer, C. (1995) *Privatisation and Economic Performance* (Oxford: Oxford University Press).

Bishop, M., Kay, J. and Mayer, C. (eds) (1995) *The Regulatory Challenge* (Oxford: Oxford University Press).

Brindley, T., Rydin, Y. and Stoker, G. (1996) *Remaking Planning: The Politics of Urban Change*, 2nd edn (London: Routledge).

British Railways Board (1963) *The Reshaping of British Railways* (London: Her Majesty's Stationery Office).

Brunner, C. (1929) *Road versus Rail: The Case for Motor Transport* (London: Benn).

Bryant, B. (1996) *Twyford Down: Roads, Campaigning and Environmental Law* (London: Spon).

Buchanan, C. (1963) *Traffic in Towns: Reports of Steering Group and Working Group* (London: Department of Transport).

Burnham, J. (2006) 'The Governance of Transport in London Then and Now', *Local Government Studies*, Spring 2006.

Burnham, J., Jones, G. and Travers, T. (1992) 'The Government of London: Transport', *Greater London Paper*, 19 (London: London School of Economics).

Carmichael, P. and Midwinter, A. (2003) *Regulating Local Authorities: Emerging Patterns of Central Control* (London: Frank Cass).

Cawson, A. (1986) *Corporatism and Political Theory* (Oxford: Blackwell).

Cawson, A. and Saunders, P. (1983) 'Corporatism, Competitive Politics and Class Struggle', in R. King (ed.), *Capital and Profits* (London: Routledge).

CEC (1985) *Completing the Single Market*, COM (85) 310 (Brussels).

CEC (1992) *The Future Development of the Common Transport Policy: A Global Approach to the Construction of a Community Framework for Sustainable Mobility*, COM (92) 494, and *EC Bulletin*, Supplement 3/93 (Brussels).

CEC (1993) *A Common Policy on Safe Seas*, COM (93) 66 (Brussels).

CEC (1993a) 'White Paper on Growth, Competitiveness and Employment', *EC Bulletin*, Supplement 6/93 (Brussels).

CEC (1998) *On Transport and CO_2*, COM (98) 204 (Brussels).

CEC (1999) *Designing Tomorrow's Commission: A Review of the Commission's Organisation and Operation* (Brussels: EC Inspectorate General).

CEC (2001) *European Transport Policy for 2010: Time to Decide*, COM (2001) 370 (Brussels).

Chester, D. N. (1936) *Public Control of Road Passenger Transport* (Manchester: Manchester University Press).

Chevroulet, T. (ed.) (2002) *Elements for Sustainable Transport Policies* [Swiss] National Research Programme, NRP 41 (Bern: Logistique, Economie, Management). See 'Auditor' (in English) on http://lem. epfl.ch/francais/informatique.php.

Conseil National des Transports (CNT) (2004) *La Lettre du CNT*, 78, www.cnt.fr.

Corbett, R., Jacobs, F. and Shackleton, M. (2000) *The European Parliament*, 4th edn (London: John Harper).

Corry, D., Le Grand, J. and Radcliffe, R. (1997) *Public–Private Partnerships* (London: Institute for Public Policy Research).

Dahl, R. (1956) *Preface to Democratic Theory* (Chicago: University of Chicago Press).

Darling, A. (2005) 'Road Pricing', speech to Social Market Foundation, 9 June: see www.dft.gov.uk.

DEFRA (2005) *Securing the Future: UK Government Sustainable Development Strategy*, Cm 6467 (London: The Stationery Office).

Despicht, N. S. (1964) *Policies for Transport in the Common Market* (Sidcup: Lambarde Press).

DETR (1997) *Developing an Integrated Transport Policy* (London: DETR).

DETR (1997a) *National Road Traffic Forecasts (Great Britain) 1997* (London: DTER).

DETR (1998) *A New Deal for Transport: Better for Everyone*, Cm 3950 (London: Her Majesty's Stationery Office).

DETR (1998a) *A New Deal for Trunk Roads in England* (London: DETR).

DETR (1998b) *British Shipping: Charting a New Course* (London: DETR).

DETR (1999) *A Better Quality of Life: A Strategy for Sustainable Development for the UK*, Cm 4345 (The Stationery Office).

DETR (1999a) *The Environmental Impacts of Road Vehicles in Use* (London: DETR).

DETR (1999b) *Towards an Urban Renaissance* (London: Spon).

DETR (2000) *Transport 2010: The 10 Year Plan* (London: The Stationery Office).

DETR (2000a) *Transport 2010: The Background Analysis* (London: DETR).

DETR (2000b) *Air Traffic Forecasts for the United Kingdom 2000* (London: DETR).

DETR (2000c) *Modern Ports: A UK Policy* (London: DETR).

DETR (2001) *Planning Policy Guidance 13: Transport* (London: DETR).

DfT (2002) *The Future Development of Air Transport in the UK: South East* (London: DfT).

DfT (2003) *The Future of Air Transport*, Cm 6046 (London: The Stationery Office).

DfT (2003a) *Proposal for a Directive . . . on Intermodal Loading Units* (London: DfT).

DfT (2003b) *Review of the Commission for Integrated Transport and Motorists Forum* (London: DfT).

DfT (2004) *The Future of Transport: A Network for 2030*, Cm 6234 (London: The Stationery Office).

DfT (2004a) *Department for Transport Resource Accounts 2003–04*, HC 222 (London: The Stationery Office).

DfT (2004b) *Annual Report 2004*, Cm 6207 (London: The Stationery Office).

DfT (2004c) *Shorter Guidance for Second Local Transport Plans* (London: DfT).

DfT (2004d) *Transport Statistics Bulletin: Regional Transport Statistics* (London: DfT).

DfT (2004e) *The Future of Rail*, Cm 6233 (London: The Stationery Office).

DfT (2004f) *The Government's Response to the Transport Committee's Report on Ports*, Cm 6096 (London: The Stationery Office).

DfT (2004g) *Transport Statistics Great Britain 2004* (London: The Stationery Office).

DfT (2004h) *Road Pricing Feasibility Study* (London: DfT).

DfT (2005) *Annual Report 2005* (London: The Stationery Office).

DfT (2005a) *Statistics Bulletin: Regional Transport Statistics* (London: DfT).

DoE (1990) *This Common Inheritance: Britain's Environmental Strategy*, Cm 1200 (London: Her Majesty's Stationery Office).

DoE (1994) *Sustainable Development: The UK Strategy*, Cm 2426 (London: Her Majesty's Stationery Office).

DoE and DoT (1992) *Transport and the Environment Study* (London: DoE and DfT).

DoE and DoT (1994) *Planning Policy Guidance 13: Transport (PPG13)* (London: DoE and DoT).

DoE and Government Statistical Services (1996) *Indicators of Sustainable Development for the United Kingdom* (London: Her Majesty's Stationery Office).

DoT (1984) *Buses*, Cmnd 9300 (London: Her Majesty's Stationery Office).

DoT (1987) *MV Herald of Free Enterprise* (Sheen Report) (London: Her Majesty's Stationery Office).

DoT (1989) *Roads for Prosperity*, Cm 293 (London: Her Majesty's Stationery Office).

DoT (1989a) *National Road Traffic Forecasts (Great Britain) 1989* (London: DoT).

DoT (1991) *Transport and the Environment* (London: DoT).

DoT (1992) *Transport and Works Act 1992: A Guide to Procedures* . . . (London: Her Majesty's Stationery Office).

DoT (1992a) *New Opportunities for the Railways: The Privatisation of British Rail*, Cm 2012 (London: Her Majesty's Stationery Office).

DoT (1993) *The Government's Expenditure Plans for Transport 1993–94 to 1995–96*, Cm 2006 (London: Her Majesty's Stationery Office).

DoT (1993a) *Paying for Better Motorways: Issues for Discussion*, Cm 2200 (London: Her Majesty's Stationery Office).

DoT (1995) *Transport: The Way Ahead* (London: DoT).

DoT (1996) *Transport: The Way Forward: The Government's Response to the Transport Debate*, Cm 3234 (London: Her Majesty's Stationery Office).

DoT (1996a) *Transport Report 1996: The Government's Expenditure Plans 1996–97 to 1998–99*, Cm 3206 (London: Her Majesty's Stationery Office).

DoT (1997) [Highways Agency and Private Finance Panel], *DBFO value in roads*, March 1997; and subsequent (undated) notices of 1997 (London: DoT).

Dowding, K. (1995) 'Model or Metaphor? A Critical Review of the Policy Network Approach', *Political Studies*, 43/1, 136–58.

DTI (1999) *Actions for Sustainable Transport: Optimisation across modes* (London: DTI).

DTLR (2001) *Planning: Delivering a Fundamental Change* (London: DTLR).

DTLR (2001a) *Major Infrastructure Projects: Delivering Fundamental Change* (London: DTLR).

DTLR (2002) *Modern Ports: Facing the Future.* Proceedings of Conference, School of Oriental and African Studies, 20 February (London: DTLR).

Dudley, G. (2004) 'The Enlightenment Function and Dimensions of Time: Evolutionary Theory and Limits in British Trunk Roads Policy', *British Journal of Politics and International Relations*, 6/3, 389–408.

Dudley, G. and Richardson, J. (2001) *Why Does Policy Change? Lessons from British Transport Policy 1945–99* (London: Routledge).

Dunnett, J. (1962) 'The Planning and Execution of Road Schemes', *Public Administration*, 40, 253–65.

Edwards, G. and Spence, D. (eds) (1997) *The European Commission*, 2nd edn (London: Cartermill).

Environment Committee of the House of Commons (2004) *Marine Environment* [Session 2003–04] HC 76 (London: The Stationery Office).

Erdmenger, J. (1983) *The European Community Transport Policy* (Aldershot: Gower).

Evans, A. W. (1987) 'A Theoretical Comparison of Competition with the Economic Regimes for Bus Services', *Journal of Transport Economics and Policy*, January, 7–36.

Evans, A. W. (1996) 'The economics of automatic train protection in Britain', *Transport Policy*, 3/3, 105–10.

Evans, A. W. (2004) 'Rail Safety and Rail Privatisation in Britain', Inaugural Lecture, Imperial College London.

Foster, C. D. and Castles, C. (2004) 'Creating a viable railway for Britain: What has gone wrong and how to fix it', unpublished manuscript.

Freight Study Group (2002) *Freight on Water: A New Perspective* (London: DEFRA).

GLA (2001) *The Mayor's Transport Strategy* (London: GLA).

Glaister, S. (1985) 'Competition on Urban Bus Routes', *Journal of Transport Economics and Policy*, January, 65–81.

Glaister, S. (2002), 'UK Transport Policy 1997–2001', *Oxford Review of Economic Policy*, 18/2, 154–86.

Glaister, S. (2005) *Competition Destroyed by Politics: British Rail Privatisation* (London: Centre for Regulated Industries).

Glaister, S., Burnham, J., Stevens, H. and Travers, T. (1998) *Transport Policy in Britain*, 1st edn (Basingstoke: Macmillan).

Glaister, S. and Graham, D. (2004) *Pricing Our Roads: Vision and Reality* (London: Institute of Economic Affairs).

Glaister, S. and Graham, D. (2005) 'An evaluation of national road user charging in England', *Transportation Research*, Part A, 39, 632–50.

Glaister, S., with Graham, D. J., Travers, T. and Wakefield, J. (2004) *Investing in Cities*, Report to Development Securities.

Glaister, S. and Travers, T. (1994) *An Infrastructure Fund for London* (London: Corporation of London).

Glen, D. with Dowden, J. and Wilson, R. (2005) *United Kingdom Seafarers Analysis* (London: London Metropolitan University).

Gomez-Ibanez, J. and Meyer, J. R. (1989) *Deregulating and Privatizing Urban Bus Services: Lessons from Britain,* Report for US Department of Transportation (Washington: Office of Private Sector Initiatives, DC 20590).

Government Office for London (2000) *Road Charging Options for London: A Technical Assessment* (Norwich: The Stationery Office).

Grant, M. (2002), 'Memorandum' [PGP64] to Transport, Local Government and the Regions Committee, *Planning Green Paper*, HC 476 (London: The Stationery Office).

Grant, W. (2000) *Pressure Groups and British Politics* (Basingstoke: Palgrave Macmillan).

Gwilliam, K. M. (1964) *Transport and Public Policy* (London: George Allen & Unwin).

Gwilliam, K. M. (1989) 'Setting the Market Free: Deregulation of the Bus Industry', *Journal of Transport Economics and Policy,* January, 29–43.

Gwilliam, K. M., Nash, C.A. and Mackie, P. J. (1985) 'Deregulating the bus industry in Britain: (B) The Case Against', *Transport Reviews*, 5/2, 105–32.

Gwilliam, K. M., Nash, C.A. and Mackie, P. J. (1985a) 'Deregulating the bus industry in Britain: A Rejoinder', *Transport Reviews, 5/5,* 215–22.

HACAN ClearSkies (2003) *The Future Development of Air Transport in the United Kingdom: South East Consultation Documents* (www.hacan.org.uk).

Hamer, M. (1987) *Wheels within Wheels* (London: Routledge & Kegan Paul).

Heclo, H. and Wildavsky, A. (1981) *The Private Government of Public Money* (London: Macmillan).

Héritier, A. and Knill, C. (2001) 'Differential Responses to European Policies: A Comparison', in Héritier, A. *et al.* (eds), *Differential Europe: The European Union Impact on National Policymaking* (Lanham, MD: Rowman & Littlefield).

Hibbs, J. (1993) *Market for Mobility* (London: Institute for Economic Affairs).

Hibbs, J. and Roth, G. (1992) *Tomorrow's Way: Managing Roads in a Free Society* (London: Adam Smith Institute).

Hillman, M. (1992) 'Reconciling transport and environmental objectives: the way ahead at the end of the road', *Public Administration*, 70/2, 225–34.

HM Treasury (1993) *Breaking New Ground: The Private Finance Initiative* (London: HM Treasury).

HM Treasury (1995) *Private Opportunity: Public Benefit: Progressing the Private Finance Initiative* (London: HM Treasury).

HM Treasury (1998) *Comprehensive Spending Review: New Public Spending Plans 1999–2002: Modern Public Services for Britain Investing in Reform* (London: HM Treasury).

HM Treasury (2003) *PFI: Meeting the Investment Challenge* (London: HM Treasury).

HM Treasury (2003a) *The Green Book: Appraisal and Evaluation in Central Government* (London: The Stationery Office).

HM Treasury (2004) *Financing Britain's Future: Review of the Revenue Departments*, Cm 6163 (London: The Stationery Office).

HM Treasury (2005) *Budget Report 2005*, HC 372 (London: The Stationery Office).

Houghton Report (1994) 18th Report by Royal Commission on Environmental Pollution, *Transport and the Environment*, Cm 2674 (London: Her Majesty's Stationery Office).

Huggett, D. (2002), 'Ports and the Environment', *Modern Ports*, Proceedings of Conference, 20 February (London: DTLR).

Kennedy, D., Glaister, S. and Travers, T. (1995) *London Bus Tendering* (London: Greater London Group, London School of Economics).

Kennedy, J. and Smith, A. S. J. (2004) 'Assessing the efficient cost of sustaining Britain's Rail network', *Journal of Transport Economics and Policy*, May, 157–90.

Kingdon, J. (1984) *Agendas, Alternatives and Public Policies* (New York: Harper Collins).

Knill, C. (2001) 'Reforming Transport Policy in Britain: Concurrence with Europe but Separate Development' in Héritier, A. *et al.* (eds), *Differential Europe: The European Impact on National Policymaking* (Lanham, MD: Rowman & Littlefield).

Labour Party (1996) *Consensus for Change* (London: The Labour Party).

Labour Party (1997) *Because Britain Deserves Better* (London: The Labour Party).

Layard, R. and Glaister, S. (eds) (1994) *Cost-Benefit Analysis* (Cambridge: Cambridge University Press).

Lindblom, C. (1977) *Politics and Markets* (New York: Basic Books).

Lukes, S. (1974) *Power: A Radical View* (London: Macmillan).

Marsh, D. and Rhodes, R. A. W. (1992) *Policy Networks in British Government* (Oxford: Oxford University Press).

Morrison, H. (1933) *Socialisation and Transport* (London: Constable).

MVA (2002) *Review of System for Making Orders under Part 1 of the Transport and Works Act 1992: Final Report to DTLR* (London: DfT).

NAO (2004) *Network Rail: Making a Fresh Start*, HC 532 (London: The Stationery Office).

NAO (2004a) *London Underground PPP: Were they Good Deals?*, HC 645 (London: The Stationery Office).

NAO (2004b), *London Underground: Are the Public Private Partnerships likely to work successfully?*, HC 644 (London: The Stationery Office).

National Assembly for Wales (2002) *Planning: Delivering for Wales* (Cardiff: National Assembly for Wales).

Newman, P. and Thornley A. (1996) *Urban Planning in Europe* (London: Routledge).

ODPM (2002) *The Government's response to the Transport, Local Government and Regional Affairs Committee's report: The 'Planning Green Paper'* (London: The Stationery Office).

ODPM (2003) *Local Government Finance Key Facts* (London: ODPM).

ODPM (2003a) *Local Authority Business Growth Incentives – A Consultation* (London: ODPM).

ODPM (2004) *Planning Policy Statement 12: Local Development Frameworks* (London: The Stationery Office).

ODPM (2004a) *Planning Policy Statement 11: Regional Spatial Strategies* (London: The Stationery Office).

Office of the Rail Regulator (ORR) (1994) *Competition for Railway Passenger Services: A Policy Statement*, December (London: Office of the Rail Regulator).

Paxman, J. (2002) *The Political Animal* (Harmondsworth: Penguin).

Peele, G. (2003), 'Politics in England and Wales', in Dunleavy, P., Gamble, A., Heffernan, R. and Peele, G., *Developments in British Politics 7* (Basingstoke: Palgrave Macmillan), 203–21.

Plowden, W. (1971) *The Motor Car and Politics 1896–1970* (London: Bodley Head).

Porritt, J. (1996) 'The Environmentalist's Conclusions', in Bryant, B., *Twyford Down: Roads, Campaigning and Environmental Law* (London: Spon), 297–309.

Potter, S. (1993) 'Transport, Environment and Fiscal Policies: On the Road to Change?', *Policy Studies*, 14/2, 36–48.

Procedure Committee (2002) *Major Infrastructure Projects: Proposed New Parliamentary Procedures*, HC1031 (London: The Stationery Office).

Public Accounts Committee (2005), *London Underground Public Private Partnerships*, HC 446 (London: The Stationery Office).

Richardson, J. and Jordan, A. (1985) *Governing under Pressure*, 2nd edn (Oxford: Blackwell).

RoSPA (2004) *Annual Review for 2003–04* (www.rospa.com).

Roth, G. (1995) *Roads in a Market Economy* (Aldershot: Avebury).

Royal Commission on Transport (1930) *Final Report*, Cmnd 3751 (London: Her Majesty's Stationery Office).

RSPB (1997) *Port Development and Nature Conservation: Supply and Demand in the GB Ports Industry* (Sandy: RSPB).

Rydin, Y. (2003) *Urban and Environmental Planning in the UK*, 2nd edn (Palgrave Macmillan).

Standing Advisory Committee on Trunk Road Assessment (SACTRA) (1992) *Assessing the Environmental Impact of Road Schemes* (London: Her Majesty's Stationery Office).

SACTRA (1994) *Trunk Roads and the Generation of Traffic* (London: Her Majesty's Stationery Office).

Sansom, T., Nash, C., Mackie, P. and Shires, J. (2001) *Surface Transport Costs and Charges* (Leeds: Institute of Transport Studies, Leeds, and AEA Technology Environment).

Santos, G. and Newbery, D., (2002) Estimating Urban Road Congestion Charges, *Centre for Economic Policy Research Discussion Paper*, 3176, University of Cambridge.

Savage, C. (1966) *An Economic History of Transport*, 2nd edn (London: Hutchinson).

SBC Warburg (1996) *Railtrack Share Offer: Prospectus*, 1 May.

Self, P. (1975) *Econocrats and the Policy Process* (London: Macmillan).

Smeed, R. (1964) *Road Pricing: The Economic and Technical Possibilities* (London: Her Majesty's Stationery Office).

Social Exclusion Unit (2002) *Making the Connections: Interim Findings* (www. socialexclusionunit.gov.uk).

Starkie, D. (1982) *The Motorway Age* (Oxford: Pergamon).

Steer Davies Gleave (1995) *Alternatives to Traffic Growth: The Role of Public Transport and the Future for Freight* (London: Transport 2000).

Stevens, H. M. G. (2004) *Transport Policy in the European Union* (Basingstoke: Palgrave Macmillan).

Strategic Rail Authority (2003) *Everyone's Railway: The Wider Case for Rail* (London: SRA).

TfL (2001) *Proposed management plan for the London Underground* (London: TfL).

TfL (2003) *Annual Report 2002/03* (London: TfL).

TfL (2004) *Congestion Charging: Update on Scheme Impacts and Operations* (London: TfL).

TfL (2004a) *London Travel Report 2004* (www.tfl.gov.uk).

TfL (2004b) *London Underground and the PPP: The first year 2003/04* (London: TfL).

TfL (2005) *Central London Congestion Charging: Impacts Monitoring: Third Annual Report* (London: TfL).

TfL (2005a) *London Underground and the PPP: the second year 2004/05* (London: TfL).

TfL (2005b) *Annual Report 2004/05* (London: TfL).

Transport Committee (1993) *The Future of the Railways in the Light of the Government's White Paper Proposals*, HC 375 (London: Her Majesty's Stationery Office).

Transport Committee (2000), *The Road Haulage Industry*, HC 296 (London: The Stationery Office).

Transport Committee (2002) [Transport, Local Government and the Regions Committee], *Planning Green Paper*, HC 476 (London: The Stationery Office).

Transport Committee (2002a) [Transport, Local Government and the Regions Committee], *10 Year Plan for Transport*, HC 558 (London: The Stationery Office).

Transport Committee (2002b) *London Underground*, HC 387 (London: The Stationery Office).

Transport Committee (2002c) *The Attendance of Lord Birt*, HC 655 (London: The Stationery Office).

Transport Committee (2003) *Ports*, HC 783 (London: The Stationery Office).

Transport Committee (2004) *The Future of the Railway*, HC145 (London: The Stationery Office).

Travers, T. (2003) *The Politics of London: Governing an Ungovernable City* (Basingstoke: Palgrave Macmillan).

Travers, T. and Weimar, J. (1996) *Business Improvement Districts: New York and London* (London: Corporation of London).

Truelove, P. (1992) *Decision Making in Transport Planning* (Harlow: Longman).

Tyson, W. J. (1989) 'A Review of the Second Year of Bus Deregulation', Report to Association of Metropolitan Authorities and Passenger Transport Executive Group.

UK Major Ports Group (2001) *Memorandum* [P 24], to Environment, Transport and Regional Affairs Committee's [incomplete] Inquiry on 'Opportunities and Development Prospects at Major Ports' (www.parliament.uk).

Vigar, G. (2002) *The Politics of Mobility* (London: Spon).

Walder, J. and Amenta, T. L. (2004) 'Financing New Infrastructures: Public/Private Partnerships and Private Finance Initiatives', in R. E Hanley (ed.), *Moving People, Goods and Information: The Cutting-Edge Infrastructures of Networked Cities* (London: Spon).

Walters, A. (1961) 'The theory and measurement of private and social costs of highway congestion', *Econometrica*, 29/4.

White, J. (1993) *Fear of Voting: Local Democracy and its Enemies 1894–1994* (Oxford: History Workshop and Joseph Rowntree Foundation).

White, P. (1990) 'Change Outside the Mets', Conference on 'Public Transport: the Second Year of Deregulation in the Metropolitan Areas', at Institute of Mechanical Engineers, London, March.

White, P. and Turner, R. (1990) in D. Hensher (ed.), *Transportation Planning and Technology* (London: Gordon & Breach).

Whitelegg, J. (1988) *Transport Policy in the EEC* (London: Routledge).

Wilson, D. and Game, C. (2002) *Local Government in the United Kingdom* (Basingstoke: Palgrave Macmillan).

Wistrich, E. (1983) *The Politics of Transport* (Harlow: Longman).

Wolmar, C. (2001) *Broken Rails* (London: Aurum).

Wolmar, C. (2002) *Down the Tube* (London: Aurum).

World Commission on Environment and Development (1987) *Our Common Future* [the Brundtland Report] (Oxford: Oxford University Press.

Index

10 Year Plan 16, 33–6, 54–5, 105,
  135–44, 159, 165, 189, 200,
  211, 220, 228, 237, 239, 263,
  268
accessibility 9, 70, 80, 85–7,
  142–3, 149, 162, 185, 224,
  235, 262
airports 21–3, 27, 36, 44, 80,
  144–5, 149, 153, 160, 180,
  183–4, 187, 233, 247, 262
  see also Heathrow, Stansted
air transport 19–22, 59, 106–9,
  112, 114, 125, 144–5, 153,
  157, 167, 173–5, 179–81,
  184, 186–7, 189, 192, 246,
  250, 253, 261
Air Transport Licensing Board 20
Alexander, Douglas xiii, 241
anti-competitive practices 108–10,
  194–5, 199
Area Traffic Commissioners
  10–11, 18
Automatic Train Protection (ATP)
  260
Automobile Association (AA) 161,
  176–7, 183, 188–9, 192

Beeching Report, *The Reshaping of
  British Railways* 18–19
Belt up School Kids (BUSK)
  169–71, 179–80, 188
Birmingham 22, 77, 92, 95, 97,
  136, 154–5, 238
Blair government policies 15–17
  buses 200
  environment 52–4, 223, 261–2
  finance 34, 36, 54–6, 87–92, 220
  integrated transport 32–4
  planning 81–3, 85–7, 135–46,
    150–2, 156–8

privatization 37–8
railways 35, 39, 65, 205,
  209–11
roads 135–6, 236–9
road pricing 241
safety 142, 260, 235
Underground 37, 212–17
Board of Trade 2–3, 5–6, 8
  see also DTI
British Airports Authority (BAA)
  22, 144, 174, 186–7, 192
British Airways (BA) 21–2, 174,
  186
British Chamber of Shipping 145,
  173–4, 181–2, 185–6, 192–3
British Rail 18–19, 45, 57–8,
  93–4, 154, 176
  privatization 21–2, 39, 45, 60–4,
    131, 200–12, 246–7, 249
Brown, Gordon 34–5, 54, 56, 105,
  188, 193, 209, 228, 232
Buchanan Report, *Traffic in Towns*
  19, 134, 240
budgetary process 28, 49–50,
  52–7, 89–92, 246–7
buses 16, 59, 92, 102, 140,
  169–71, 262
  competition and deregulation
    20, 24–6, 194–200
  impact of bus deregulation
    195–7, 247
  licensing 10, 20
  predatory behaviour 199
  tendering 99, 197–8, 200
Buses White Paper 194
Business Improvement Districts
  (BIDs) 226
Byers, Stephen 36, 68, 74–5, 162,
  209
bypasses 27, 34, 154, 184, 237

Cabinet 52, 67–8, 159
Cabinet committees 55, 68–9
Cabinet Office 68–9, 73, 120, 127, 143
canals 1–5, 12, 15, 250
cars 33–5, 168, 176, 179, 221, 242, 248, 255, 264–5, 267
  company cars 52, 265
  see also congestion; emissions, fuel tax; parking; tolls; VED
Central Railway 155–6
Chancellor of the Exchequer 6–8, 28, 35, 42, 52–6, 105, 188, 193, 209, 223, 228, 232
Channel Tunnel 51, 156–7, 268
Channel Tunnel Rail Link 49, 154, 156
Civil Aviation Authority (CAA) 20, 22, 37
Clarke, Kenneth 185, 228
coaches 1–3, 10–11, 23–6, 58, 169–71, 247, 269
Commission for Integrated Transport (CfIT) 34, 165, 167
competition 21
  anti-competitive practices 194–5, 199
  bus and coach 25–6, 194–200
  rail 26, 200–12
  see also market mechanisms
Competition Commission 51, 59, 61
Confederation of British Industry (CBI) 35, 80, 171–2, 180, 185–6, 192–3
Confederation of Passenger Transport (CPT) 169–70
congestion 11, 28, 30, 34, 54, 70, 85–7, 112, 135, 142, 163, 180, 204, 257
  charging 29, 33, 36, 53, 72, 190, 240, 248, 265
  urban 19, 136–9, 228
  see also London congestion charge; road pricing
Consensus for Change 32

Conservative government transport policies
  see Major government policies; Thatcher government policies
coordination of transport 3, 9, 11–12, 14–17, 19, 42, 60, 66–73, 199
  lack of 75–6, 197
  with other policies 93–5, 97–9
cost–benefit analysis 143, 163, 169, 232–6
Council of [Transport] Ministers 108–9, 114–17, 120–1, 125–7
CrossRail 140
cyclists 6, 73, 84–5, 90, 101, 176, 235, 267

Darling, Alistair xiii, 36, 68, 188–9, 258
Department for Communities and Local Government (DCLG) 49, 90
Department for the Environment, Food and Rural Affairs (DEFRA) 49, 71
Department for Transport (DfT) 36, 42–7
  airports 144–5
  budgetary process 54–6
  buses 200
  coaches 169, 171
  environmental policy 249, 261
  executive agencies 47, 69
  mobility unit 47, 189
  planning 72–3, 83, 85–7, 143–5, 150–1, 156–8, 252
  ports 145–6, 168–9
  rail 62, 66, 209–12, 251
  regional offices 44, 70
  roads 168–9, 186–8, 235–8, 241, 257
  statutory powers 42–3, 74–5
  transport policy unit 45, 47
Department of the Environment (DoE) 28–9, 47, 70–1, 83, 157, 168–9, 187

Department of the Environment,
Transport and the Regions
(DETR) 32–3, 36, 51, 76,
80, 137, 140–1, 145–7, 168,
248, 252
and roads 135–6
Department of Trade and Industry
(DTI) 50–1, 71, 185
Department of Transport (DoT)
51, 128–9, 134, 183, 248
environmental policy 28–32,
47, 234
planning advice 83
deregulation
air 19–20
buses 16, 21, 25, 194–7
coaches 20–1, 23–6, 247
road haulage 18, 23
shipping 22–3
Design, Build, Finance, Operate
(DBFO) 239, 256–7
Disabled Persons Transport
Advisory Committee (DPTAC)
162, 166, 176, 189
Dunwoody, Gwyneth 74, 190–1
Durham 243, 265

Earth Summit 28, 104, 134, 223
see also Kyoto
East London River Crossing 134
economy and transport 28–31,
52–3, 56, 93, 142, 162–3,
182–3, 192, 235, 258–9
emissions 28–9, 35, 50, 53, 56, 71,
101, 113–14, 134, 136–7,
141–2, 223, 235, 249, 255,
261–2, 265, 267
environment 180, 183, 261–2
costs 163, 233–5
green indicators 29
road–building 17–18, 27–8,
134, 178, 184–7
road traffic 29, 141–2, 255
taxes 53–4, 265
transport policy 22, 27–33, 71,
113–14, 248–9, 252

see also Houghton Report;
sustainability
environmental impact assessment
132, 157, 184, 234
European Commission 110–11,
114–19, 122–7, 136, 164,
178, 184, 234, 251
European Court of Justice 108–9,
116, 122–5, 184
European Parliament 28, 108–9,
115–17, 121–3, 125–7, 187
European Union
competition policy 108–11
environmental policy 113–14
handling by DETR/DfT 114,
128–30
handling by UK parliament
127–31
transport policy 107–15
executive agencies 47, 69

Fennell Report 58
ferries 21–2, 51, 182
finance *see* fuel tax; funding;
London congestion charge;
private finance; road pricing;
taxation; vehicle excise duty
forecasting 135–46
Fowler, Norman 20, 23
Franchising Director 61–4
see also rail franchises
freight 3, 12–14, 110, 151, 164
rail 8–9, 61, 110, 136–7, 139,
142, 155–6, 201, 206
road 14–15, 18, 23, 131, 168,
179, 181, 188
sea 22–3, 111, 145–6, 164, 182
fuel tax 7, 10, 34, 52–4, 56, 145,
178
funding 52–3, 268
budgetary process 53–7
central government 49–50,
54–7, 200, 202–3, 211,
219–20, 237–8, 256–7
European Union 112–13

funding (*cont.*):
  local government   79, 87–92,
    94–6, 198, 228, 231–2
  see also finance

Gladstone   2, 3, 14, 246
global warming   28–9, 71, 113–14,
    134, 142, 261–2
  see also emissions
government, central   *see* Blair;
    Major; Thatcher; *and under*
    individual departments and
    ministers
government, local   *see* local
    authorities
Greater London Authority   70,
    79–80, 97, 105, 150, 213–17,
    232
Greater London Council   78
Guidance on the Methodology for
    Multimodal Studies
    (GOMMS)   235

haulage   *see* freight
Heathrow   22, 36, 132, 153, 155,
    157, 179, 183, 186–7, 192
Herald of Free Enterprise   58,
    182–3
Heseltine, Michael   49, 133
Highways Agency   43, 46, 48, 51,
    70, 84, 152, 237, 239, 257
history of transport   1–39
Home Office   51–2, 70–1, 91,
    104
Houghton Report   29–31, 134,
    149, 261

inspectors   2, 47, 66, 153–4,
    156–8, 160
integrated transport policy   32–8
International Maritime Organization
    107, 112
international transport   106–7,
    110–12, 124–5, 164
issue network   169

Jubilee Line extension   133, 154,
    224

Kyoto accords   104, 114, 261
  see also Earth Summit; global
    warming

Labour government policies   *see*
    Blair government policies
land-use planning
  central responsibilities   49, 68,
    70, 147–60, 255–7
  local responsibilities   80–5,
    149–52, 255–7
land value capture   224
Leeds   77, 92, 103
licensing
  air   19–20, 59
  bus and coach   10–11, 20, 24,
    59
  rail   62–3
  road freight   11–12, 18, 23, 59
light rail   90, 92, 96–8
Livingstone, Ken   38, 92, 99–103,
    105, 214–17
Lloyd George   6–7
local authorities   5–7, 49–50, 70,
    72–3, 77–105, 147–52, 224–8,
    231–2
  see also land-use planning; *and*
    under individual authorities
local–central government
  financial   49–50, 79, 87–92,
    231–2
  on local planning   70, 83,
    149–51
  relationships   72–3, 78–80,
    85–7, 99, 104–5
Local Transport Plans   81–2, 85–7
London boroughs   85, 227
  see also local authorities
London Buses   21, 26, 140,
    197–8
London congestion charge   54,
    94–103, 140, 219

London mayor *see* Greater London Authority; Livingstone
London Transport 11–12, 19, 24, 45, 78
see also Transport for London
London Transportation Studies 140
London Underground 12, 75, 98, 102, 140, 154, 189–90, 233
Public–Private Partnership 37–8, 54, 60, 93, 212–17, 229–30, 247, 254
lorries *see* freight

M6 154–5, 238, 257
M25 237
Major, John, government policies 17, 26–32, 134, 201, 206
Manchester 22, 77, 92, 95, 97, 136, 155, 157, 184, 263
maritime transport *see* sea transport
market mechanisms 20, 22, 24, 50, 75, 123, 194–5, 200, 209, 218
see also competition
Mawhinney, Brian 30, 248
metropolitan districts 81, 85, 94
Ministry of Transport 7–8, 14–15, 43
Mobility Unit 47, 162
Monopolies and Mergers Commission 199
monopoly 2–5, 8–9, 11–12, 15, 20–1, 26, 63, 195, 199, 201–2, 211, 215, 243
Morrison, Herbert 2, 10, 12

National Air Traffic Services (NATS) 37, 230
National Bus Company (NBC) 21, 24–5, 198
nationalized industries 2, 12, 20–1, 24–5, 37, 57–8
Network Rail 39, 64–5, 210–12
New Approach to Appraisal (NATA) 235–6, 248

Newbury 154, 184
New Roads and Streetworks Act 154–5
Nottingham 97

Office of the Deputy Prime Minister (ODPM) 49, 71, 82, 89–91, 132, 150
Office of Fair Trading (OFT) 50–1
Office of Passenger Rail Franchising (OPRAF) *see* Franchising Director
Office of Rail Regulation (ORR) *see* Rail Regulator
Oxleas Wood 134, 186

package approach 72–3
Parliament
European legislation 127–31
House of Lords 44, 74, 128, 130, 154
Public Accounts Committee 189, 216, 230
Transport Select Committee 74, 82, 105, 142–3, 146, 148–9, 157, 190–1
see also European Parliament
parliamentary bills 154–7
parliamentary train 3
parking levy 227–8, 248
Passenger Service Requirement 62
Passenger Transport Authorities 19, 78–9, 93–9
pedestrians 10, 19, 73, 84–5, 97, 143, 161, 176, 234
planning *see* 10 Year Plan; land-use planning; Local Transport Plans; regional planning
planning gain 227
planning guidance 29, 70–1, 76, 83–6, 149–51
policy communities 168, 251
policy networks 168, 251
pollution *see* emissions
ports 22–3, 145–6, 164, 168–9, 173–4, 182

Prescott, John   32–3, 35, 37, 48–9,
    67, 80, 87, 104, 114, 145, 165,
    186, 188, 213, 229, 255, 263
private bills   *see* parliamentary bills
private finance
    Private Finance Initiative   32,
        222, 228–30
    Public–Private Partnership   32,
        222, 228–30
    toll motorways   239
    see also London Underground,
        NATS
privatization
    British Airports Authority   22
    British Airways   21–2
    British Rail   21–2, 26–7, 39, 45,
        60–4, 131, 200–2, 246–7, 249
    ferries   21–2
    London Buses   197–8
    National Bus Company   21–6
    ports   22–3
public consultation   163–4
public inquiries   153–4, 156–8, 178
Public–Private Partnerships   *see*
    private finance
Public Service Agreement   55–7
public service commitment or
    obligation   230

rail franchises   61–2, 64, 201
    revenues and costs   202–6
rail investment   204–12
rail network construction   1–5
rail privatization   *see* privatization
Rail Regulator   61–6, 202, 208–11
rail services   200–10
    charges and fares   62–4
    history   1–5, 8–11, 14, 18–19,
        26–7
    see also competition;
        deregulation; freight;
        privatization
Railtrack   35, 39, 60, 64, 201–2,
    207–10
    access charges   62–4

Railway Accidents Investigation
    Branch   66
Railway Administration   209
Railway and Canal Traffic Acts   2,
    3, 5, 8–9
Railway Rates Tribunal   8
Rees Jeffreys   6–7
regional offices   7, 73
regional planning   147–52
    see also planning guidance
Regional Transport Strategy
    150–2
regions   7, 73, 79–80, 148–52
Ridley, Nicholas   25, 67, 74, 185
Rio *see* Earth Summit
risk transfer   205–6, 229
Road Board   6–7
road construction   27, 34, 36,
    134–5, 142, 153–4, 161, 178,
    186, 222, 236–9
    cutbacks   28
    history   5–8, 14, 17
    private financing   239, 257
Road Fund   7–8
road haulage   *see* freight
Road Improvement Association
    6
road pricing   31, 239–44, 257–8
road vehicle tax   *see* vehicle excise
    duty
Royal Automobile Club (RAC)   6,
    161, 169, 177, 183
Royal Commission on
    Environmental Pollution   *see*
    Houghton Report

SACTRA   *see* Standing Advisory
    Committee on Trunk Road
    Assessment
safety   111–12, 259–60
Scottish Executive   43, 146–9, 163
sea transport   21–3, 51, 58, 107,
    111–12, 145–6, 164, 168–9,
    173–4, 181–3, 185–6, 192–3
Sheen Inquiry   58, 182–3

Society of Motor Manufacturers and Traders   168, 172, 174

Standing Advisory Committee on Trunk Road Assessment (SACTRA)   30, 69, 23–4, 258

Stansted   36, 157, 179, 184

Stevenage   49

strategic environmental assessment   82, 148

Strathclyde   78, 92–5, 97

sustainability   28–33, 46–7, 71, 75, 83, 113–4, 132–3, 142, 144–5, 147–9, 151, 248–9, 256–8

targets   31, 52, 55–7, 86–7

Tax Increment Finance   226

taxation   52–6, 87–9, 222–8, 265
    see also fuel tax, tolls

Thatcher, Margaret, government policies   17, 20–6, 33–4, 94, 194–5, 197–8
    see also deregulation; market mechanisms;

tolls   239, 257

trade unions   170, 174–6, 180–1, 186–7, 192, 198

Trans-European Networks (TENs)   112–13

Transport 2000   161, 176–7, 179

Transport and Works Act 1992   155–7

Transport for London (TfL)   79–80, 95–99, 101–3, 214–5, 232, 247

transport funding   *see* funding; private finance; tolls

Transport Research Laboratory   48, 233

Transport Select Committee   *see* Parliament

Transport Working Group of EU   120–1

Treasury   7, 14, 28, 52–7, 66, 71, 73, 154, 159, 184, 191, 202, 209, 211, 213, 217, 222–3, 228–9, 232, 241

Turnpike Trusts   4–6

Twyford Down   178, 186, 189

Tyne and Wear   95–7

vehicle excise duty (VED)   31, 53, 223

vehicles
    see emissions

Virgin   186, 205

walking   *see* pedestrians

Welsh Assembly   43, 147–9

workplace parking levy   227–8, 248